MY AMY

MY
AMY

TYLER JAMES
with Sylvia Patterson

MACMILLAN

First published 2021 by Macmillan
an imprint of Pan Macmillan
The Smithson, 6 Briset Street, London EC1M 5NR
EU representative: Macmillan Publishers Ireland Ltd,
Mallard Lodge, Lansdowne Village, Dublin 4
Associated companies throughout the world
www.panmacmillan.com

ISBN 978-1-5290-4215-3 (HB)
ISBN 978-1-5290-4217-7 (TPB)

1 3 5 7 9 8 6 4 2

A CIP catalogue record for this book is available from the British Library.

Typeset in Sabon LT Std by Palimpsest Book Production Limited, Falkirk, Stirlingshire
Printed and bound by CPI Group (UK) Ltd, Croydon, CR0 4YY

Visit **www.panmacmillan.com** to read more about all our books
and to buy them. You will also find features, author interviews and
news of any author events, and you can sign up for e-newsletters
so that you're always first to hear about our new releases.

This book is for the two most important women in my life,
Amy and my mum.

CHAPTER 1

Friday, 22 July 2011, 1 p.m. The phone rang and her name came up.

'AMY.'

Her voice said, like it always did: 'You alright darlin'?'

I wasn't alright. Because she wasn't alright. Nothing was alright. Last night I'd walked out of our home in Camden Square, the last of countless homes we'd lived in together since Amy was eighteen years old. We'd been best mates since she was twelve and I was thirteen, inseparable soulmates forever. Walking out was a new tactic for me. I'd tried everything else. After years of trauma, of trying to save Amy, I was running out of ideas. So now, every time she relapsed, I'd leave because I wouldn't support her drinking.

'If you're drinking, I won't be here.'

Sometimes I *was* there but she wouldn't know it. I'd sleep under a blanket on the treadmill in the gym downstairs to get away from the noise: she'd scream my name, blare music, play the zombie film *Planet Terror* on a loop all night long, blasting it out of her speakers.

But mostly I'd go to my mum's in Essex for two, three, four days. Then Amy would ring.

'T, please come home.'

And we'd make a deal.

1

'I'll come home. We'll start the process again, withdrawal, stopping drinking tomorrow.'

And it worked. *It was working.* She was getting better. She went three weeks without a drink, four days back on it, three weeks off again. Every day she was sober she was in the gym, on the treadmill, rebuilding herself. It was a pattern but she was close. *So close.* She was even writing music again. She hadn't touched hard drugs, despite what the tabloids said, for three years.

So I'd walked out of Camden Square, again, at ten at night. I sat, exhausted, outside a local pub and was about to call an Addison Lee taxi to my mum's. But this particular time I had a feeling that I shouldn't just leave like I usually did. Something in that moment was different; there was some awareness that wasn't on the surface. I was usually calm with Amy, I never wanted to make her feel bad because I knew that didn't work with alcoholics – back in the day, if someone screamed at me when I relapsed, it would only make me want to drink more. But this time? I thought *fuck it.* I need to be something else: hardcore.

I opened the door with my keys, went upstairs to her bedroom on the top floor and she was doing all the stuff she normally did when she relapsed: listening to music really, *really* loudly from speakers linked to her laptop. It was usually Mos Def; right now it was The Specials' 'Ghost Town' blaring out. I stood at her open door; she was pottering around, drinking wine, going in and out of her en suite bathroom, singing, obviously feeling normal and good again because that's what alcohol does when you've been craving it. I just lost it. I flipped.

'None of this is normal, none of this is good, none of this is funny, it's all bollocks!'

I knew I'd piss her off. I was never really angry with Amy, I always supported her, helped her, *loved* her – but I'd had enough. I went over to her laptop and slammed the top down, shut everything off.

'What the *fuck* are you doing?' she yelled. 'I was listening to my music!'

I sat on the end of her bed and this time I was screaming.

'You *can't* drink, this can't happen anymore! We can't just keep going through this process! Relapsing, relapsing, relapsing, we've been in and out of hospital so many times, the doctors have said you can't drink anymore or you'll *die*. They've sent you *letters* telling you that. This is no longer an option! Do you realize what you're doing to *me*?'

I was the only friend she had left by then, the only person around her all the time who wasn't paid to be around her. Everyone else in her life had bailed out. However much they loved her they couldn't deal with her. No one else was there every day supporting her. I went to a level I'd never been to before.

'Forget *you* for a minute, do you ever contemplate what will happen to *me* and my *head* and my *life* if you're not here anymore? If you die? You love me, your best friend in the world. But you'll blow me to pieces. You may as well get a fucking *shotgun*.'

She had a little living room off her bedroom where I was pacing round, pulling my own hair out the back of my head.

'I dunno what to *do* with you anymore! I'm out of ideas, you don't seem to get it!'

She tried to convince me everything was alright.

'But T, I'm in the studio downstairs, I'm doing music again.'

She was always trying to be the person she thought she had to be: this character called 'Amy Winehouse'. And by now I had a mantra: 'It's better to be alive being Amy than to die trying to be "Amy Winehouse". *Fuck* Amy Winehouse, it's a character, *fuck* that persona!'

And then she said what she always said: 'T, I'm not going anywhere.'

All I had left was my new tactic: 'Unless you stop drinking *right now*, I'm going.'

'Well,' she snapped, 'fuck off then.'

'Well, fuck *you*.'

It was all so routine. I just picked up my case and left. I *had* to. I couldn't let her think any of this was OK or just put up with it and do nothing. Like some people around her often seemed to.

The next day there was the call. 'You alright darlin'?' I knew it would be a long conversation, so I walked down to the end of the road at my mum's where there's an enclosed field surrounded by bushes. There was no one there but me. I could tell she'd only had a couple of drinks. It was lunchtime.

It was a weird conversation. She talked to me about *me*. I think she was trying to say sorry. She knew how much I gave to her. I gave her my life. She was grateful and part of her felt guilty. She was telling me again, 'I'm not going anywhere T, I'm gonna be alright.' But this time she was also saying, 'But this is what I want for *you*.' She wanted me to make music again and I wasn't interested. I'd no desire to be famous after everything I'd seen. She'd said herself for years, anyone who wants to be famous must be mad. She always used to say: 'Fame is like terminal cancer; I wouldn't wish it on anyone.'

Amy had never wanted to be famous. She wanted to be a jazz singer. More than anything else she wanted a family, to be a wife and have kids. All Amy ever wanted was normality.

And she wanted that for me too. She wanted someone to

love me. She said, 'T, I want you to fall in love.' She'd never seen that happen for me because I was always looking after her. I was twenty-nine and I'd never had a proper relationship – when would I have had time to meet anyone? I barely had any other friends because Amy always came first.

'T,' she said. 'Come home.'

'Well I'm not coming home *now*. I'll come home tomorrow.'

There was no point going back that night – I could tell she was just going to carry on drinking. She rang me again much later very drunk, maybe eleven o'clock, chatting nonsense. I fell asleep on my mum's couch.

Around 2.30 a.m. she rang again. I was exhausted and just didn't answer. Pointless, she wouldn't even remember it. I went back to sleep.

The next day, I went home to Camden Square. Before I went in, I sat on a bench in the square for ages, preparing myself for the days ahead. I rang my friend Chantelle and all we talked about was Amy. I was exhausted and she was trying to help me. 'You need to start looking after yourself,' she kept saying, 'I love Amy to bits too but you can't do this anymore.' But this was what I *did*. And I'd keep doing it until Amy had cracked it.

I got up, keys in hand, and walked up the steps to the front door. This hadn't been any different to any other relapse and I knew what was coming next: she'd wake up, she'd want to be sober, I'd take her to hospital for alcohol withdrawal and we'd start the whole process again. Amy rebuilding herself for weeks, on the treadmill, being healthy again, being funny again, back to her brilliant self. And maybe this time would be the time she stayed sober forever. It would happen to her like it had happened to me, that was her goal, she said it a million times: 'If Tyler can do it, I can do it.' Our lives were parallel like that, they always had been, since we were kids. We did everything together, me and her. It was *always* me and her. So I knew she'd get there eventually.

I *knew* it.

I turned the key in the door and stepped inside. It was Saturday, 23 July 2011.

CHAPTER 2

Canning Town in 1982 – the year I was born, a year before Amy – was typical working-class East London. Everyone's a hard nut and if you're a boy, you've got to be able to fight. I wasn't a fighter, I was a reader. I grew up in a council house with my mum and big sister. I'd be upstairs in my room reading Shakespeare plays, listening to music and writing poetry when my family was downstairs watching *EastEnders*. I was always sensitive, different. I didn't want to go out and play football with the other boys. I was very into school, into learning, and in my environment that was *weird*. My parents weren't academic. I was an East End boy whose tracksuits came off the back of a lorry.

Most boys I went to school with ended up in prison for dealing drugs, robbing cars, all sorts. A lot of my family were gangsters, they owned East End pubs and some of them were in prison.

Growing up there was funny too: there were drink-fuelled family barbecues in our five foot by nothing concrete 'garden', endless games of knock down ginger and every New Year's Eve, the whole street would be out banging dustbin lids at the stroke of midnight.

Amy glorified where I'm from. My maternal grandad Albert Reading, a twin, was a real gangster, a hit man for the Krays. Amy had a book about my grandad on a shelf in our first flat in Jeffrey's Place in Camden. I can't stand the man, I only ever saw him twice.

Amy always wanted to be a gangster's wife, that was her fantasy. She loved *The Godfather* films and Scorsese movies, like *Goodfellas*. She loved gangster's molls, who always had loads of kids, even if they usually got beaten up. Part of the fantasy was being a gangster's mother: in Amy's head she wanted to give birth to the Krays, have two sons she could tell off. I'm due twins genetically, they skip a generation in my family, so she'd call me 'Twin Spunk' and say she wanted to have my kids. We used to laugh about how I'd impregnate her with two naughty bastards, twin boys we'd name after Marlon Brando: Marlon and Brandon.

She loved my fucked-up East London family so much she'd fantasize about marrying *into* the family. Because I was like a brother to her she'd go on about my cousin Dan instead, everyone used to say we looked like two sides of my grandad Albert and Dan was the naughty one, a bit of a gangster. She'd say to me a lot, 'I'll probably end up marrying your cousin Dan.' And she never met him once in her life.

One of the reasons I was so close to Amy is because she reminded me so much of my mum, Tina: mothering, strong, traditional – both full-on characters who like to look after their men. My mum had been in a damaging relationship when she was a teenager, which was one reason why she and Amy were so close: she got married too soon at sixteen to a wrong 'un, so she understood about Blake. They divorced and she met a good man, my biological dad, and had my older sister. Four years later I came along. But my mum and my dad were from completely different worlds. He was a sensitive poet, creative, musical, an actor and my mum just woke up one day and thought, 'What the fuck?!' They divorced when I was two.

I've only two memories of seeing my mum and dad together in the same room, ever. The first was at Christmas, when I was about nine, and my dad came round with presents. And a decade later after I was violently attacked – a life-changing incident that led to me moving in with Amy permanently. I came round in a hospital bed, my mum and my dad were in the same room and I actually thought I was hallucinating. But they didn't have any bad feeling towards each other and the divorce didn't really affect me. I saw my real dad regularly so I had a father figure and, by the time I was nine, I had a stepdad, Danny, a big East London personality who had loads of jobs, did a bit of painting and decorating, but was mostly a scrap metal dealer with a working man's white Transit van. Then I had a little sister.

The family set-up maybe made me an outsider. It maybe made me feel special. It maybe gave me the confidence to try and do something different with my life. Or think I could be a recording artist. I was the only boy and my mum always made me feel special. I'm still my mum's prince. But for years I grew up with a single parent, surrounded by amazing women, my aunties – even my mum's best friend lived with us for a while. It gave me a lot of respect for women and for mothers.

As a kid, I don't remember not singing. It's weird, because I don't sing now, ever. My mum's got a tape of me at five singing Kylie's 'I Should Be So Lucky' and 'Wouldn't Change a Thing'. And Stevie Wonder's 'Isn't She Lovely'. CDs were a big thing then and my family listened to loads of music, especially Motown – all the women dancing with their vodka and coke in their hands. My mum was into Fleetwood Mac, UB40, Kate Bush and so much soul. She and my nan and aunties loved Otis Redding, Stevie Wonder and The Supremes. My Aunty Sharon was obsessed with The Supremes: at parties she'd think she was Diana Ross. That's the stuff I loved.

We didn't have loads of money but I never went without. Because my family loved music so much and so did I, I even had my own record player for a while when I was only six. I had Michael Jackson on vinyl, loads of 7" singles and then, at ten, I had a ghetto blaster which I *loved* and bought loads of CDs for: Lauryn Hill, Brandy, Monica. And like every other kid at that age who wanted to sing, I was obsessed with Mariah Carey. And Whitney Houston. I spent my whole childhood in my bedroom because I wanted to be alone with my own music and books and thoughts. By the time I was a proper teenager it was always Black music I loved: American R&B and soul, Eric Benét and Donell Jones.

Not being funny, but I was a pretty kid, with blond hair and green eyes. I was the spit of my mum, a very attractive woman. When she was young, she had stunning eyes and ridiculously high cheekbones. I did some modelling as a kid for a Sanatogen billboard, and also for Toyota. I was only around six when I was in an *EastEnders* Christmas special where they went back to the Second World War and the blonde woman from *Birds of a Feather* played my mum. I got bullied at primary school but I think everyone did where I was from. The boys I went to school with could just about read and write and I was like my real dad, creative and insular. Amy was the same. She never mixed with her family, not because anything deep was going on, she was just a geek. We both were.

By the time I was eight, I'd already started going to theatre classes on Saturdays, in Plaistow in East London, just wanting to sing and learn about singing. I went to secondary school in East London as well, but only for a year. And then I was at Sylvia Young's Theatre School. It was all encouraged by my biological dad. I would see him every other weekend when he'd take me for a McDonald's. He felt bad about him and my mum splitting up, in particular knowing I was basically like him and was now growing up in this hard-nut fighting environment. He'd been in musicals, movies in Hong Kong – nothing big but always artistic. I missed him; we had quite a bond. I'd go to his on a Saturday and we'd play the piano. He knew the arts world and encouraged that side of me, he knew it was important. And he worried that if he didn't, by the time I was sixteen, I'd be another one involved in crime.

We were close and then, when I was around sixteen, our relationship came apart, like it typically does at that age. My dad was manic depressive, what we'd now call bipolar.

It became my big fear because I suffered from depression a lot when I was a teenager – I was afraid that I would be next. It was the same with my alcoholism. My dad never drank but my grandad, my dad's dad, who died before I was born, died of alcoholism. My great grandad did as well. Years later, when I was going through all my alcohol problems, my dad's view was: 'It's in your genes, it'll be a problem in your life.' Luckily, I've got a bit of my mum in me as well, the East London fighter. So I always thought, 'Hang on a minute – what? I'm doomed? Fuck that!' I know it can be genetic but I don't believe there's no way out of it.

Because my family owned a couple of pubs there were always parties. My nan made chicken curry for all the fellas at the bar and I'd just run around. Motown was always on. I didn't know anything about jazz, I only knew the obvious stuff, like Frank Sinatra's 'Fly Me to the Moon'. It was Amy who introduced me to jazz – she was a proper jazz scholar.

I don't know what it is that makes someone love music as much as we did. I think it's just in you. Being a singer was all I ever wanted to be from the age of four. I just knew I wanted to be an artist, I didn't want to be a boy in East London with a normal life and a nine-to-five job. I'd watch *Top of the Pops* and say, 'I wanna be on that one day, I wanna be like them'. I was headstrong, determined; I knew exactly what I wanted and was prepared to work hard for it. Everyone listens to music but not everyone is *obsessed* with it. Anyone who ends up with a record deal, your connection to music is just off the charts, it's *who you are*.

You don't end up going to Sylvia Young's when you're thirteen by accident.

CHAPTER 3

I knew about Sylvia Young's Theatre School through the Saturday stage school in Plaistow; if you're involved in the performing world in any way, and I was from a really young age, you know about Sylvia Young's and you know it's the best. If you're serious about becoming an artist in some way, and I was, that was *the* route. At ten I'd started going to Sylvia's part-time classes in Marylebone, central London, on a Saturday. It was brilliant, you got to spend the whole day there just singing and doing bits of drama. Sylvia herself would always be mooching about watching the talent. One Saturday, she walked in while I was singing a solo and she asked me if I wanted to go to the school full time. She liked my voice and suggested that I should. I didn't, straight away. We couldn't afford full time; it was £10,000 a term. My mum struggled to give me the £2 pocket money to go to secondary school every day.

The Stage newspaper gave an annual scholarship and 20,000 people would apply. I got an audition. The editor of *The Stage* was there, as well as Sylvia, along with the school's head of drama and head of singing – terrifying. I did a little modern acting piece with a northern accent from *Kes*, some sight reading, a piece of poetry and a dance routine which was so hideous Sylvia stopped me halfway through. I couldn't do *theatre*-type dancing and couldn't have cared less about *any* dancing. My last thing was singing and after the dancing embarrassment, Sylvia calmed me down, sat in her chair, put her elbows on her knees and announced, 'Oh, I'm looking forward to this!' I sang The Bangles' 'Eternal Flame' in my little unbroken voice, which my family called 'the voice of an angel'. I just liked that song the week of the audition. It was the mid-nineties and I couldn't have given a shit about Britpop; they weren't singers to me – I thought Liam Gallagher's voice was awful. Singing that Bangles song got me the scholarship.

It was hard for my parents to find the money for my posh school uniform and my mum had to give me a fiver every day for the travel card into central London. My real dad was worried he'd encouraged me into the most insecure profession there is and wished he'd encouraged the side of me that could've been a lawyer. He played a trick on me, to find out how determined I was: 'If you go I'll never speak to you again.'

'Fine!'

I was a very good student. At theatre school, there are people who are only creative and good at performing, and no good at maths or English. So that made me one of the brightest boys there. I got four A*s and four As in my GCSEs. There were certain exams, like science, where I'd get 100 per cent. Letters were sent to the school saying I was in the top one hundred of the highest-scoring pupils in the country for those exams. I ended up being head boy.

Monday, Tuesday, Wednesday we did academic stuff. Thursday and Friday was vocational – singing, dancing, acting – and in those classes you could be with kids older or younger, whatever stage they were at. We had a cool singing teacher called Ray Lamb who'd always say, 'Just do your own thing'.

One day he suggested recording 'Happy Birthday' for his nan. He picked two kids to sing it: one was me and the other was this tiny girl I'd never seen before. She was twelve, nearly thirteen, but she looked about nine, barely five feet with long dark hair, a little Jewish girl from north London. We were only in the same vocational class because we couldn't dance to save our lives – high kicks from the corner with big grins and jazz hands just weren't our thing. She stood up first. She was wearing what we all had to wear, the school uniform of grey trousers with a big V-neck jumper in what they called Lollipop Red. Then she started singing.

I could not believe my ears, or my eyes. This tiny girl was singing like a forty-year-old jazz veteran who drinks three bottles of whisky and smokes fifty Marlboro Reds a day. She probably *was* smoking Marlboro Reds already. Her voice was something else, like Nina Simone or Dinah Washington. Because I wasn't big on jazz, the only thing I'd heard like it was Marilyn Monroe singing 'Happy Birthday Mister President' to JFK. She finished her version and sat down. Then I got up and did my Stevie Wonder rendition.

When the class ended we walked out of the room together. I blurted it out, 'Who the fuck are you? Your voice is absolutely sick.'

She came right back.

'Your voice is absolutely mental.'

Those were our first words. I heard her sing before I heard her speak; it was love at first listen. Then it was love at first sight. You know how it is sometimes, you meet someone and it's instant, you click, it's like you've met before, like you were supposed to meet: *there* you are, where have you been? That's how I felt the day I met Amy. The day I met my soulmate. The girl you know as Amy Winehouse.

Our friendship blossomed instantly, not only fuelled by music but a deeper connection: we were both fucked-up teenagers and we saw that in each other. We were depressed, anxious, insecure. The biggest hole in Amy was her missing father, Mitch. Her parents split up when she was nine; her dad cheated on her mum, Janis, with a woman he knew at work, Jane, and all the family knew about it. Amy and her brother Alex used to call her 'Daddy's work wife' (she was to become his second wife). It wasn't just that, though. Most people at theatre schools like to show off, camera in their face, and Amy just wasn't like that, she was never happy-go-lucky, she was complicated, solitary and reclusive, like me. At lunchtime in the lunch hall – they called it the Green Room like you were at the BBC – you'd have kids learning their dance routines in one corner, other kids harmonizing in another corner and me and Amy would be sitting at some table just *depressed*. She'd say to me, 'You get depressed like me, don't yer?'

I was a very unhappy teenager with terrible acne who'd cry himself to sleep. I would sit on a chair at lunch breaks and put my head down on my arm on the table, hiding away from all the other kids with their over-the-top enthusiasm and full-beam teeth. Amy just had an understanding of me, like I had of her. We'd sit in the corner and she would play with my hair. I had blond curtains in the first year which went to the end of my nose, like Nick Carter from the Backstreet Boys but not stylish at all. The curtains were so long I'd tuck them behind my ears and Amy would pull out a bit of curtain and wrap it round her finger, round and round, like ringlets. She'd play with my legs too. Amy was obsessed with big legs. The boys at school did loads of dancing so they had muscular legs and I was six foot, the tallest boy in my class, bigger than the rest of them. She'd make a joke, kind of flirty, 'you've got lovely big legs!' But mine weren't the only boys' legs she played with. There was a black boy in my class called Junior, he had *very* big legs and she definitely played with his!

She was gifted, ridiculously smart. She loved words: Amy would watch *Countdown* and get every single conundrum right. She'd sit by herself doing Sudoku, faster than anybody else, was always doing word puzzles, book after book. She occupied her mind, she needed stimulus or her thoughts would wander off to some naughty place, like what boy she fancied or what tattoo she might get or if she would dye her hair pink. Where I was academic, Amy wasn't interested. She was a rebel, which pissed off the headmaster, Mr Muir. He was Scottish and thought he was gorgeous, like Sean Connery. Amy came in one day with her nose pierced. I asked her if she'd got it done in Camden.

'Nah, I did it myself, just put some ice cubes on it.'

I was tall and she was so short that I'd sling her over my shoulder and carry her around for a laugh. Amy fancied me at first but then Amy fancied loads of boys. She was in love with love. She kept this book at school of compatibility ratings with notes for the boys in our age group, rated one to ten. Mine said: 'He's perfect, he likes music.' I had a girlfriend at school called Claire so at the end she put, 'but he's with Claire!' so my rating dropped to nothing. She still had that notebook in the house years later; we'd read over it, pissing ourselves laughing.

It's not like romantic thoughts didn't cross our minds. Trying to define what we were, friendship is not the right word. I can only describe it as soulmates: she loved me and I loved her. We were like non-blood brother and sister, but also like I was her dad and she was my mum. Something in my gut told me I had to look after her, like I had a responsibility. We just made each other make sense. We weren't normal teenagers and there was an understanding that relationships would come and go, but I was her boy, she was my girl and we'd be there for each other forever. It was like that all through Amy's life.

I'd always felt different to everybody else and the first time I didn't feel that way was the day I met Amy. I thought, *I'm actually not that weird, am I? I'm nothing like my cousins, nothing like the other boys in my area, but there's nothing wrong with me, cos you're just like me. And it's OK to be fucked up, we're both sound and we've got each other.*

She was also really funny, she'd do impersonations of everyone, a comedy Jewish one of Sylvia and a brilliant one of our speech teacher Jacqui Stoker going mental. She was a great teacher but if you didn't pronounce your 't's at the end of a word she'd flip out.

Most of the kids were into their show tunes and so were the singing teachers. There were three of them as well as Ray Lamb, the one who picked me and Amy to sing 'Happy Birthday' and he was the only one who'd encourage ad-libs and freestyle. All the others were about technique and singing 'Why, God, Why?' from *Miss Saigon* and 'There Is a Castle on a Cloud' from *Les Mis* and all that bollocks. He'd always ask me and Amy to freestyle. We did a cabaret show at school and ex-pupils came back to watch it – Emma Bunton, the boyband Damage – and while everyone else was singing Michael Jackson's 'Earth Song', bawling 'What about us!?', I came out and ad-libbed all over it, riffing, and then Amy did her thing, jazz ad-libs, off-the-scale harmonies, mooching around on stage in her black joggers and white Sylvia Young t-shirt, sounding like someone from the forties. No one else was like her.

We did loads of cabarets together. Whenever there was some soiree at the Dorchester Hotel we'd be asked to do a big cabaret. The whole school rehearsed and rehearsed and we'd rehearse our little off-the-wall solos. Then we'd hide away from everybody else; I'd shoot out and get a box of twenty nuggets from McDonald's and we'd eat them in the corner by ourselves.

Another thing she loved was the school lighting box. There was a main room downstairs where shows were put on, it wasn't a theatre but the closest we had, with a ladder at one end. You went up the ladder to this big box at the back where the technical guy controlled all the lights. That was the lighting box, it was the only private space in the school and it was known as The Place. And that's where you went to get off with someone. Just snogging, being a teenager. Amy was up and down that ladder more than most!

By fifteen, I was changing. I couldn't get out of bed and started to turn up late every day. My mum would come into my room at night and sometimes I'd be crying, saying I just didn't want to wake up in the morning. *Proper* depression, something chemically wrong. It terrified my mum and she shared that information with my real dad, a manic depressive on antidepressants and, just like he said about the alcoholism in his family, he responded, 'Well, he's my son, his head's starting to go, he probably needs tablets.' He took me to a doctor who suggested antidepressants, but it didn't happen and there was a hoo-ha about it. My mum, in her East End way, wasn't having it: 'Fackin' hell, what d'you mean putting him on tablets? He's fifteen!'

Amy was put on antidepressants at fourteen. It wasn't my place to say, but I don't think fourteen-year-olds should be. I don't know if they helped her or not but she wanted to go back on them in the future so perhaps they did. All I know is that she was taught at a young age that chemicals were how you fix your head. Not 'go and talk to somebody'.

Amy had been put up a year because she was so bright but

she didn't care about academia. She was too intelligent and got bored. I understood that. I took my maths GCSE two years early, teaching myself at home because you weren't pushed enough there. So Amy stopped doing well. She was under-achieving and Mr Muir thought she needed to go to a normal school. He suggested to Janis and her stepdad she could be an intellectual. She was asked to leave and they agreed to it. Amy was really unhappy about it, she liked the school, she liked the discipline and it was full of nutters in its way. There's a myth that Amy was expelled, and she never was, because Sylvia would never have asked her to leave, it was all from Mr Muir, who Amy never got on with. And I don't know how she wangled it but she never did go to a normal school after that, she went to BRIT School in Croydon – the one the media called Britain's Fame School – and told me she thought it was shit. I found out years later Sylvia was furious about Amy leaving, that she'd rung Janis to ask her to rethink, convinced Amy wouldn't be happy elsewhere. And she was right.

After she left Sylvia Young's we got even closer, it was like being forced apart made us appreciate each other even more.

We'd spend weekends in her room, which was in the base-ment of her stepdad's house in Totteridge & Whetstone. The room was a converted garage and her mum, stepdad, step-brother and stepsister were all upstairs. She was like Cinderella, the odd one out, the rebellious character in a serious, conven-tional family. I used to climb through her bedroom window, sneaking in, because her stepdad was strict and would never let a boy go round a girl's house at eight at night, even though we were just friends. He was like a Victorian dad almost, he'd knock on the door every five minutes, 'Turn the music down!'

while they were watching *Question Time* upstairs. Most of the time he didn't know I was there. A couple of times he caught me and turfed me out. He wouldn't have a go at me, he'd have a go at Amy, 'I told you, no boys are allowed in this room! Get out!' We'd just laugh. Sometimes I'd wait round the corner for half an hour and sneak back in through the window again. We'd listen to our idols, jam together and 'self-medicate', as it's called now. We were just being teenagers: guitar in one hand, a drink or a spliff in the other.

I was still at Sylvia's, she was at BRIT School and every night after school we'd talk on the phone about music, her parents' divorce, everything. Mobile phones were new and free after six o'clock so we'd sit on the phone from six till midnight. I was a terrible insomniac and Amy would sing me to sleep every single Friday night; it was like a way of starting the weekend. 'I'm Only Sleeping' by The Beatles. Or her favourite, 'So Far Away' by Carole King.

I was friends with her other close friends too. Amy had been best friends, like sisters, with a girl called Juliette Ashby since they were four years old. They went to the same primary school, Osidge, and by age ten invented a little hip-hop duo Sweet 'n' Sour – Amy called them the white, Jewish Salt-N-Pepa. There was another good friend from that primary school, Lauren Gilbert, who was like the baby of our circle, whose stepgrandad was Amy's great uncle, so they were like cousins. We were all close and hung around together all the time, from fifteen, even more so when I left Sylvia's at sixteen. Juliette was a singer too and we were all into Eric Benét, Boys II Men and Brandy. My mum would always chuck me a tenner at the weekend and we'd all go out for a meal.

Amy had a very heathy attitude towards food back then. She loved Chinese and a tapas restaurant in Camden we always went to, Jamon Jamon. There were sleepovers and house parties at each other's family homes and it was obvious even then how me and Amy were different: people would have two Bacardi Breezers and be smashed; we'd be drinking vodka straight from the bottle. We just had that nature. And at that age it's funny.

Where I'm from every family had a static caravan, you went on weekend holidays, you never went abroad and I loved it. Ours was in Clacton-on-Sea. Every Friday in the summer season I'd get in my stepdad's van, lie under a blanket and we'd head to the caravan site, a proper seaside caravan park with arcades. The very first time I drank was in that caravan, I was thirteen, with a bottle of K cider and it felt absolutely brilliant. It was the very first time in my life I felt aaah, everything's alright now.

Amy started drinking before me, she was maybe twelve, she was smoking weed the whole time I knew her. By fifteen, sixteen, when we were depressed, we'd have bottles of Hooch at sleepovers and we'd recognize we weren't depressed anymore, at least temporarily. For Amy especially, chemicals were now always the answer, I'd tell her I was really depressed and she'd say, 'Come to mine tomorrow and we'll have a drink, have a spliff.' She was like that forever. If these things made you feel better, why wouldn't you?

One night we all got in someone's bed. Lauren, Juliette and Amy used to spoon. Because they were all a bit Jewish they called it Bumschnigs. That sleepover, we were *all* Bumschniging – me, the three girls and another boy. We were sixteen, seventeen and just passed out. The next morning, when everyone else was up and back in the living room, Amy walked into the bedroom and this party girl I didn't know was leaning over me with her tits hanging out. Amy went mental. 'You're disgusting!'

She kicked her out and they had a proper fight. She was always looking out for me, like I looked out for her. A couple of years later we'd be out clubbing and because I was such a bad insomniac, I'd randomly fall asleep and Amy would always say, 'Come and sleep on my lap.' We'd be in a corner in a little booth and she'd protect me, wouldn't let anyone come near me, she'd shout over the music, 'Don't you come near this boy, don't you realize he never sleeps?!'

We were both very distinct characters. Where she was rebellious, I was a lost soul, but in deeper ways we were so similar, two complex introverts obsessed with music. My mum always used to say we were 'two peas in a pod', meaning we were inseparable, like two very different peas living in exactly the same pod! We even had a Jewish connection: my real dad's Jewish and my mum isn't, so I'm not, but my real name is Kenneth Gordon and Gordon was Amy's nan Cynthia's maiden name. That was a big thing when I first went round to Cynthia's. I was sixteen, seventeen, coming out of my ugly acne phase, and Cynthia said, 'He looks like that DiCaprio boy!' I thought, *I fucking love this woman*.

Amy loved her nan, Mitch's mum, and Cynthia loved me, she'd cook Jewish dinners for me on a Friday night, salt beef and latkes, a cross between a roast potato and a chip, lovely. Amy called her nan Cynthie, she lived in a little maisonette in Finchley ten minutes away from Amy's. She was tiny like Amy, with big hair, not a beehive but bountiful, glamorous hair. I can still see us now, getting off the bus in Finchley, me and Amy, like two little scallywags going up to this maisonette on the high street, going into the kitchen and there's this woman cooking and she's done up to the nines. Full make-up, black hair, a black dress on with sequins and sparkles, smoking a fag. She was stunning, like a movie star, like Joan Collins in *Dynasty*. And classy with it, not like she was trying to look younger than her age. A lovely, very good-looking older woman who put herself together so well, even to cook salt beef – she really was something else. She'd been a singer herself and Amy liked to remind me Cynthia had gone out with the famous London jazz club owner Ronnie Scott. That's where Amy got her fifties pin-up girl obsession from, she looked up to her nan more than anyone.

Amy was much closer to her nan than to her mum, who was lovely but a very mild-mannered personality, Amy's complete opposite. Amy could've rung Cynthia up and said, 'Nan I had sex last night and now I'm pregnant,' knowing her nan would listen without judgement and help. She couldn't do that with her mum, she just wasn't open and modern like that. My first dinner with Cynthia was also the first time I met Amy's Aunty Mel – she was so beautiful, like the woman in the Scottish Widows advert – and Mitch, who was sitting at the table with his big belly and his big personality – funny, like you'd expect from a London cabbie. Him and Amy had a good banter between them, normal dad and daughter stuff. Amy brought all the food in and me and Mitch felt like kings that night, the only boys there being fussed over and fed by women.

Amy would come to mine in Canning Town and stay over sometimes when my mum was away for the weekend in the caravan. By sixteen I'd grown out of the caravan, so me and Amy stayed indoors playing computer games; she'd smoke her spliff and we'd have little parties. She even stayed over when my mum was there, I'd sleep on the couch. The first time she was there my mum asked her to sing to her, in the living room, while she was having her usual breakfast: a boiled egg and a fag. She asked Amy to sing 'Fly Me to the Moon', the only jazz song she knew. Amy smashed it and my mum was shouting 'Oh my God!' They just clicked. Amy knew she could tell my mum anything and they had conversations about things Amy wouldn't even talk to me about: in years to come, a lot about Blake.

MY AMY

If Amy stayed over at mine when my mum was away we'd sleep in my bed and she'd sing me *awake*. The loveliest way to wake up, with her sitting on the edge of my bed, singing. It would usually be Carole King's 'So Far Away'.

That became our song.

CHAPTER 4

In the last fifteen years it's been possible, even encouraged, to be famous for no reason, to be 'famous for being famous'. You can be famous for being an idiot now. When me and Amy were teenagers that didn't exist – you had to have a talent for something. Amy never wanted to be famous but she wanted to be successful and to be an artist. I was the same. So in a way, we kind of did want recognition, but Amy *definitely* didn't want to be as famous as she became.

Theatre school normalizes the idea of fame. Your mate at school who can't add ten and eight is suddenly on *Top of the Pops*, so you don't think there's anything special about anybody famous. Sylvia's probably created more famous pop stars than most in the mid–late nineties era – Emma Bunton in the Spice Girls; the Appleton sisters and Melanie Blatt in All Saints.

It also makes you grow up fast. You get up every day, commute maybe ninety minutes into central London, have lessons all day, finish at four, then between four and six you have auditions. It makes you disciplined. Casting directors came to our school as it was easier than bringing us to them. People putting a boyband together would come and see our sixteen-year-old boys. At thirteen, when I went from pretty blond child model to ugly acne boy, it really affected me. I hated having my picture taken, I had panic attacks, grew my hair really long. Then, suddenly, at sixteen, when my acne cleared up, it was a given I'd be in a boyband. I could sing and I was alright looking. I was in the same class as Lee Ryan, who went on to be in Blue, and John Lee from S Club 7. I got lots of boyband offers, I could very easily have been in Blue. But by now I was into my music seriously, with an attitude: *No way I'm gonna be some shitty little pop star in a boyband.* Amy was like that too, even though behind all that attitude we were just insecure, had no confidence: the kind of people who never would've gone on stage or sung in a studio without alcohol.

Billie Piper was in our class, who did the *Smash Hits* advert where she popped a piece of bubble gum and ended up with a record deal. She really wanted to be an actress and no wonder: she must have been the worst singer in the school. Everyone was shocked. 'How's Billie got a record deal?!' I've heard a journalist say Amy was into being weird at school, pretending to be a witch, and she put spells on Billie Piper. Brilliant story but it's not true!

When you leave Sylvia Young's you're still on their books, so they're like your agent. This young guy, Nick Shymansky, was looking for a singer, his first find as an A&R Talent Scout. He was working for Brilliant PR who did the publicity for the Spice Girls. Nick was basically the teaboy hoping to get into A&R, like his uncle Lucian Grainge, who was (and still is) head of the major label conglomerate Universal Music Group. Sylvia played him my tape and he took me on straight away. I suddenly had a manager and started going to studios and meeting producers. Nick was two years older than me and seemed about twenty years older, like a dad, he was never youthful. He was sensible, responsible, he had a *mortgage*. We'd all be kipping on sofas and he had his own flat in Bayswater. He was never boring though, he was so passionate about music. Even if he'd have one drink and fall to pieces.

Amy, meanwhile, was still in the basement at her stepdad's smoking too much weed. I begged her for a tape of her singing. I'd tell Nick about Amy and he'd roll his eyes, thinking if she was a jazz singer she must be 'a bit jazz hands'. I knew how talented she was. She was still only sixteen but I knew she needed to be an artist, knew she needed some direction and so I begged her again, for months and *months*. Eventually she made a tape and sent it to my mum's house, singing jazz stand-ards she'd recorded with the National Youth Jazz Orchestra, who she'd worked with for a few months on Sylvia's recom-mendation. I played it to Nick in his car and he was blown away, said she was 'off the charts unique'. He wanted to meet her and I set up an introduction near the Brilliant office, in Turnham Green park. She got off the train, met us, he did his spiel, 'I wanna be your manager, I can really develop your sound' and they started talking, so I left them to it. When I came back Nick looked weird, Amy got up to leave and basically went in and snogged him! Nothing else happened though, they got over it and Nick was now her manager. She was still so young I think her parents had to give permission. I can imagine Mitch would've been excited about it.

I've often thought about that chain of events, how me badger-ing Amy to make that tape led to her being discovered. How without that tape the public might never have heard of her. But that means it led to everything else, too.

Simon Fuller, the man who managed the Spice Girls and who created *Pop Idol* in 2001 – which pretty much invented all the contemporary TV talent shows – had a management company, 19 Entertainment. Fuller merged 19 with Brilliant PR and auto-matically began overseeing everyone on the Brilliant roster.

Loads of people lost their jobs but Fuller was interested in keeping Nick because Nick had me and Amy. I was signed to 19 first in 2001, Amy in 2002, so Simon Fuller was now our overall management boss. He was a very powerful man and I was excited to meet him, and nervous. He was lovely and he knew his shit, he was the kind of persuasive entrepreneur who'd say, 'When you've had your first No. 1 . . .' and you believed him. Back then, you *made* stuff happen; it's not like that now. If you had a powerful manager you had the best chance of being massive. As long as you got on the right radio station and *CD:UK* on a Saturday morning, you'd probably smash it.

I was well into jazz by now, through Amy, and Fuller had an idea: the two of us would star in a jazz movie set in the 1950s. We even rehearsed for it for four days in a pub in Putney, pissed on Jack Daniel's, singing jazz standards all day while Simon Fuller's minions filmed us. The idea just disappeared, like lots of grand ideas do.

Amy wasn't ambitious. She would've sat in her room playing guitar, singing and smoking weed for the rest of her life. Nick would spend a good two hours trying to coax Amy out of bed to get her to the studio. She just loved smoking weed. And it had to be what she called 'natural weed', nothing synthetic, definitely no hard drugs. I'd tried pills a couple of times, which didn't agree with me, and Amy told me off.

'You don't do that!' she scolded. 'Don't do chemical, only do natural.'

'Oh yeah, Amy and the first thing you do in the morning is roll a spliff.'

'Yeah but that *is* natural.'

That was her stance at the time, she was righteous: do not do hard drugs. *Do not, do not, do not, do not!*

We were both going to studios, writing and recording. I was

sent off to work in a shed in someone's back garden in Perivale in residential Ealing. Through Nick, I sang for producers Danny D and Tim Blacksmith, who managed the Norwegian songwriting duo Stargate, who've since worked with Beyoncé and Sam Smith. I sang Stevie Wonder's 'Isn't She Lovely', which I'd been singing since I was five, and three days later I was on a plane to a studio in Norway. It was my first proper studio experience, my first plane to another country, my first songs produced by professionals instead of jamming in a shed. Simon Fuller was having new ideas, saying I needed to be a proper pop star. Amy needed to go down the cool, interesting jazz route but me – and by this point I'm changing, I'm nineteen, a pretty white boy who sings like a black boy – I was the commercial one. It's hilarious to me now: *I* was the money shot!

Amy was offered a publishing deal with Guy Moot at EMI for £240,000. Suddenly she was financially independent, she moved out of her family basement and rented a flat in Finchley with Juliette. I pretty much lived there too. Amy was eighteen, I was nineteen, the start of us living together. Juliette had a boyfriend, she was out a lot, but when we were all in together we'd jam and sing and play music, drinking, Amy smoking weed (I never liked weed) – just normal kids loving their first burst of freedom.

Amy then signed her deal with Island Records. Another £250,000. She was terrible with money and behaved like most people would do at that age, like she'd won the lottery. It was 2002: the wise thing to do with that kind of money would've been to buy a little apartment in Shoreditch that would now be worth two million. But you don't. You do what Amy did – you buy a load of Louboutin shoes, a load of dresses, endless guitars and music books, you order expensive Chinese and Indian food, buy a spectrum of Superhero dolls and comics and all the shit you like because you're a geek and you're nineteen.

Amy loved a bath. The Finchley flat had a big, spacious bath and she was always in there with a face mask on, a hair mask on, exfoliating her skin. She could spend £80 in Boots in minutes. One guitar she bought she called Cherry – there's a song about it on her debut album *Frank*. She wasn't great on guitar, so she bought chord books and the two she learned from most were *The Beatles' Greatest Hits* and *Carole King Tapestry*. She'd still sing those songs to me, The Beatles 'I'm Only Sleeping' and Carole King's 'So Far Away', but now she could accompany herself properly on guitar.

With her new record deal Amy was in her element. She was finally away from her family and could be what she always wanted to be: *free*.

CHAPTER 5

In 2001, the first series of *Pop Idol* brought in the era of Simon Cowell. People said to Simon Fuller at the time, when I was newly signed to 19, 'Why don't you just put Tyler in the show and make him win it?' Of course he couldn't really do that but I still worried about it. I was ambitious but I wanted to be a proper artist. *Popstars: The Rivals*, which produced Hear'Say, had been so successful I knew this new show would be massive too. Fuller teased me. 'No Tyler, it won't affect what you're doing. I promise you I won't let a boy win. I want a girl to win.'

The first series of *Pop Idol* was won by Will Young.

I had a production deal with 19 which meant I was making music for him and was in development working with other artists. I used to see Fuller every week but when *Pop Idol* took off, I just wasn't as relevant to him anymore. I also went to college for a year, Duff Miller in South Kensington, opposite the Natural History Museum. It's private and seriously posh, most people go on from there to Oxbridge. I won a scholarship for there too, through my GCSE results, and studied English literature, theatre studies and maths. I was determined to do my own thing while still working with 19 but, by year two, I'd already been recording in a multimillion-pound studio in Norway with Stargate. I got three As in my mock

A-levels and dropped out. I'd made my mind up: I was going to be *an artist*.

I had several publishing deals offered to me that Simon Fuller turned down, including a £500,000 deal. He said, 'Don't do it, we'll wait till it's a million.' I believed him entirely. I thought that by the time I was twenty-six, I'd be able to retire and travel the world. The industry was like that then. After Britpop and dance music in the nineties, in the noughties pop was now the dominant force again. Daniel Bedingfield wrote the garage single 'Gotta Get Through This' and Sony gave him a million quid publishing deal. That wasn't unusual.

I loved pop music. I had a real admiration for a catchy song, for songwriting pop genius. I'd go to the studio and try to write a hit. Amy wasn't like that at all. She'd be in the studio writing about the fella she was fucking or the argument she'd had with her friend. She was always writing things down – diaries, poetry, plays, doodles. She really liked *Sex and the City* and she wrote songs about the show. She also wrote a song called 'Tyler in Cashmere', about dressing me up in a cashmere jumper – I've still got it. The song was about how great life could be. These songs were her learning process. None of them were recorded, she was just writing and writing and writing.

We were both obsessed with Lauryn Hill. Salaam Remi co-produced The Fugees album *The Score* in 1996 and Commissioner Gordon was the engineer on *The Miseducation of Lauryn Hill* in 1998. Now, through Island, Amy was working on her debut with Salaam and Commissioner Gordon, flying off to America.

Fuller could see I was good at writing pop songs for other people. I could see music in mathematical sequences and I could use the Pro Tools software programme. He was also looking after Cathy Dennis and he started seeing me as that kind of songwriter, grooming me to be his male Cathy Dennis. I was only around twenty so his thinking was, I'd do that for two years and then afterwards become an artist. It was a good way of breaking an artist too, becoming known at a young age for working on other people's songs.

In 2002, I was sent round the world with Nick, to America, Europe. I was a jobbing songwriter working with Merlin in Sweden, who wrote for Jennifer Lopez; I did a week's writing with Robyn when she was an unknown songwriter and wrote with Rob Fusari, who'd worked with early Destiny's Child. *Pop Idol* had now evolved into *American Idol*. Kelly Clarkson won the first series and a guy called Justin Guarini came second, and Fuller gave me the job of writing and producing half of Justin's first album, even though I thought he was totally up his own arse. He was doing the American Idol tour so whatever city he was in, I'd go there. In the end Simon took all the work I'd done for him back; my second single, 'Foolish', came out of that. I felt good about my life, I was a jobbing songwriter flying all over the world and Simon Fuller paid for everything. Brilliant!

Me and Nick used to sit in our hotel rooms all over America and fantasize about the future, everything seemed possible then. We fantasized about when Nick would be a big manager and I'd be a massive artist. And today he *is* what he fantasized about – he always knew what he wanted to do. He always knew me and Amy were a bit fucked up, though, even before the chaos began. He'd say, 'You two should have therapy.' He'd say about my younger self, when he first met me, 'It's funny man, I always used to think you were gonna top yourself any day.' That was his joke! He saw me as the most fragile person. Before I came out of myself through drinking and being creative, I was an insecure little mess. The first gigs I did, I used to get told off –

'Open your eyes!' I *couldn't* open my eyes, I didn't want to see the people. Amy was the same. We liked singing, Amy liked strumming her guitar but we didn't want to do it in front of anyone else. Then we started drinking and it solved it all.

The next year, me and Amy were both working in America and Nick came too. I was working with a few people, including the girl who came third on the first *American Idol*, Nikki McKibbin, and Amy was working with Commissioner Gordon in New Jersey and Salaam Remi in Miami on the music that would become *Frank*. Nick coordinated it so we'd all be in the same place at the same time. Salaam was based in Miami and that's where I'd work with Nikki, so we were in Miami for weeks, staying in The Raleigh, this ridiculously glamorous art deco hotel. Amy chose it because it's in a big scene in *The Birdcage* with Robin Williams, a movie about drag queens and Amy was obsessed with drag queens, she loved gay culture. Right next to the hotel was the beach. We were in the studio every day and out every night clubbing. There was so much Miami night life; we were young, our heads were full of R&B and hip hop, we had a convertible company car and we were driven around.

We were obsessed with the film *Sister Act 2*, where Lauryn Hill first became a star. The little boy in it who sings the high notes, Ryan Toby, was in the group City High and I worked with him too, he was now a writer and producer and wrote a lot of Will Smith's music when he was huge. He had this mansion villa on the beach and, after a day in the studio, we'd be driven round to his in the convertible. Amy would smoke weed, we'd go out for dinner, then a club, have a few drinks and then go back to the studio and start recording in the middle of the night. Or we'd get back to the hotel, where Amy's guitar and lyric book would come out, she'd roll her spliff and we'd all jam.

One night, me and Amy wrote a duet together on the beach called 'Best for Me'. We'd written together professionally once before, in the studio in London, two songs that eventually went on my debut album, one called 'Procrastination', which was about not wanting to be in the studio and another, 'Long Day', which was about . . . it being a long day in the studio! We worked well together: I was all melody first, whereas Amy was all poetry first. But being on the beach made it all so special, next to the lapping ocean at four in the morning, me drinking, Amy smoking weed – you don't get to do that very often, you're usually in some dungeon in East London. We went back to the studio, recorded it and I was so pissed I couldn't even put my vocal down. She scolded me: 'For fuck's sake T, we'll do it tomorrow!' I went outside at 6 a.m. and passed out in the convertible with the top down. It was all so lovely, being young and creative and free like that. We'd stay up all night on the beach to watch the sunrise, me, Amy and Nick, going to bed after dawn. Everything just felt perfect.

One of the people we were working with took me to a hotel once to see his friends. They were all sniffing coke in the middle of the day. I was stunned. They offered me some and I said no, I'd never taken cocaine and I never thought I would. Especially not in the afternoon! Two and half years later that would be my life. *Perfectly normal.*

There were stupid nights out. There was an *American Idol* movie made, *From Justin to Kelly*, typical Simon Fuller trying to rinse every penny out of it, a hopeless musical romantic comedy which won four Golden Raspberries for Worst Movie. But we all went down to watch the last scene being filmed, met Kelly Clarkson and went on to the wrap party. There was a blonde girl there who worked with Simon Fuller, she wanted to meet his English crowd and Nick had a crush on her. The party had a free bar, and me and Amy were all excited: 'It's free, let's get absolutely fucked!' Nick had to be the sensible one, the manager, but because he fancied this girl we decided to ruin him, embarrass him, knowing if he had two drinks he'd be slaughtered.

We plied him with drink, which was really wrong, he looked so irresponsible. Me and Amy had to literally carry him back to his hotel room between us, one arm around him each, all lopsided because Amy was so much shorter than me, dragging his feet along the corridor. We laid him down on his bed and dressed him up in Amy's headscarf, her pink woolly cardigan and a big pair of sunglasses. And took pictures, as evidence. He was really sick the next day, he couldn't even *speak,* he was vomiting, the lot, which me and Amy found hilarious.

We were chancers, too. One night in New Jersey, we all decided to ring up Clive Davis, the American music industry big-wig, who was CEO of RCA Music Group at the time. I'd written a song with Rob Fusari the year before in America, 'She Doesn't Even Know I'm Alive', which sounded like a Christina Aguilera hit, we all thought it was brilliant, so did Simon Fuller. Nick decided he would ring up Clive Davis, pretend to be Simon Fuller and get him to agree to listen to it. He got the number, was giving it the spiel, 'I've managed the Spice Girls, I've got this cool young white guy, sounds like a black guy,' and the receptionist said, 'OK, I'll put you through to Clive . . .' Nick panicked: 'Oh God I've gotta sound professional!' So to make it seem authentic, he put the phone on hold and said, 'Amy, you should be my receptionist.' She was well up for it, got on the phone and said in this posh voice, 'Hi, yes, my name's Sandra, I'll just put Simon Fuller through now . . .' He agreed to listen to it when we sent it and we thought Clive Davis would ring me up the next day and give me two million quid. We never heard back!

Simon Fuller was well pissed off with us, especially with Nick: 'You don't do that, you don't pretend to be me!' I was twenty, my thinking had been, 'I'm getting old, I'm not a teenager anymore, I *have* to make things happen.' Me and Nick were fiercely ambitious – and Amy just wasn't.

Everything happens so fast in that world. You don't have time to think about how different reality is, to how it was just a year ago. In 2003, Amy and me were driving around Miami in a convertible, top down, both with deals, working with these talented people, making our own money. Amy was out buying shoes and dresses every day; we went to all the fancy delis and restaurants and bars and parties. Two years before this, I was in my council house in East London. Amy, similarly to me, was beginning to lose touch with all her other friends. You start to live in a different world because you just don't get to see anyone from your previous life. You're thousands of miles away, you're out clubbing, drinking, shopping and in the studio every day.

In Miami, I saw Amy come into herself. To me, she was always mature for her age. The day I met her she seemed like an old soul trapped in a kid's body, trapped in a basement in this alien house with a strict stepdad, looking around her as a teenager thinking, 'What is this bullshit?' What Amy wanted and needed was independence. And now she finally had it. She had money, confidence and she looked amazing too. She had big tits, an arse, she was fit and sexy, buying dresses that showed it all off. In her *attitude* she was sexy. One of the biggest videos in the world since the late 90s was 'Genie in a Bottle' by

Christina Aguilera, who had the body of a teenage boy, nothing womanly and sexy about that, and now so many female pop stars were skinny twiglets. When Amy walked down the street in Miami, swinging her shopping bags in her dresses and high heels, men couldn't take their eyes off her.

In New Jersey, where she was recording with Commissioner Gordon, we watched the Grammys together in the hotel where we were staying. The three of us were sitting on the edge of the bed, Amy in the middle, right in front of the TV. Norah Jones won loads that year and it prompted me and Nick to have a massive argument about the sudden decline in the Grammys generally and Alicia Keys specifically, who'd won five Grammys the year before. I thought Alicia Keys was good but she wasn't as good as everyone said she was. Myself and Nick didn't disagree about much but when we did, we really did: we're both passionate and stubborn. This time, before we knew it, we were calling each other cunts, standing either side of the bed, pointing at each other. I threw the hotel phone at him and we swung at each other. By now, tiny Amy was standing on the bed so she'd be the same height as us, arms outstretched, right in the middle, shouting 'Break it up, boys!' like a Jewish mother. She *loved* that role, looking after misbehaving men.

When we went to delis after the studio at five in the morning, Amy would make sure every boy had his meal and his salt and pepper pots – me, Nick, Salaam sometimes – she was always mothering, it was the way she was brought up. In the morning at the hotel when me and Nick went down for breakfast, Amy would be putting our breakfasts out on a plate. At restaurants, with the crew from the studio and sometimes Salaam's dad, she was always the only girl with loads of boys and she'd make sure everything was right.

One time, we were in a restaurant where they cook the food

in front you and I was really tetchy about it because they served seafood. I've always had a severe fish phobia and I can't control how I'll react to it, I've been in restaurants before where someone's put a lobster head on my plate and I've tipped the table over. Amy being Amy decided to tell Salaam about it. Salaam is a lovely guy, like a living teddy bear and also a bit of a joker. Salaam picked up a crab – Amy put him up to it – he put it on my shoulder and started playing with the crab in my face. I flipped out, smashed everything on the table in front of me, freaked out crying. Amy was *pissing herself.* I left the restaurant, went out into the parking lot and had to sit on a wall, I was shaking. Amy came out, trying to hold in her laughter, and sat down beside me. 'T, I'm soooo sorry . . .' She was still mothering me – even though it was her fault!

The whole Miami trip was some of the best times we ever had. I saw her turning into the person she always wanted to be. The person she *really* was.

CHAPTER 6

Mitch started to reappear in Amy's life, a lot. She'd always wanted to live in Camden because she thought it was the coolest place on the planet. Now she was buying her first Camden home, a one-bedroom, top-floor flat in a little mews called Jeffrey's Place, on the border of Kentish Town, the rougher end of Camden. It was officially a two-bedroom flat but the second bedroom was the size of a Rizla – with no bed in it – it was a box-room full of rails of clothes. Buying property was not the kind of thing Amy would do – she would've happily rented – so Mitch had gotten involved, which was sensible. Amy had money now.

We didn't see much of her mum, Janis, maybe at the odd gig with her husband. She was diagnosed with MS in 2003 and there was an understanding from then on that sometimes Amy's mum just wasn't that well. There was no judgement towards her for that obviously, and all I knew was that she was very floaty on the rare occasions I saw her. I felt sorry for Janis, it probably had an effect on her and Amy's relationship but much less so than the fact they were just completely different types of people.

Amy loved Jeffrey's Place, everything about it showed her character. In the living room, she hung portraits above the mantelpiece in different-sized frames: vintage *Vogue* covers, including a Marilyn Monroe, some family snaps and fashion illustrations.

Her VHS video collection included the very first video single, Madonna's 'Justify My Love' (so good it was banned by MTV in 1991) and Marilyn Monroe's 1956 film *Bus Stop*. She loved Marilyn, and had one of those rectangular mirrors embossed with Marilyn's face.

Her bookshelves were always full, from Hunter S. Thompson, Bukowski and Dostoyevsky to Jackie Collins, Dr Seuss and Claudia Rosen's *The Book of Jewish Food* – the book she learned to make Jewish chicken soup from. There was a suitcase of family photos and another silver case filled with CDs and vintage vinyl, including film soundtracks like *Dr Zhivago*, loads of jazz (her brother Alex introduced her to Thelonious Monk, who she loved), Frank Sinatra, Sarah Vaughan and *Remember Marilyn*, released in 1972, the first vinyl compilation of Marilyn Monroe's music. Her Superhero dolls were on display on the bookshelves too, alongside her prized collection of WWF figures.

She was obsessed with Smeg fridges and there was one in the kitchen which she covered in stickers of 1950s pin-up girls, long before her pin-up girl tattoos. She still had puzzle books on the go, lying around the flat, and she still watched *Countdown*. When it came on, she used to jump up off the sofa to sing the opening theme tune – doo-roo, doo-roo, doodle-oo-doo, dum! – and do a stupid dance to it, wiggling her bum. I'd stay there loads, usually sleeping on the couch, which is what insomniacs do anyway.

Every day, she'd go out and buy fresh flowers from a Camden flower stall and go shopping round the market. She would regularly bring back moody Calvin Klein boxers for me, and every day she'd have a sunbed. There was a sunbed place on Parkway and she was good mates with the girl who ran it. Amy was naturally very pale but she always looked brown as a berry, everywhere. She'd tell me she'd literally bend herself over, split herself every single way so the UV light would hit, as she'd say, 'every single part'. I wondered what she meant and she took a picture to show me. She'd spread her bum cheeks – not so I could see her arsehole, she wasn't that crude! – so it would get in there. The whole picture was violet and she only had her goggles on, smiling. Sometimes she'd come out after *hours* in there, knowing she'd gone too far, and say, 'I look like a Barbie gone wrong!'

Amy was a real character and that's exactly what was missing from the original photo shoot for *Frank*. Amy and Nick were really unhappy with it, the photographer just didn't get her. He'd tried to make her look pretty, and fashiony, just boring, no personality – this wasn't the girl who wrote 'Fuck Me Pumps' in Miami. He'd taken photos in a launderette, which was too obvious. Me and Amy always used to go to the launderette in Camden. We could easily have bought a washing machine but we'd go there every three days, Amy loved sitting in the launderette having a fag and reading the *Sun*, that was always her paper. Sometimes it was the *Star*, for a laugh. And this whole photoshoot was just bland: it could've been any girl in London.

I had a mate called Charlie who was into photography; he lived in Shoreditch and I asked him if he'd do us a favour – just take some pictures. So a few of us went to Shoreditch – me, Amy, Nick and a friend of mine, Catriona, who I met in college, a posh Scottish girl with a rough side, another real character. We were crossing the road, there was a man with two dogs and Amy knew how much I loved dogs: 'Tyler look, two schnauzers!' She asked if she could hold the dogs as a treat for me, Charlie took the picture and that's the image on the cover of *Frank*.

Amy still had a healthy attitude towards food. Coming from

a Jewish family and being a traditional girl, food was a big thing. Now, in the months before *Frank* came out, she began saying, 'I've started on this diet.' At the time it was so ridiculous it was funny. The OXO cube/Haribo diet. She invented it herself. If you fancied something savoury you'd have an OXO Cube dissolved in a glass of hot water, beef or chicken. If you fancied something sweet, you'd have one Haribo sweet. She had a real sweet tooth, loved Haribo anyway and she'd take ages to get through one Tangfastic. But she'd cave a lot, give in and eat a pizza.

This was the proper start of Amy's eating disorders, an ongoing struggle with anorexia and bulimia. If it started earlier, in her mid-teens, that was something I never saw myself, which doesn't mean it didn't happen. But it was there in a significant way from now on, which coincided with her suddenly seeing pictures of herself all the time.

It's different now of course: kids stick their phones in their faces all day long, taking or creating idealized pictures of themselves and sending them out into the world, asking to be looked at. But we were both suddenly thrown into this world of photoshoots and videos and you become self-conscious overnight: *hyper-conscious*. You develop an unhealthy obsession with your physical self which you never had before. In Jeffrey's Place, Amy was always doing promo, flying all over the country. She'd have the glam squad round – hair and make-up sent by Island Records – and emerge looking like a completely different person. Her skin was naturally quite bad when *Frank* was released and all of a sudden her skin was perfect. It was the same situation for me when I started releasing music a few months later. I'd look in the mirror with make-up on and think my skin before must've been terrible. We would both come back from a day of promo, take the make-up off and be totally depressed because you think you look like shit. You just look *real*. Those things affect you.

It was 2003 when I was signed, like Amy already was, to Island Records. Nick took me to Darcus Beese, the A&R director who signed Amy. It felt like a new achievement for me because it wasn't orchestrated by Simon Fuller, who was now a TV talent show entrepreneur.

In October 2003 *Frank* was released, a month after Amy turned twenty, and the media called her 'curvy'. She interpreted that as 'fat'. We'd call it 'fat-shaming' now. I didn't see bulimia then. You can't be bulimic and not eat. What I saw was basically anorexia, the OXO cube/Haribo diet. I understood, I wanted to be thin myself. We had a phrase: 'Eating is cheating.' I wasn't anorexic but I didn't eat an awful lot, which isn't unusual when you're twenty-one and going out drinking and partying. I saw Amy losing weight but I wasn't worried. When *Frank* came out she wasn't stick thin and it wouldn't have been cause for concern if she said she wanted to lose half a stone. Even though she didn't need to, she was perfect the way she was. I'd say to her, 'You've got tits and an arse, you look sexy.' But she wouldn't listen. She'd say, 'I can say the same to you, why d'you like being thin?'

Frank was critically acclaimed and shortlisted for the Mercury Music Prize. Amy wasn't a household name yet but she had the media interested in her from the start. She was funny, she liked a drink and a smoke, she was sweary and she was gifted. Sometimes she found interviews incredibly boring when journalists always asked the same questions. She'd come home to Jeffrey's Place, I was usually there, and she'd tell me what she'd been thinking through the boring ones: 'I wonder what they'd say if I just jammed a pencil in my eye right now?'

She had an industry-only show one night at the Cobden

Club in west London and I bought her a Pringle dress for it. It was like a big boy's jumper you'd wear after you'd just had sex. She was the kind of girl where you wouldn't be able to find your shirt or your jumper because she'd be wearing it. The dress was pink, baby blue and black, V-neck, not too low cut, quite short. She looked absolutely stunning and there was nothing about Amy that wanted to be thin that night. As insecure as she was, I knew she felt sexy. I could tell she loved all of it that night: it was intimate, she'd had a drink, she wasn't famous, she was enjoying just being herself.

We'd done open mic nights by then in this club in Soho near Piccadilly Circus, next to Chinawhite's, which was a place Amy hated, always full of the 'celebrities' of the day. Our club had a Sunday night for R&B heads and, one night when it was my show, we sang the duet we'd written on the beach in Miami, 'Best for Me'. Amy was my guitarist that night too – I was the lead singer and Amy was in front of me with her guitar! It was lovely, but I was nervous. Amy had four months' more live experience than me and her advice was, 'Get some drink down yer and don't think about it.' At least I could open my eyes on stage by then. Whenever we came out of that club, Amy would look at the Chinawhite crowd outside on the pavement and announce, 'Dickheads.'

The 19 Christmas Party was on 19 December 2003 – Simon Fuller was obsessed with the number nineteen. It was held in the R&B club near Piccadilly Circus. I'd done coke once before by now at a party and it didn't feel like a big deal. I just thought, 'I'm growing up.'

I took a moment to look around: I was at my top management's Christmas party where no expense had been spared, there were chocolate fountains and all kinds of stupidness. David and Victoria Beckham were there. Simon Fuller said to me, 'This is Emma,' and it was Emma Bunton – the whole place was full of people on TV. I was laughing, I thought, 'Here I am, I'm signed to a major label, I'm a priority act, I've got my album to make, next year I'm probably gonna have a number one single and now I'm going off to do coke in the toilets . . . life is *fucking brilliant*.'

Then I got the shit kicked right out of me.

CHAPTER 7

The day after the 19 Christmas party, I had the worst hangover ever and didn't get up till 4 p.m. The only solution was a few drinks with my mates in Shoreditch. I was now living at my stepsister's in Bow, Nicola, my dad's daughter from a previous marriage. I'd lived in the same council house my whole life but then my mum, stepdad and baby sister had moved to the country, which I was never going to do. I'd always got on well with Nicola, she treated me like an adult, and Bow was the first time I'd flown the nest. I'd had my £200,000 record deal advance so now I was independent and could afford rent, had nice clothes and could fully look after myself.

Walking to the bus stop, I'd already clocked this gang of boys, about ten of them, and I knew they'd clocked me. It was obvious I had a bit of money: well-dressed, maroon Pringle jumper, alright-looking, *scarf*. I didn't look like a boy who would fight. I'd been mugged before in Canning Town for my mobile and just thought, 'Have it, I'll buy another one.' But this lot, I knew in an instant. *They're gonna fuck me up.*

I made a decision: as soon as I turn left for the bus stop, if it's empty I'm gonna run. If there were loads of people there I'd be safe; it was rush hour, obviously they'd leave me alone. I turned left, there were a good eight adults at the stop, cool.

I sat down on the little red plastic bench. And they carried on coming. And just burst through all the people. They didn't ask for my phone, money, anything. I wasn't mugged, I was *attacked*. Every single adult just disappeared.

They beat the living shit out of me. I was on the floor, getting kicked everywhere, trying to protect my body, tight with adrenalin, kicked by four boys either side, kicked in the face, the back, it was like they were trying to kill me. A week later at that very bus stop, a boy did get killed and it would've been that gang. I thought, 'Any second now, I'll know what it feels like to have a knife go into my body.' They let up, I got away, started running back to my sister's – running, running, running, people looking at me in horror, covered in blood. I battered on the door, my sister opened it and screamed, 'Oh my God!' I went straight to the toilet and vomited and vomited, the shock of it. Then I thought, 'I'm filming a video next month.' I was aware of my battered face, I could see it was all swollen while I was vomiting. I looked at my sister. 'They've broken my nose, haven't they?' She nodded. She drove me straight to hospital, past the bus stop where my scarf was lying on the ground splattered with blood. I knew then I couldn't live there anymore.

I was put into a wheelchair because I couldn't even stand. I had all the scans: two broken ribs, a fractured spine, a broken cheekbone, broken jaw, broken nose. The police came, asked me loads of questions and I wouldn't tell them anything – the old Canning Town way of never talking to the police. I wasn't going to bother my mum, I thought she'd have a breakdown. Then the hospital said, 'You've got internal bleeding.' I thought 'Shit . . . I'm gonna die, I wanna see my mum.' Nicola rang her and she turned up in minutes. She walked in, saw I was black and blue and burst into tears.

'I could've been putting my boy in a box tomorrow morning.'

Then my real dad turned up. It was so surreal – the first time I'd seen him in a room with my mum since I was nine years old. I'd seen him loads since then but never the two of them together, my biological mother and my biological father, the two people who created me, who are chalk and cheese, were in the same room right in front of me. I thought, *I don't know how this is gonna go down, thank God there's a drip in my arm full of morphine!*

Uncles turned up: who did it? I didn't care about retaliation, nothing could reverse what had happened. All I knew was it had fucked me right up.

I was in hospital for five days. They wanted me to get my nose done in there and I refused; I'd pay for it to be done by an expert, I could afford it. It sounds ridiculous but I was thinking about my career. I discharged myself and just *left,* went to my mum's and that's when I started taking painkillers. I'd been prescribed my own painkillers but because I discharged myself, I wasn't given any medication. My nan always had stashes of co-proxamol, she had a repeat prescription for an old ankle injury in the war but only took them on an 'as needed basis' so they piled up.

Co-proxamol was eventually banned for causing serious side effects, like an inflamed pancreas. I thought they were fucking lovely. That's when my painkiller addiction started. For years afterwards, I'd just raid my family's first aid boxes, everyone had painkillers, co-codamol, tramadol. My mum has a place in Spain and they're very lax there, you can buy 30mg codeine tablets you'd need a prescription for here, and they're cheap, so she'd stock up on them and soluble, fizzy codeine. She didn't know I was taking them for years.

The tablets definitely eased the pain in my back but what they did to my head felt a million times better. I felt relaxed, and I wasn't used to feeling relaxed. 'Magic pills' I thought. I had all these insecurities growing up anyway, about not being like the other hard nut boys, about wanting to listen to music and read poems, and that had left me feeling scared for years. And now the attack just shook me to the core. My confidence collapsed; I felt vulnerable. And because I'd been mugged before, although not violently like that, I started thinking, 'Why are people always picking on me?' I felt like that for *years*. I still do to this day. Over time, the physical pain went but the emotional pain kept me downing those magic pills like smarties, for years. I couldn't stop until I eventually went to rehab.

I already knew I was an addict – I'd *always* been an addict. McDonald's was my first addiction and Amy found it hilarious. When we were out drinking, I'd suddenly randomly disappear for forty minutes. Friends wouldn't worry. 'Oh, he's gone to McDonald's.' When you fancy a McDonald's, you fancy *a McDonald's,* that specific, addictive taste. When I was a kid my real dad took me to McDonald's and me and Amy used to talk about the psychological attachment. It reminded me of being loved by my dad. If I got a craving, I'd book an Addison Lee on the management account, the cab service everyone in the music industry used, to the nearest drive-through and get loads: two large fries, a chicken sandwich, Big Mac, six nuggets, couple of cheeseburgers. The taste of the mayonnaise when I was pissed, I absolutely loved it. I'd be drinking so much I'd usually vomit everything up when I got indoors so it was perfect, I'd wake up and feel alright.

In early 2004, there was a Brits party in the West End. I was there with Nick, Amy and our rapper mate John Lacey, known as JtWR (John the White Rapper); we were all absolutely smashed. I needed a McDonald's so I went down to Leicester Square. John walked with me and it wasn't like me but I was rowdy, talking to strangers, hyped and happy, a nice drunk. I got to McDonald's . . . and it was *closed*. Just missed it. I was fuming, started shaking the doors, being silly, shouting '*Please* can I have a cheeseburger?!' I could imagine them inside, cleaning up, thinking, 'No chance mate, I've been working twelve hours for three pounds an hour, go fuck yourself.'

There were wheelie bins outside and I started kicking them over, being ridiculous. I felt a policeman's hand on my shoulder. I'm obviously drunk and disorderly. He said, 'You need to come with us.' There were people around watching and I was pissing myself laughing, saying, 'This is hilarious, you don't understand, I'm such a good boy, I'm a boffin!' They put me in the back of this meat wagon, punched me about, kicked me and I was so drunk I just kept laughing. All I could hear was John on the phone to Amy going nuts, 'They're taking Tyler to prison!' Then shouting to me, 'Don't worry, we'll bail you out!'

We got to the police station where they put me in this cell. It had one of those benches built into the wall that flips out and I just passed out. They let me out next morning and only then did I realize I was in Victoria, with millions of missed calls on my confiscated phone. I must've still been half cut and said to the policeman, 'Can you get me a car?' He said, 'Fuck off and get the fuck out.' I signed something, it was obviously a fine and I actually said, 'I'll give this to my accountant.' I'm surprised they didn't kick the shit out of me. This wasn't the working-class boy from East London!

Amy *did* get me a car. I got home, got into bed and she told me what happened.

'We came down! We tried to bail you out, I offered them money, pressing the intercom in the middle of the night, "You've got Tyler in there, we're gonna bail him out!"'

Amy talked about that for years. 'The only time this boy ever got arrested was trying to break into McDonald's.' That all seems so innocent now. It was the least of the trouble my addictions would get me into.

The day the plaster came off after having my nose done, Nick Shymansky advised that the best thing to do was just crack on.

'D'you still wanna go on tour with Amy tomorrow?'

I definitely did. We had a five-date UK tour lined up, our first tour together, me as her support act doing a twenty-five-minute acoustic set of the songs that were about to be released on my debut album. I'd spoken to Amy a lot when I was at my mum's recovering. She was really worried, even though I downplayed it, but she knew me better than I knew myself and she knew how badly it had affected me.

Island arranged a tour manager for us, Sean, an ex-marine. He was told, 'Don't ever leave Tyler on his own, make sure you even take him up to his room.' I was constantly nervous, anxious, scared, even with the painkillers. That led to me drinking in the morning. Not much, a shot of Jack Daniel's. But *every morning*. It started my drinking problems, alongside a codeine dependence. Amy saw it all up close. She actually said to me, 'T, you're gonna end up an alcoholic.' She wasn't totally serious but she wasn't joking either.

Amy was very wary of these things and always aware of what was going on. She'd mention I smoked too much, too, when it was *her* fault I hadn't given up! One of the worst things Amy ever did to me, and she did some pretty bad things, was after I got the plaster taken off my nose. You had to have it on for ten days and for those ten days I didn't smoke, I *couldn't* smoke. And I'd been smoking for years like a trooper. The first day of the tour, I said to Amy in the car, 'I haven't smoked for ten days and I'm not craving it so I'm just gonna give up.' I was young, it was the perfect chance. She looked at me, said 'Shut up T, give it a rest,' put a fag in her mouth, lit it and handed it to me. And I haven't stopped smoking since! She never smoked fags like I did, she was a weed smoker, she'd just put a bit of tobacco in her weed. She smoked about seven Vogue cigarettes a day and was genuinely concerned about how much I was smoking. So every time she had a go at me from then on I'd throw it back in her face, 'It's your fault!'

After the tour we were in Jeffrey's Place and she had an idea.

'Why don't you just stay here properly? I'll look after you, we're both doing the same shit all the time, touring, going to the studio. Just stay with me. Stay as long as you like.'

I moved in. I never moved out of Amy's from that moment on. We never *decided* to live together, it came out of that extreme situation and it drew us even closer. She could see I was messed up: JD in the morning when I wasn't on tour anymore; painkillers every day when I wasn't in physical pain anymore. And living together was easy, we just got on. She was always trying to make me laugh. I'd been a vegetarian teenager and she knew I was squeamish. So when she was making me chicken soup one day, she came in with a spoon while I was lying on the sofa. 'T, look at this!' It was the chicken's eye on the spoon!

Had I not signed a record deal, gone on tour and had an ex-marine looking after me twenty-four hours a day, I might have had time to deal with being so badly attacked, but I didn't. I've done the therapy now: it happened almost as soon as I'd flown the family nest and that's why it affected me so profoundly. I was frightened to live on my own and it made me emotionally dependent, I guess. It's part of my nature, too. I've always felt so loved and protected by my mother and it affected me when she moved to the country. Within a week or two I was living at my sister's. Then the attack happened. Me and Amy had already formed our bond but her saying, 'Stay with me, stay as long as you like,' put things on an extra level. She smothered me, became a surrogate mother figure. And like I've said, she reminds me so much of my mum.

There was a load of nonsense going round when we were on tour about how we were boyfriend and girlfriend. At school, we saw each other that way for a while but it became very clear that that wasn't what we were about and then there was no more of it. It was never that and it was never going to *be* that. We did used to snog – at that age, between friends, there's always that kind of shit. Amy used to go to the Heaven nightclub a lot, she loved her gays, and she took me and Nick one night. She'd taken a pill, I hadn't and she just went for me, snogged the face off me! But nothing sexual ever went on between me and Amy. There were headlines and quotes about us because Amy encouraged it, for a laugh. There was only one bedroom in Jeffrey's Place and sometimes I slept on the sofa, sometimes in the bed with Amy; it was like she was my sister. We were both insomniacs and used to listen to a Soweto Kinch jazz album together every night to try to send us to sleep. The intricate jazz melodies occupied the mind, which was much preferable to staring at the ceiling hoping to drift off. Music was our religion, it was like praying before bed.

Sometimes I'd wake up in the morning, still half asleep, and Amy would be doing promo on her phone. One time they were asking what she was up to and she said, 'Oh, I'm just lying in bed with my boyfriend Tyler, we've just had a bit of breakfast.' Amy invented it – it was fun, it was silly, I backed it up and it was all bollocks. When I started appearing in *Smash Hits* magazine, doing interviews and photoshoots, I was touring with

Natasha Bedingfield. They printed that Natasha Bedingfield fancied me and Natasha Bedingfield was scared Amy would beat her up!

In the record industry it's all about who's with who so we just thought this was easier, we're together, end of story. Anything that was ever written or talked about to do with me and Amy having sex, it was all fabricated: that shit would never come out of my mouth. Amy had a proper band with her on tour and she was seeing a friend of one of the musicians, the sweetest, nicest fella. Amy really liked him and I always wonder what would've happened if they'd stayed together. He was cagey around me because he thought he was fucking my girl-friend. It was all really awkward.

It all came to light one particular night. I was in bed in Amy's hotel room and woke up to them snogging on the sofa. I didn't take a blind bit of notice but when he saw me get out of the bed he jumped out of his skin. Stunned! Amy was pissing herself laughing, saying 'Surely you know T ain't my fella? I ain't that fucking bad!'

On that first five-date tour the venues were a good size, mostly the Carling Academy 2 venues round the country: Birmingham, Manchester, ending at Shepherd's Bush Empire in London, a couple of thousand people. In Birmingham, after the sound check, after a few drinks, me, Amy and her trumpet player Ben saw a Toys R Us and Amy had an idea. She bought a load of pretend toy instruments – saxophones that blew bub-bles, trumpets with silly little buttons on the side that make noises – and snuck them onto the stage in place of the real instruments. The rest of the brass section didn't have a clue. So the drummer started playing drums, the bass player started up, Ben started pushing the buttons on the comedy trumpet, and the saxophone player got into it, blowing out all these bubbles.

It was only for a minute but the audience found it funny and so did we, just us lot, not fucked up, having a laugh.

We both had to do a load of press and Amy had the same attitude in the beginning as she always did, she found it *really boring*. Whenever she had to go off and do interviews she'd say, 'I've gotta go'n do all this shite now.' We had to do lunchtime university gigs as well, before you did the proper promo, and that was always so dry; you'd have to talk some head boy doing the university magazine.

All our early tours together were hilarious. Sean would wake us up at 8 o'clock, me and Amy would take our pillows out of the bed in our hotel rooms, take them straight into the people carrier and just go back to sleep. A moving car was one of the few places I *could* sleep. Some mornings we'd barely bother to get dressed and just stayed in our pyjamas or joggers. Amy once had the duvet still wrapped around her from the bed and went straight into the car. We'd do radio tours at the same time as the actual tour. We'd be lying under our blankets in the people carrier, pull up at a radio station and Amy would whip off her joggers, put her jeans on. We'd been asleep and three seconds later were singing live on the radio. As soon as we were done, straight back in the car, jeans off, joggers back on and go straight back to sleep. Sean used to call us Human Mattresses.

It was great, all we had to do was travel, get there at two in the afternoon, give a few radio interviews, hungover from the gig the night before, have a little beer to settle the nerves, go and do the university gig, do more radio interviews, do the whole thing again on a loop. Backstage in the dressing room we'd listen to Minnie Riperton and Musiq Soulchild, drink whisky and have a sing-song to warm ourselves up. Nowadays you get your throat steamed and drink honey and lemon, but that wasn't us. Amy would sit there curling her eyelashes, putting her eyeliner on and her hair in bows while I put wax in my hair. When we performed, we'd both stand at the side, watching each other, smiling. In 'Fuck Me Pumps' there's the lyric, 'I'd love a man six foot two or taller.' She'd sing, 'I'd love a man six foot two or Tyler.' Everyone used to sing it, a running joke throughout the band. We were just the best of friends.

The summer of 2004 was the first time Amy played Glastonbury. I wouldn't play there till the following year but in 2004 I was going anyway, a Glastonbury virgin, with my sister and my friend Catriona. I had passes for VIP hospitality and my sister had a mate who'd drive us. She told me he was a nutter, that he'd drive at 110 miles an hour so she gave me a bottle of whisky to calm our nerves. Me and Catriona had polished off the whisky by the time we arrived. We pulled up and my sister blagged it like we were two pop stars in the back, half inebriated under these blankets.

I walked in and, straight away, slipped on my arse. It was a wet, muddy Glastonbury and I got covered in mud, all over my nice clothes, no wellies. I looked at Cat, I was all excited, a bit pissed and went, 'Fuck it, we're here now!' I put my hand into the mud and smeared it all over my face, it felt like the party had started, I was just a mud monster already, brilliant.

Within the first five minutes I lost everyone. Three hours later, I had pockets full of MDMA crystals from the stash of drugs I'd been given by some random to 'look after'. Who I then lost. I had no idea I'd been given MDMA crystals and it was the first time I was ever entirely off my face, walking around Glastonbury licking my fingers. That was my supply for three days. Unsurprisingly everything was a blur. I offered strangers my pockets, where they dabbed their own licked fingers and two northern girls put a tablet in my mouth. I freaked out, which was ridiculous, because I was already out of it on MDMA, but I wasn't a drugs person. I was on my own, I thought, *Fuck, I've just taken this tablet, it might kill me, I don't know these girls, I should never have done that on my own, I need help!*

I knew I'd know people in hospitality and somehow found the way, had somehow not lost my pass. Nick 'Grimmy' Grimshaw, the radio and TV presenter was there, a friend of mine by then, it's a small circle in the industry. Somewhere in the daze I saw Paul McCartney wafting in weird colours on screens. I've never experienced drugs in that way before. I ended up staying in Grimmy's tent and he looked after me, one of the funniest people I've ever met in my life.

Towards the end of the weekend, I remembered I was supposed to see Amy's show, meet up with her afterwards and then we'd go home together. By now I'd lost Grimmy and everything else – phone, wallet, money – I was stranded, lost. All I knew was Amy was on at a certain time so if I managed to get there I'd be safe. I was still completely covered in mud, found the small stage where Amy was singing and barged through people to get to the front. It was pissing down, brollies everywhere; she was on stage in a pink knitted top and a little denim skirt, and I looked like I'd rolled out of a dustbin. (The day before I *did* wake up in a dustbin.) The show was being live streamed on the BBC, she stopped singing for a second and I heard her:

'Tyler, is that you?'

I wasn't waving but I was right at the front. I thought, brilliant, she knows I'm here, I'm safe! I got backstage and Amy looked in my eyes, laughing: 'Look at the state of you, you're high as a fucking kite!'

I was laughing too. Sean, the ex-marine tour manager,

refused to let me get in the car in the state I was in. He started stripping my clothes off, stripping me down to my boxers, the only part of me that didn't have mud on – I'm MDMA'd off my tits and Amy's video recording the whole thing. They put black bin bags in the back of the people carrier, I got into the car, lay down on Amy's lap and fell asleep. And woke up at home.

There has been no other time in my life that was so mental and carefree. It was epic. It was funny. Most of all, there was no problem. Everything was just normal and fun, behaving like everybody else who's ever gone to Glastonbury at twenty-two and been off their face. I had the best weekend of my life.

That was the first summer after *Frank* was released, when me and Amy were just kids having a ball and I've often thought about that time. About how the level of fame she had with *Frank* was perfect for her. She was known, critically acclaimed, she could go about her business and the odd person would come up and tell her they loved her music. If only we could go back in time and hold it there. But that's not how it went. Because she was just a bit too brilliant.

CHAPTER 8

You don't really know the nature of the music industry until you're in it. If you're an artist, you have many months, even years, when you don't have any time at all, not for yourself, your friends, your family. I'd be in the studio till 4 a.m., get in a car, get home half an hour later, Amy would be getting up, going to Germany, wherever. She wasn't commercial, she wasn't having number one singles, but she did a *lot* of promo for *Frank*, much more than she did for *Back to Black*. Amy's mind needed to be occupied and the music industry is very good at occupying your mind for you. For a time, until it stops. You go from being on tour every day, constantly being with your band, meeting a hundred different people every day – you're overly stimulated, every night's a party, you're doing what you love, you have people telling you twenty-four hours a day how brilliant you are, how talented you are – and all of a sudden, you have nothing to do. The cycle is over – album, promo, tour, all finished – and you're expected to just go back to your flat in Camden and do nothing and be normal.

Very quickly after the *Frank* cycle ended, Amy started to lose the plot. She wasn't happy. She was *really bored*. She'd always been a clean freak and now she was seriously OCD. Then she became nocturnal. She was never an early riser, she wouldn't get up till eleven, but this was *fully* nocturnal. She was awake all night cleaning in her Adidas tracksuit, listening to music with her Marigolds on and her cleaning sprays, dusters and mops. It was relentless, she couldn't leave a cup on the dresser.

She wasn't stupid, she noticed the changed behaviour in herself and tried to do something about it. She rang her mum and I heard her ask her straight: 'Mum, I need to go back on them tablets,' meaning the antidepressants she was on when she was a teenager. Amy came off the phone, didn't say much about what was said but she never did go back on the tablets. But she still thought, like she always did, that chemicals were the answer.

So, every night, the bottle of Dooley's started to appear. With her sweet tooth she loved Dooley's, a toffee cream liqueur made with Belgian toffee, Dutch cream and vodka. It's like Bailey's Irish Cream, so delicious people don't think they're *really* drinking. She had superhero shot glasses, hers was Wonder Woman, mine was He-Man. I'd come in from the studio, walk into the living room, with the shelves with her books and videos and WWF dolls, with one little sofa and one little table, and the Dooley's bottle would come out from under the table, it was never *not* there. She'd recognized she needed help, didn't find any, so she did what anyone does through boredom and an unhinged mind: she self-medicated.

Amy was changing. For the very first time, she'd get up at eleven in the morning and say, 'Let's go to the pub.' Daytime drinking. She was never, *ever* like that before. The person she was before, who'd get up, go and get fresh flowers from the market stall, get the *Sun* from the newsagent and write her to-do list – shopping, sunbed, launderette – would now get up late every day and say, 'T, let's just go to the pub and play pool.' I was getting pissed off hearing her say it. I could drink Jack

Daniel's all day and not be paralytic. I could do it for two days, but on day three I'd want to do something else.

Before, we'd always gone drinking in different places – Shoreditch, Primrose Hill, even 'normal' West End clubs but by now she'd never go there again. She'd fallen in love with The Good Mixer. It was a proper drinkers' pub, with a pool table, where she didn't have to get dressed up. She went there in her jeans and ballet pumps with no make-up. She was amazing at pool, she'd kick the arse out of hard-drinking men who were always shocked that this mouthy, tiny girl could *ruin* them. She'd drink all day and wouldn't eat much. Amy wouldn't drink pints, and neither would I, she'd have a black Sambuca shot every twenty minutes. Juliette and Lauren were still around but doing shots in this piss-stinky pub with cokeheads in the toilets and wandering toothless wonders on heroin and crack just wasn't their scene.

Nick was as worried as I was. He cared a lot more about Amy as a person than he did about her career, which is ultimately why she sacked him. We were hearing stories about her staggering home. One night she fell and hit her head on the steps to Jeffrey's Place. I wasn't there but Juliette and Lauren were and Amy ended up in A&E. They were both saying, 'This shit can't go on.'

With daytime drinking you start to mix with a different crowd. It wasn't unusual for people in our unconventional world to party through the day. If you were twenty-two years old and someone said, 'Here's a couple of hundred grand, you've got the year off work, just think about a new album,' what would anyone do? Amy, being normal, not wanting to be famous – she wasn't behind VIP velvet ropes like one of Atomic Kitten – would get up, put on her Fred Perry, her Pink Ladies jacket from *Grease* (she loved that film) and go to her normal pub around the corner. And she found out, if you just drink steadily throughout the day and you stay just a little bit drunk, then everything's soft focus and everything's dandy. That's where alcoholism starts. And if you're daytime drinking, you start to meet people who do hardcore drugs.

And it led to Amy meeting Blake.

Amy met Blake Fielder-Civil in the Old Blue Last pub in Shoreditch one night I wasn't there. He was just a guy she fancied at first but addictive personalities can also become addicted to people and it wasn't long before she didn't just fancy him, she was *obsessed* with him. And *he's* an addict. Where the Amy of before was methodical with her lists, always writing things down, which led to her being a songwriter, now she was becoming random and messy. And Blake was chaos.

I didn't know anything about Blake but Amy would tell me. He was messed up, druggy. He told Amy he'd had a traumatic childhood in some ways. Amy would say, 'He's done not bad considering.' She admired him, how he'd struggled, a hustler surviving any way he could. He was also charming, handsome, dishevelled, did coke in the toilets, was a bit of a wrong 'un and a hard nut who knew how to fight. He played pool, he was a geezer, always talking to this girl, that girl, 'Alright darlin'? Wanna drink? I'll look after ya . . .'

So we started constantly going to the Old Blue Last because Blake was usually there. Amy would sit and stare at him, salivating. I saw that look countless times: she was in *awe* of him. If you're a young woman who's starting to like trouble, he was your dream boy. Amy was also searching for something, her idea of a proper man, and Blake represented a lot of the qualities she looked for. The sort of man who, if another man said something dodgy to his woman in the pub, would knock them out. That was Blake. She was infatuated; he went from being this guy she'd go on and on about to him suddenly being there, so quick, like young love is.

Before Blake, Amy only had one proper relationship, in her late teens with a guy called Chris. I never met him but 'Stronger Than Me' on *Frank* is about him – a song which says, 'You should be stronger than me, because you're a man.' I knew what she was thinking, 'Please be a geezer, please be a man, take charge and tell me when I'm out of line' – that's what she always wanted. She had a thing about always listening to your man, like someone from the 1950s. At that time, the biggest female pop stars in the world were singing about independence, making their own money – Destiny's Child's 'Independent Woman', TLC singing 'I don't need no scrubs.' Amy hated all that. The only love songs she cared about were ones that said, 'I will throw myself under a bus for you.'

When she first met Blake, there was a side to Amy that was very girly. She'd have her hair all done, dress immaculate, make sure he always had his food. But as time went on, they were like two lads. She adopted his mannerisms as well as his life-style. I'd never heard Amy use cockney rhyming slang but Blake used it constantly and she picked it all up. 'He ain't got a Danny' – he hasn't got a clue, a Danny La Rue. 'Do me a lemon' – don't get smart with me, lemon tart, smart. 'Are you 'avin' a bubble?' – bubble bath, laugh. They had this Bonnie and Clyde thing; the gangster, criminal, bad boy side of him, she glamour-ized all that. They immediately became one, started dressing alike. Amy bought him clothes and, being in the industry, she got loads for free. Amy loved dressing a boy up and there was a style in Camden then, with the Fred Perrys and the trilby hats, the Libertines look. She adopted Blake's geezer mannerisms too:

when Amy was a bit rowdy, raring up, she'd roll her sleeves up, grab her bollocks that weren't there, as if she was gonna square up to you for a fight. She reminded me of Scrappy Doo, the puppy from *Scooby Doo*, tiny but brazen and mouthy.

In Jeffrey's Place, Amy loved being in the bath for hours, like a ritual. I don't know why but there was no lock on the bathroom door. I'd sit on the toilet seat for three hours while Amy was in the bath, talking about life – that was a big part of our social time, Amy putting a bit more hot water in, bubbles everywhere. I'd wash her hair in the bath. 'Could you put this conditioner in my hair?' Amy was a very naked person. I don't mean everything was out! But she'd walk downstairs in her knickers and it was nothing to either of us. Now, I always saw Amy and Blake in the bath. I'd walk past and they'd be chilling in the bath. Having a fag in the bath. I saw Blake's cock a million times.

I wasn't worried about Blake, or his habits, I just knew he was a survivor. He was still with someone else when he started seeing Amy and it was no secret. By fifteen, he was already looking after himself, already in bad places and already taking drugs. Survivors like that use people when there's money and food around, but not in a conscious way. It's their natural instinct. If he was selling drugs, robbing, hustling, he didn't talk about it. Amy would say, 'It doesn't matter he's with this other girl, we can't ever be anything serious anyway because he's messed up.' She'd brush it off but it hurt her. She'd just pretend.

I didn't buy it. I thought, no, you've fallen head over heels in love with him. But the biggest problem between them, and she wrote it in 'Back to Black', was 'You love blow and I love puff.' When I was sitting on the toilet seat and she was in the bath, she'd say, 'It's never gonna work, we can never really *really* be together because he's a heroin addict.' She was still sensible to some degree. She knew it was doomed but you can get addicted to doomed romance. She didn't even believe in healthy relationships, she said it a million times. 'If it's healthy, it's not love.' She thought true love could only be chaos, drama and madness.

Amy would *die* for somebody.

CHAPTER 9

I didn't see Blake smoking heroin at first. He was always doing coke. He'd do coke when he was watching *EastEnders*. He watched it avidly, pull the coke out like it was a fag, and go on about the Mitchell brothers. Amy didn't do coke with him, she was already drinking her arse off and had been smoking weed since she was in nappies. It was no big deal to her. She lived in Camden where you're exposed to cocaine all the time and she wasn't malleable like that. She was still very natural-versus-chemical about drugs, still had her morning ritual – cup of tea, roll a spliff.

Blake was still seeing his other girl and Amy was seeing someone else too, our friend George, a black dude. George was very good looking, an A&R boss, lovely bloke, but it wasn't serious, she just fancied him. Amy fancied black guys more than white guys. That was the biggest shock with Blake, that he was white. 'Me and Mr Jones' is about George (with a nod to Nas the American rapper, who she loved but didn't know yet, who has the same birthday as Amy) and so is 'You Know I'm No Good'. The lyric from that song, 'upstairs in bed with my ex-boy', that's a real story. I was in the living room in the early Blake days; Amy was upstairs having sex with George. She came downstairs and told me Blake was coming round and could I sit with him for a while and watch TV? My response was, 'Are you 'avin' a laugh, Ame? Are you seriously putting me in this situation?!' She said, 'Just turn the telly up!'

Blake came round, I hardly knew him then, I thought, *This is well risky*. I didn't know he was seeing someone else as well. He wasn't an idiot, you could hear them upstairs. We were watching *EastEnders*, Blake was sniffing coke and I was sneakily turning the volume up – 'So . . . you like *EastEnders* then, Blake?' – thinking, *Jesus Christ, how long is this gonna last?!* Amy came back in, started talking loudly to Blake and I saw George sneaking out the door. It's was hilarious and so awkward.

Sometimes I'd wake up and it wasn't just Blake there, his friends were too. I'd go to make toast in the morning and there'd be heroin foils on the kitchen worktop. Amy wasn't doing that shit then but she didn't care, she didn't judge anyone. Jeffrey's Place was where the house parties happened. When the pubs shut, loads of randoms came back, a lot of wrong 'uns. There'd be people downstairs doing coke till six in the morning. At that age, there weren't many people who had their own place, so Amy's place became *the* place.

By now, I was filming videos and doing heavy promo. There were two Nicks at 19 Entertainment, Nick Shymansky and Nick Godwyn, and they both looked after me. They were worried about me doing promo for squeaky clean magazines. They'd notice I was always shattered and they wanted me to look alright. They told me: 'You shouldn't live with Amy anymore.' Nick Godwyn made me move in with him for a while, into his little posh flat in Kensington, which I hated. One night I was hammered and spilt a bottle of Baileys on his pristine carpet. I saw him cleaning the carpet in the reflection from the bathroom mirror while I was throwing up in the toilet. I felt bad. I told Amy about that and she pissed herself.

Island Records had been the right label for Amy but it wasn't right for me. Darcus kept saying to me, 'Are you ready? To become famous?' Which I thought was *weird*. Things started to go wrong. My first single, 'What Do I Do', was supposed to be released in summer 2004; Capital Radio predicted a summer smash, a proper reggae pop song. Something happened logistically and they kept putting it back and back, into November, when I'd be up against the biggest names for Christmas, including Eminem. I kept saying, 'Can't we release it next year? I've been waiting for this since I was five years old singing Kylie Minogue songs, I can wait another four months!' But they wouldn't listen. They said they'd done all the work, so it was going ahead.

Island were doing well: Keane were smashing it and they also had the Sugababes so they were a bit full of themselves at the time. They had a lot going on so I wasn't their top priority. The single went in at number twenty-five, with no airplay, which was decent but I felt massively let down. For the second single, 'Foolish', they went all guns blazing with a very expensive video. There was a soundstage with a mic stand in the middle, a huge band in grey suits, seven half-naked supermodels and when I play piano there's a girl's crotch in my face. I was bricking it. Amy was there. I encouraged her to do stuff with me so she wasn't in the Mixer on her own when Blake wasn't around. I made sure there was a pool table there so she wouldn't leave. And she encouraged me . . . to drink! She said, 'Have a drink, you'll be alright' and it helped. Four drinks down, I was up on the soundstage throwing the microphone around and that wasn't *me,* I was shy, insecure. That's the beauty of alcohol.

I went on summer road shows up and down the country and Amy would get up in the morning, depressed, get in the car and travel with me. She was still nocturnal so she'd sleep in the car with my hoodie over her. We pulled up in Wales once and Kelly Clarkson was there. She was on before me. We'd met Kelly before, in Miami, at the movie wrap party, even though Amy thought *American Idol* was scum. She came up to me to say hello and was asking about Amy so I went out to the car.

'Ame, Kelly's here.'

'Kelly who?'

'Kelly Clarkson, we met her in Miami, she wants to say hello.'

Amy pulled the hoodie back over her head.

'T, I couldn't give a flying fuck.'

'Foolish' came out in March 2005 and went to number sixteen, which was OK but the joy was taken out of it because of the expectations. It'd been number one on music TV show *The Box* for two months, voted for by the public. I did *Top of the Pops* for the first time. I wasn't excited but I tried to appreciate it: from when I was five I'd always said, 'I wanna be on *Top of the Pops*' and how many people actually see it happen? 50 Cent was performing as well, he came over during the run-through and said, 'You've got some sick voice, I had to come over, who are you?' He was a cool guy and that's all that day meant to me.

For the third single they insisted I do a cover, and you know you're screwed then. It was White's Town's 'Your Woman', a number one in 1997. It never made sense to me that I'd be singing, 'I can never be your woman.' There was no meaning for me at all, so I just went through the motions. It charted at number sixty. I knew what was coming.

Island Records dropped me. I lost my deal. My album, *The Unlikely Lad,* never came out on CD; they released it on digital download only (long before music streaming took over). What happened to me was typical then. Island spent significant money on the second single when the first single hadn't quite worked. So they'd blown my best song and then the cover was a disaster. I was still seen as a talented little dude so the thinking was, 'We'll let him go, write off the costs, Nick can take him to someone else.'

I was in the pub with Amy in Shoreditch when I got a call from the tour manager. Work was still scheduled in the diary so the show was going on for now. He said, 'Tomorrow morning eight o'clock, picking you up at the flat . . . and I'm sorry by the way to hear about it.' I said, 'About what?' They tell everybody else before they tell you. I got off the phone, Amy was at the pool table. I went over.

'I've been dropped.'

She was furious. 'Darcus is a fucking idiot! Let's not even think about it, fuck it. Gimme your phone.' She rang someone up. 'I need five grams of coke.'

These were my early coke days and it wasn't a big deal. Cocaine just kept me awake for drinking. Then I'd always just stop. This was Amy's way of giving me a hug.

I'd known it was coming but it still fucked me up. I felt lost. *Lost.* It's not just losing your job, it's losing your dream and losing everything you are. I'd been waiting for this since I was *three,* when I first started to sing. A boy who grew up in a council house in East London, who was different to everybody else, who won a scholarship to Sylvia Young's, who started writing in studios at fifteen and by eighteen was managed by one of the biggest managers in the world. It's a fairy tale. *The Face* magazine had called me 'Britain's answer to Justin Timberlake'. It felt like everything I'd done since the day I was born was all leading to this moment, and now the moment had been ripped away.

I still had Nick. He was devastated but he dealt with it like he dealt with everything, with a genuine, positive spin, so you didn't just lose the plot and go off and do loads of drugs. He said I still had plenty of time. People told me I'd be back in a couple of years, but two years at that age is a lifetime. I felt the same way Amy felt. I was down, I was bored, I had money, I could go out every day and every night. I'd been such a good boy, I'd never really done all the partying chaos. The fun times I'd missed out on through travelling, promo, never seeing my friends. I'd get off the plane sometimes in London and kiss the ground. I'd only been to Glastonbury twice, the second time to perform. So it was time to be naughty and drink and do drugs. I thought, 'Fuck this world, I'm off!'

But before I could escape I had one more commitment for Island. They'd gone to the base level, realized little girls fancied me and put me on tour with McFly.

That's when I *definitely* knew everything was over.

CHAPTER 10

I had to do the tour with McFly otherwise I'd be sued. I *hated* doing it. The last date was in Dublin, 'Why Do I Do' had been number two in Ireland for months, everyone was singing it. So I drank myself into oblivion most of the time, other than when I had to be sober enough to go on stage.

My sister was living in Thailand at the time. Amy knew where my head was at and we were talking on the phone.

'T, why don't you just fuck off to Thailand? Stay with your sister. Get wasted for four weeks.'

Great idea. There was a wrap party in Dublin and I wasn't going; I'd even heard McFly's manager was interested in taking me on. I'd had enough. I got in a car, flew back to London, went to a warehouse party in Soho, did a load of ketamine and, by 6 o'clock in the morning, I'd somehow booked a flight and was sitting on a plane to Thailand, coming down off ketamine. One of the worst flights of my life.

I'd gone through duty free, grabbed two bottles of Jack Daniel's and 'Foolish' was on the big screen in the airport. The woman I bought my drink from was embarrassed seeing the video. She said, 'I really like your song,' a glimpse of what it would've been like to have a proper hit – bitter-sweet. I just wanted to *get the fuck away*. I couldn't get a flight to Phuket where my sister lived, so I'd booked a flight to Bangkok instead in a blur. I landed in Bangkok a mess, coming down, hungover, ringing Amy.

'I'm in Bangkok.'

'What's it like?'

'I'm stuck in the airport, I can't get a flight to Phuket for eight hours, I've gotta sit here all day, I'm dying, I'm gonna have a panic attack, you have to stay on the phone with me.'

I found one airport bar like a little jungle-forest, with an outside area. I had The Fear and needed to smoke. They said they weren't open yet.

'Please! I need a drink.'

They gave me bottles of beer. I sat there smoking fags and drinking beer on the phone to Amy till I was ready to pass out in the terminal. And woke up with a really bad back. It was always bad, ever since I was attacked.

I spent three and a half weeks in Thailand, went to full moon parties, it was everything I wanted it to be. You could buy a hundred Valium for 50p. I called Amy from this little hut on the edge of a beach, there was a stunning sunrise. I'd got myself a magic mushroom smoothie to calm me down after loads of amphetamines and there were all these little Thai boats dancing on the water. Beautiful. I'd lost my deal, I'd gone crazy and as fun as this was, I told her how I felt.

'I'm lost, Ame.'

'T, don't worry, you're just in a mental place right now, you're working shit out, stay as long as you want and then just come home.'

While I was out there, my bank came on the phone: we need to alert you to fraud. I'd been in the pop machine, I had no idea what money I had in my bank account, I just used my card. I had an accountant so I didn't think about it. The bank woman asked where I was.

'Thailand.'

'Yes we can see that. But you're also in Camden.'

'Am I?'

There were all these transactions for £50 in a Chinese in Kentish Town. I thought, how much crispy duck can you buy? I rang Amy.

'Ame, my bank's saying there's fraud going on, all these fifty pounds to this Chinese restaurant.'

'Oh yeah that's me babe, I've been getting a bit of Chinese and they sell coke, for Blake.'

'Alright cool, better ring the woman back, I won't tell her that though!'

Amy had my card number, I didn't care, she could have anything she wanted from me. You could do fifty quid cashbacks in pubs on a Friday night, which was normally bullshit, it was for cocaine and this Chinese was a dealing place. Amy wasn't flush with cash anymore. I lent her money around then, £10,000. While I was away, Blake was in Jeffrey's Place every night doing coke, even though Amy had spent all her money. She was reckless. She'd call cabs to go and pick Blake up a kebab.

Amy and Blake split up. It had lasted less than a year. Blake fobbed her off, she got dumped by him, even though it kind of phased itself out. He was with his other girlfriend and, anyway, she'd been fucking George. It was always tumultuous. But now she was drinking even more, to forget Blake.

Nick was more worried than ever. 'She needs to go to rehab. I'm gonna drive her into a field and tell her she's got a problem.' So he drove her out to this field, where she couldn't escape, and told her: you're drinking too much, I think you're depressed, I think you need to go to rehab.

This was ridiculous to her.

'Nick, what the fuck are you talking about? I'm a bit down, I'm going out and playing pool, having a few too many drinks . . . like you do!'

I was worried but I didn't think she needed to go to *rehab*. Crazy people in Hollywood went to rehab. But Nick drove her to a rehab place and got her to speak to a counsellor for twenty minutes. To Amy it was laughable. She just did it to appease him. The rehab guy told her she was depressed and she said, 'No shit Sherlock.' She told me, 'I'm not having some prick who's studied psychology telling me how I feel.' She knew all about that kind of self-analysis and she did not think she had a problem. And neither did I, not then.

Now Nick was starting to think he couldn't manage her like this. There was already talk of the second album but he thought it couldn't happen – not when she just wanted to drink and forget.

Amy's taste in music was changing because the Camden scene was changing. The Good Mixer, the Hawley Arms had jukeboxes and they didn't play modern pop, it was all retro, like the original '69 Toots and The Maytals' 'Monkey Man', before The Specials cover made it famous (it was Blake who brought The Specials into her life). And she discovered the 1960s girl groups. She loved the high drama, the romance, especially the Shangri-Las and specifically 'I Can Never Go Home Anymore'. That song is how Amy felt about Blake. If she was in a bad place that song was *always* on at home.

And it changed everything.

CHAPTER 11

In the mid-2000s, the music scene in London *was* Camden Town. It was all about bands, a new guitar band era the Libertines started. Every Joe Bloggs was trying to start a band and every fella in every bar had a guitar and a trilby hat. In every pub and every venue someone was doing a gig, pretty much everybody was young, having fun and doing drugs. It was perfect timing when Koko, the old Camden Palace, opened in 2004.

It was a scene dominated by blokes in bands but also a type of character, which Amy fitted like a glove. She was a female solo jazz singer, but she was also a bit of a fella. Basically, it was all about being a full-on rock 'n' roll nutcase. You'd always see Kate Moss, Pete Doherty and Fran Cutler, who did their PR – she was always right up my arse in case I was with Amy, just doing her job I suppose.

The Good Mixer had been the central Camden pub in the nineties Britpop days but the Hawley Arms was the central pub for our generation. It was only a few minutes' walk from where we lived off the bottom of Kentish Town Road and two minutes away from the old MTV studios, so there were always characters and people from bands in there. I'd see Noel Fielding from The Mighty Boosh, Johnny Borrell from Razorlight, the Kaiser Chiefs, Arctic Monkeys, Sadie Frost, Peaches Geldof. Some nights, before she was proper famous, Amy would jump behind the bar and serve pints for a laugh. Anything normal like that she loved. She would've absolutely *loved* to have been the woman running a busy workman's caff.

Our circle was really young; we hung out with Grimmy and the other presenters of Channel 4's 'youth' strand T4, as well as Kelly Osbourne and Tom Wright, the son of Radio 2 DJ Steve Wright, my buddy to party with, and talk about the meaning of life all night. He was incredibly intelligent, witty, and all round good fun. Amy loved him. She called him Tom Wrong. If I wasn't at home and had gone missing, she'd ring me up, 'Where are ya? With Tom? I'll see yer in a few days then!' Then she'd be with us by the end of the night.

Everyone knew everyone and we moved around in crowds, ten-, eleven-handed, one place to the next, like the Stables, then some pub after hours where someone would always get their guitar out and start jamming. That's when Amy got into 'Valerie', the Zutons song she covered in 2006, which she heard in the middle of the chaos. We'd end up in the Good Mixer at five in the morning with Donny Tourette from the band Towers of London; he always used to get me and Amy singing 'Creep' by Radiohead. The singers in the bands were all shouty types – 'wooooooourgh!' – and Pete Doherty would say about me and Amy, 'These are proper singers!'

Pete was and still is one of the softest, most gentle, intelligent people, as well as an unapologetic heroin addict. He's like a poet from 300 years ago. That's what Amy loved about him, she was always into poetry. If you were in a hotel room at three in the morning, Pete would suddenly sit down with a piece of paper and start writing, quietly, and that was Amy all day long. She liked what the Libertines stood for as much as the music, the freedom they represented – an up-the-revolution attitude Pete used to describe as 'firing pistols in the air!' The whole scene influenced the way Amy presented herself as a character, as 'Amy Winehouse'.

She was still working too, when she had to. We were on a pub crawl one day, it was 2004, after *Frank*, and we were in the Mixer. She was supposed to do a cover for the latest Bridget Jones film, *Bridget Jones: The Edge of Reason*. It was a request from Island Records, a cover of Carole King's 'Will You Still Love Me Tomorrow', which she knew inside out. She wasn't interested: 'I just wanna play pool!' I had to encourage her, 'Come on Ame, we need to do it!' Island had even organized it so it was recorded in Primrose Hill, around the corner.

We got to the studio – me, Amy and Cat. Amy went into the glass booth, we could see her. Before she went in, I'd begged her to do her falsetto. I knew Amy's vocal capacity and she never showed it off, not really, real singers don't. So I begged her, please Amy, do some falsetto. She said, 'Why would I do that? I never do that.' I listened to her perform it perfectly – it's Carole King, after all, one of her standards. I was sitting on this big black leather sofa, every note was perfect, it was a lovely, sunny day and she was singing it like she sang it when she was sixteen years old.

She got to one particular bit in the song and I looked at her as if to say, 'Come on, bitch, do it!' She looked at me through the glass and sang, 'and will my heart . . . be broken!' She did the fucking falsetto! I'd heard it a million times and she'd never recorded it. She did the whole thing in one take, walked out the booth and smiled at me as if to say, *well there you go*.

Every single day was a party. We'd never stay in, always be going to gigs, always end up on somebody's floor at four in the morning. Sometimes the party was in Jeffrey's Place. We made a few friends for life. When we first lived together unofficially, before Amy had even written *Frank*, long before she was 'Amy Winehouse', I met a girl at a house party who I just clicked with. Her name was Chantelle and Amy became her friend too, pretty much the last new friend Amy made before she became famous. Most of Amy's friendships came out of partying and drinking from then on, but Chantelle's friendship with Amy was never just about that; Chantelle was a party girl who was also very caring, a spiritual soul with a massive heart. She was a student then and went on to be a great writer.

Amy met her stylist through the Camden scene too. Naomi was studying at the London College of Fashion. Her boyfriend was dodgy, she was in a bad situation, so Amy helped Naomi get away from him, gave her the job of her personal stylist, which she was from then on, sorting out all her dresses.

Amy and Kelly Osbourne became good mates. Kelly was looking for some normality in her life, she'd just done *The Osbournes* TV show and was back in London getting away from the LA world that messed her up with drugs in her late teenage years. Kelly was now all about sobriety, even if drink and drugs were a central part of everything around her in Camden. She was hanging out with Tom Wright which is how we met. She and Amy had a strong girl friends' connection, something I obviously never had with Amy. Boys can't provide that, however sensitive you are. I loved that she had that friendship. Especially since Juliette and Lauren, who had been like her sisters when we were kids, were now on her dick all the time about drinking. That was only because they were worried, of course, but Amy wasn't listening.

So many of us were addicted to *something*. I was still having my shot of JD in the morning, still constantly taking strong painkillers. There was cocaine and drinking to excess, which I fully indulged in. I was blocking stuff out, I had no real purpose in life but this was fun. Tom Wright ran a few venues in Camden and we'd go from one to the other, me buying cocaine on my card. We'd be at house parties and if I fell asleep – and sleep will come at some point when you've been awake for two days – a random would put one finger on one of my nostrils, make me breathe in through the other one and that's how I'd wake up. Tom thought it was hilarious. I loved it – I'd never roamed around like a carefree tramp before.

Finding drugs was easy. You could buy drugs in some of the pubs, they had private upstairs rooms, for the little VIP lot anyway. The Hawley Arms had those rooms: someone in our group would make the call and everyone waited for the dealer to arrive. Either that or you were sitting in someone's house, everyone put their money in and someone turned up. We'd walk into the Mixer mob-handed – Amy, Pete, Kate – walk straight up the stairs to the private room and the people downstairs would look at you like you were Camden royalty, ridiculous. Tom would be putting on a gig at some pub and me and Amy would be security on the door and take it seriously, like a proper job. We both loved having a task.

Cocaine was something I could do for two, three days but it never took over my life. The problem was alcohol. Cocaine was just alcohol's facilitator. You can't drink the amount I was drinking and not fall asleep. Two bottles of vodka a day. Some people get angry with alcohol, I was just more confident, less anxious. Alcohol made everything better, made *me* better. And of course if you're doing coke you're not gonna fall asleep. So I'd do anything to eventually get some sleep, I would've drunk a whole bottle of whisky. You learn the tricks – a big swig of Night Nurse, the insanely strong cold 'n' flu medicine, a load of codeine, whatever is around. My drink of choice was a glass of whisky with ice and two fizzy codeines, effervescent tablets, near bedtime. I got into sleeping tablets, every night. And then, very quickly, the drug scene started changing.

It was public knowledge that Pete Doherty was a heroin addict and now heroin started to spread throughout Camden. To me, it's the drug that you just don't do: it's not sociable, it's *Trainspotting*, you're just going to end up dead. We know how addictive it is; you can try it on a Saturday night, by Wednesday you're robbing out your nan's purse.

People were dabbling. It was just *there,* becoming normalized. There were many times I'd drag one of my mates out of a bathroom when I'd caught them with a foil, smoking away, and tell them straight, 'What the fuck are you doing, you're becoming a heroin addict!?' And they were, even if they could all still function. And it was changing Amy's perspective. Only a few years on from 'don't do chemical, only do natural', she convinced herself heroin was alright. Not that she was doing it herself yet. But other people were, people she liked and admired.

Amy wasn't always just partying though, far from it. She was also writing new songs. Mostly in the middle of the night. On the kitchen floor.

CHAPTER 12

'd heard Amy write loads of songs. She'd write her feelings down first. There was no song that started with melody or chords first, it was always words. For a songwriter that's very unusual. I was in awe of that, this page of poetry and no chords. She was still nocturnal and she'd sit on the floor in the kitchen, with a bottle of Dooley's or Jack Daniel's, her guitar out, with a piece of paper and a pen.

Upstairs in bed, I could hear her clearly. I knew those songs before they sounded like those songs. The first thing I heard was what would become 'Back to Black', the song, I knew the chorus for weeks; the words to the verses were written down but weren't in any musical form yet. At first she had the same chords going through the entire chorus: 'We only say goodbye with words . . . You go back to her and I . . . go . . . back . . . to . . . black . . .'. The melody went down but the chords didn't go down with it and so didn't support it, all of that wasn't there. I hated those original chords to the chorus so I told Amy I thought she should change them. She did, which makes me sound like a right cock, but it's true.

She wrote most of the songs on *Back to Black* through spring 2006, through months pining for Blake, going out on the piss, coming home and writing into the night. I'd get up in the morning and she'd ask me: 'What d'you think of this?' There were fragments of verses, songs not formed yet, with loose titles which changed. Songs that would become 'Wake Up Alone', 'You Know I'm No Good', 'Love Is a Losing Game', which was originally called 'Gutter', and 'Me and Mr Jones' about George. The line 'what kind of fuckery is this?' I heard her say that a million times, that's just how she spoke.

She wrote most of the lyrics in a special notebook, a retro comic Catwoman journal, the pages embossed with Catwoman's hooded face. The opening spread was where you fill in your name: 'This Journal Belongs to . . .' She wrote Amy Jade, her name and middle name, like you would do if you were about twelve. She'd doodle in between the lyrics, rows of hearts and sketches of pin-up girls' faces, alongside her immaculate hand-writing. It wasn't a mess, it was beautiful. The lyrics were rude, funny and so mature and yet the doodles were naive and sweet. I think people forget: when she wrote *Back to Black* she was only twenty-two years old.

To me, *Back to Black* isn't funny like *Frank* is. It's a heart-ache album. When she was sitting on the kitchen floor she was depressed. Amy didn't do things by half, she wasn't sitting down with her bottle like she was in the studio writing lyrics, she'd be crying her eyes out. She'd be just about to pass out before I picked her up and put her into bed. It was upsetting. She'd always say about songwriting, 'You get a pen and slash it into your arm and bleed all over the pages.'

She *was* slashing her arms by now. One night in Koko, she asked me to come into the bathroom with her. She had a vest on underneath her top and took the top off. Without saying anything, or making a big deal of it, she was showing me the cuts on her arms, something she wanted me to know. I was concerned of course but it's not like I hadn't seen self-harm before. I didn't say anything either, she wouldn't have wanted me to, but now she knew I knew. And she knew I'd keep an eye on it from now on.

I thought her new songs were maybe *too* depressing. Not only did I not know *Back to Black* would be what it became, I had no idea what the album would sound like. I didn't even know if these songs were ever gonna *be* on an album. I also heard from Nick that Island were thinking about dropping her. From a record company's perspective, they wanted a second album and it wasn't coming. They knew she was drinking a lot. It doesn't mean they didn't think she was a viable artist but when she was writing those songs they weren't hearing them. She was indoors with her guitar, not in the studio.

The actual recording was very quick: two weeks in Miami with Salaam Remi, two weeks in New York with Mark Ronson. Amy loved the 2003 song 'Ooh Wee' that Mark Ronson did with Ghostface Killah and Nate Dogg but she also had a crush on Mark and that's really why she wanted him to produce the album. I thought they'd end up together – he was a bit of a sexy nerd – but they became good friends. He was the musical equivalent of Amy, the pair of them would sit and talk about music for four, five hours at a time. When she left for America she was in a good-ish place again, excited to work with Mark for the first time, excited to be creative again – the only part of being 'Amy Winehouse' she liked. She was focused, she'd sorted herself out, not least because she had a deadline.

It was Nick Shymansky who played me some of the finished *Back to Black* in his car. Amy would never have played anyone her new album. There was a song originally called 'They Tried to Make Me Go to Rehab', which she'd written about Nick driving her into the field and his attempt to take her to rehab. Typical Amy had made something hilarious out of that scenario: 'They tried to make me go to rehab, I said *no no no . . .*'

It was written in New York with Mark and it was weird for me because I didn't hear its creative process at all. I heard it finished like everyone else. I was shocked. 'This is a massive pop song!' I didn't tell her how much I liked it cos that would've made her hate it, so I just said it would be a huge hit. She shrugged it off. 'I wrote that in ten minutes, it's not really my favourite.'

The scenario which inspired the 'Rehab' song wasn't typical for a manager. Nick was trying to help Amy more out of friendship and it created all this tension between them. Amy knew she was drinking too much. She was out all the time at house parties and gigs and her career was taking off, so when he said he was worried she didn't want to hear it.

In 2006, her management contract came for up for renewal: after three years both sides decide if they want to renew. That was another tension. Amy was starting to not like that she was, on paper, managed by Simon Fuller. She hated what he stood for: shiny mainstream pop, idiots on talent shows. So she was done with 19. But she still, even with the tension between them, wanted Nick to manage her on his own, not through 19. Nick, being sensible, was not going to leave 19.

When I was signed to Island, we both had a live booking agent, Raye Cosbert, from MJM Productions. I didn't know an awful lot about him, it wasn't a personal relationship. But when someone takes off, if you're a booking agent, you turn up a lot more. He wasn't especially appealing to Amy but compared to everyone else he wasn't constantly on at her about sorting her life out.

Nick and Amy had an argument in Nick's car. He was saying, 'I can't manage you like this, you're drinking way too much', and her response was a threat.

'Well, you know what? I'll get that Raye fella.'

She wouldn't have known his second name. It was frivolous and completely random. Raye came out of nowhere. Out of a 'fuck you' attitude. Nick called her bluff and handed her his phone.

'Alright, here's my phone, ring him.'

She rang Raye and asked him to be her manager. *Back to Black* was already written, everything was in place. Raye became Amy's manager because of two young people having a silly argument and them both being stubborn motherfuckers. Raye was a big black man with dreadlocks and Amy, all her life, had a natural affinity with black people and black culture, especially Black music, obviously jazz, soul and hip hop, that played a part. But most importantly, Amy thought Raye wouldn't object to the way she was living her life. She thought that as long as she did the work, she could do whatever she wanted and Raye wouldn't interfere.

Raye was suddenly *there*. Things were very different. There wasn't the closeness she'd had with Nick, there was no history, no relationship built up through the years. He was with her most days but it always felt like he was just her manager, not so much her friend which was the way she wanted it. As her manager, I'm assuming he would've earned 20 per cent of the royalties on *Back to Black*, the industry percentage standard. I often heard Amy say, 'I'm giving him twenty per cent.' That's quite an incentive. Not that he knew how big the album would be and it's not like he asked for the job. But he knew the album was written, all the work was done. He would also, I presume, earn 20 per cent of her next recording advance. I could imagine him thinking that if he let her go and lost this incredible opportunity for his career and his life, she would just give the job to someone else anyway, so it might as well be him. Many others in his position would have done exactly the same.

*

Mitch came round to the flat to have a word but it wasn't about drinking.

'Ame, you should go and see me mum soon, she hasn't got long left.'

Amy went to see Cynthia, and not long afterwards she passed away from lung cancer, another reason she would have a go at me about smoking so much. Amy never spoke about her nan's death, at all, which means it really affected her. She didn't even speak about it when it happened. She didn't even tell *me* she'd died: Mitch told me. I knew instinctively not to ask her about it either. She had the famous tattoo done, of the fifties pin-up girl in the tiny shorts, the name Cynthia around it on her right upper arm, a tribute to the nan she loved so much, who she always said looked like Sophia Loren in her day. But she wasn't even saying that anymore. Amy always talked, she talked and talked and talked, and she *never* talked about the death of her nan.

2006 was also the year my mum and stepdad Danny got married. They'd been together twelve years by then. My mum wasn't bothered about getting married, she'd been married twice before, but Danny was up for it. 'Come on, let's have the party!'

Amy was made up about it. She idealized my mum and stepdad's relationship – he was her man, she was his woman, an unbreakable duo, she always admired that. Amy's heart melted when I told her I was going to give my mum away and walk her down the aisle. I made all these jokes to Danny: 'I might not give her to yer.' When the wedding came up, Amy was in a bad place with drinking, after Blake, before *Back to Black* came out, with Cynthia not long passed away. The wedding was a big thing for her, she didn't want to embarrass herself or anyone else. But it was an East London wedding and a lot of people made a lot more of a show of themselves than Amy did. It was *raucous*.

It was out in a hotel in Chingford. We all stayed there the night before. Danny drove there in his scrap metal van and hung my mum's wedding dress in its zipped-up hanger sleeve on the back of the van, such a pikey. My mum was mortified. 'Why have you stuck my wedding dress on the back of your van?!' He wasn't even supposed to see it.

There were 200 people on the day. I made a speech; Amy was sitting next to me and I made her cry. I thanked Danny for raising me: 'Thank you for treating me like a real son. And my mum is my world.' Danny's mum cried, everyone cried. Amy loved that day, she just got to be herself with my family, the kind of people who would never judge you, who would say, 'We're all here and we all love you.' There was dancing to Motown: me, Amy and my mum all dancing to The Supremes together on the dance floor, a proper celebration. My friend from college, Catriona, was there as well. At four in the morning, I was sitting out on the lawn with my cousins, Amy and Catriona. Amy was obliterated, she couldn't form words – it was funny but she needed to go to bed. I encouraged her, 'Darlin', the sun's coming up!'

Next morning, phones were blowing up. Amy hadn't even mentioned she had a photo shoot the next day. I answered my phone and it was Shane, Amy's PR from Island Records.

'Tyler, are you with Amy? I know it was your mum's wedding, she's got a photo shoot today, mate, I'm down at the shoot, everybody's here, please *please* tell me you're in England?'

'We're in Essex!'

'Cool, we'll get a car . . .'

For years afterwards, Amy was asked about the cover image

At the Sylvia
Young Theatre
School where
we first met.

On the beach in Miami.

After a duet together with our manager Nick Shymansky.

Crashing in the Raleigh Hotel, Miami.

In the studio with Salaam Remi.

Amy with the band in 2003. MD Dale David is pictured far right.

Top left The 19 Christmas Part
shortly before being beaten up.
Top right The Pringle dress I
bought for Amy.
Left Amy on stage in the
early years

OPPOSITE PAGE
Cut-out Amy performing
Frank at HMV in 2004.
Top A photo shoot when we
were living in the Jeffrey's
Place flat.
Bottom left At the Saatchi
& Saatchi Gum Factory
Launch Party.

Mustique
Above At Basil's Bar.
Left Amy driving a buggy around the island.
Bottom left Leaving on the plane.

OPPOSITE PAGE
Main picture Amy with Kelly Osbourne at the Elle Style Awards in 2007.
Inset left With Dionne, Pete Doherty, Amy and myself at K West Hotel.
Inset right Blake and Amy being stalked by paparazzi after leaving rehab.

Left Amy hugging
her Mum at Henley.

Above Leaving Amy's flat in Prowse Place.
Left With Mitch going to see Blake
in court.

OPPOSITE PAGE
Amy at the Grammys, where she
won five of the six categories
she was nominated for.

of *Back to Black*, those photos where she looks all crumpled and forlorn with a thousand-yard stare. She'd always laugh.

'That's how everybody looked the morning after Tyler's mum's wedding!'

'Rehab' was the first single and Island needed a video. Amy didn't want to do a video, she hated doing videos. Other than going out and performing her songs, once they were written and recorded, she was done with them. She met a few different directors and didn't get on with them and they couldn't get her to do it. So I had an idea. When all my shit with Island was going down, I'd met video director Phil Griffin. He was a ballet dancer, he'd done choreography and he'd done loads of poptastic videos – his first one was Billie Piper with the bubblegum – he'd done Westlife and he did my last video for the cover of 'Your Woman', which I did not want to do. Before we filmed it, I told him: 'No offence but I couldn't give a fuck.' He laughed and said, 'Let's just do it.' He was frank and real and we went out for a drink. I persuaded Amy to meet him. They got on and we all got smashed in the Soho club Jazz After Dark.

Nick was still my manager, he heard Phil had got the 'Rehab' job and rang up. 'What have you done, the label's saying he does Westlife videos?!' Phil sold Amy his idea by saying, 'I'll stick you in a nut house and you can sing on the bed.' He went on to do nearly all of Amy's videos. He went from poptastic to working with Paul McCartney, Rihanna and Prince.

'Rehab' went to number seven in the UK charts, an actual smash hit single. Amy still wasn't ambitious but she did care about how her music was being received, cared if people liked it, cared she hadn't sold herself out. She'd see people like Natasha Bedingfield doing well with weedy pop songs when she was writing brilliant, clever songs like 'Fuck Me Pumps', which got nowhere in the charts. She'd see a Nas song get nowhere either, and it pissed her off, the state of the music world. But 'Rehab' was a true crossover hit. Girls Aloud covered 'Rehab' on Radio 1's Live Lounge, a crossover statement in itself.

Amy was in a good place. She was healthy, happy, glamorous and full of life. After all that time off in the Good Mixer, which led to Blake, depression and eventually *Back to Black*, she was wiser, more confident, had more of an edge to her, with new tastes in music, especially the 1960s girl groups. She'd been creative again, she'd been to Miami, New York, she'd proved to herself she was resilient, she'd cracked on and written this amazing album.

It was the first time she really showed off all the tattoos she'd had done over the last eighteen months: the horseshoe, 'Cynthia', the Blake pocket over her heart. The beehive had arrived. It was just a little one, for now, a fixture pinned into her hair, with her actual hair woven around it. There would be loads of beehives to come, of various sizes; I have one to this day. It was both a retro style statement and her comfort blanket and I understood that. We both had comfort blanket hair, a distraction because we didn't like our faces: instead of worrying about yourself, you worried about your hair. I'd hear Amy say, 'If it's not big hair, it's not working.'

Alex Clare was Amy's rebound after Blake. He was different to Blake but still rough around the edges: dirty white t-shirt, chain smoking Marlboro Reds, always playing the guitar. He had a great voice and I think being an artist himself might have been an angle for him, wondering if Amy's success might rub off on him. His day job, for now, was a chef. He seemed scared of letting her go anywhere and wouldn't let her out of his sight. He was intimidated by Amy's relationship with me.

After the top ten success of 'Rehab', Island Records started to spend money. The second video from *Back to Black*, 'You Know I'm No Good', was a high production number shot by Phil Griffin in a lot in East London with four little sets representing Jeffrey's Place; by now, Phil was friends with Amy so he knew the flat well.

Alex was invited to the 'You Know I'm No Good' shoot and he was due to turn up in the afternoon. That morning, everything was going great, everyone was pleased. Amy came over to me.

'Guess who's coming in a minute?'

'Who?'

'Blake.'

'You're having a laugh.'

'No. Blake's coming.'

CHAPTER 13

Blake rocked up to the video shoot for 'You Know I'm No Good'. I didn't hate the dude, had nothing against him. I knew so much about him I almost felt sorry for him. There was no sign of the Amy who hated video shoots that day, she was happy to be there, which was definitely something to do with him. Even though she was with Alex at the time. When she told me Blake was coming, she knew it was wrong. She was smiling. This was mischievous Amy, a side of her I loved. I could understand it. It was Blake who dumped her. Then, all of a sudden, Amy's up there, people are talking about her, she's the shit. It's all there in the lyrics to 'Back to Black': 'He went back to his old *safe bet.*' Boring! Nothing like what they had, which was tumultuous and unhealthy and *real love.* They might have been in contact for weeks for all I knew. I didn't pry.

She'd just had a top ten single and here she was making an expensive video. Blake had never seen that side of Amy. When they met, she was that girl running around Shoreditch and playing pool in the Mixer. Imagine: 'Hello fella who wasn't that interested and palmed me off, we're at my video shoot and I wrote this song about *you* actually, mate. All my songs are about you! And look, there's an entourage of thirty people who are here because of *me.* Oh and by the way I'm wearing a nightie and my hair's all done and I'm wearing loads of make-up.' I don't blame her: she felt good, she felt sexy and she wanted the man who broke her heart to see it.

Blake was a random that day. Phil Griffin didn't know who he was. Amy had said to me, 'Will you stay with Blake? He doesn't know anybody.' He was overwhelmed.

'Faaaackin' hell Tyler, this is serious, can you believe it? And she wrote all these songs about me! I should be asking for royalties . . .'

It was banter but there was a part of him that meant it. I knew Amy wasn't serious about Alex, so asked her what was going on with Blake. She said, 'Oh nothing, we're just mates.' I thought, don't lie to yourself and don't lie to me. Anyone could see the lust between them. I was thinking, *Get a room!* She insisted, 'It's not like that, Alex is still coming this afternoon.' With another big smile on her face. Neither of them knew about the other, of course. Blake left, Alex came down in the after-noon and there were very strict instructions from Phil to everybody on the set: do not say that boy Blake was even *here*. It was all very tongue in cheek and very funny.

When the shoot ended, Phil dropped us all home. Phil was happy, Amy was happy, I was happy. I knew I'd played a role in getting Amy's career started and it was a moment for me too, I was so proud of what she'd done. Especially when only months before, all Amy was doing was dragging me to the Mixer the moment I opened my eyes.

We were joking and laughing together, Amy cuddled me and it pissed Alex off. He started an argument. Phil let him have it. 'Mate, I'll let you out the car, I don't know who you think you are but these two have been friends for years, they won't even remember you in a month's time and they'll probably get mar-ried and have babies.' Alex said something stupid like, 'Tyler wouldn't even know how to do it.' Amy went mental and stuck up for me. His days were numbered.

Alex went with Amy to the Brits in February 2007, when she won Best British Female Solo Artist. *Back to Black* was nominated for Best British Album too, though they gave it to the Arctic Monkeys' *Whatever People Say I Am, That's What I'm Not*. I'd had to do some corporate gig in Europe and flew back to be with Amy for the aftershow. There were a few us, all staying at the Covent Garden Hotel in two rooms, and we all saw Alex arguing with Amy. He was just immature, lots of people were like that around her, wanting to keep her to themselves. I couldn't deal with Alex and took Amy aside by myself.

'Ame, you do know you've just won a Brit? Fuck this little prick getting annoyed at you for no reason, you've just won a Brit so tell him to shut his mouth and you just appreciate it.'

Me taking her away made him even more annoyed: 'Where are you going with her?'

'Mate? She's just won a Brit! I just wanna talk to my friend and appreciate the moment, can you just fuck off?'

That ruined the night for me, and Amy knew it.

Two days later, Amy was in Paris doing promo for *Back to Black* and Alex was there with her. Me and Chantelle were in a bar in the afternoon in London when she rang up. 'Come out here!' I looked at Chantelle. 'Fuck it, let's get on the Eurostar!' We got there in time for dinner that night, Amy fancied the Buddha-Bar, she'd been told the food was amazing. It was also well expensive. It was the beginning of Amy becoming 'somebody', the beginning of a world where, suddenly, your best friend has a lot more money than you do. I had plenty money of my own but I would never go there through choice.

'Can we go somewhere normal, Ame? I know you've got money but I can't afford to spend four hundred pounds on a meal!'

We went anyway. Amy insisted and said we wouldn't have to pay. Alex was annoyed *again*, this time that Amy was buying dinner for her friends, especially me. Raye was there and when the bill came to the table he turned to the tour manager and said very quietly, 'This is definitely going on Amy's company account.' Amy was on the other side of the table. It's standard practice in the music industry, to charge expenses to the artist, but it was the first time I saw him see Amy in a way I didn't, as the person who pays the bills.

Raye turned to me. 'Maybe you should leave a tip?'

I thought, what a wanker. He didn't ask Alex. Or Chantelle. When you're friends with someone who's famous you're judged for it, like you're some hanger on. It was the first time I realized that, overnight, everybody wants to get up my friend's arse. In many cases because they're intimidated and impressed by fame. I felt very quickly that they didn't want me around, that I might get in their way. They just wanted this girl to keep working. Things were going so well. There was an agenda. It was business. None of this existed during *Frank* when it was fun and innocent and real and felt like everybody was there to support her and her music.

Raye ruined that Buddha-Bar meal for me, by making me feel like I was freeloading. I was sitting there with all these people who were making me, someone at the table who actually knew Amy, who she'd actually be upset about if they dropped down dead, feel like some sort of ponce. Amy would never do that to me. She hadn't changed, she hadn't gone up her own arse. She was real, she was exactly the same. Yeah, she was pleased she had a nice hotel room but she didn't give a shit as long as she had somewhere to put her head down. It's like they say: it's not you that changes, it's everybody else around you.

I learned very quickly not to take it personally. There were many times I'd hear people ask Amy, 'Oh, is Tyler your PA?' Sometimes, in the future, I'd be at home in one of the many homes we shared, in my own bedroom, and some random would walk in and ask me, 'Who the fuck are you?'

'Who the fuck are you and why are you in my bedroom?!'

They didn't know me because they didn't know *her*. These things happened countless time and I got used to it: you grow a thick skin and it becomes funny.

The day after the Buddha-Bar meal in Paris, me and Chantelle were getting the night train to Italy, having a break. I was still intent on having all the fun I'd missed. Amy wanted to come with us and couldn't.

'I gotta stay with these lemons and do more fucking promo.'

We got on the train to Venice, there were two Chinese girls sharing our cabin. They lost their iPod and thought we'd stolen it, which we did not, so we ended up in a police cell at six in the morning. We were protesting our innocence, stinking of drink, with these two innocent little backpackers who couldn't understand a word and it looked like we'd robbed them blind. They obviously didn't find their iPod on us so had to let us go.

We rented a little apartment. We were lying on the bed, hungover, switched the TV on and there was Amy on Italian MTV doing an interview and her voice was dubbed in Italian. She was standing there and all we could hear was 'pasta, pasta, pasta'. It was one of those 'wow' moments – our friend is getting famous *everywhere*, she's really doing it. It wouldn't be long until *Back to Black* was number one in nineteen countries.

CHAPTER 14

I knew Blake was back in Amy's life because he was just *there*. She would never have said, 'Me and Blake are back together.' I could see that: they were both back in the bath, having a fag! After the video shoot for 'You Know I'm No Good', he was constantly around. Amy was buttoned to his lap, arms always around him. Very rarely would they not be *on* each other. They were both romantics, young and in love. He was an addict but he was also empathetic and caring, they were similar that way too.

In early 2007, when *Back to Black* was number one in the UK, I was still living in Jeffrey's Place but I was AWOL a lot, staying on sofas or at my mum's. I was a mess, drinking, in chaos. When I did stay there, Amy and Blake both looked after me. They knew about addiction: we were all fucked up people. Blake treated me like I was Amy's brother. I'd sit on the sofa between them, crying, drinking, talking.

The flat was getting trashed now. Amy was drinking heavily, Blake's friends were always round with their heroin foils and crack paraphernalia. There'd been a fire. Amy had left all the candles burning above the fireplace and gone to bed one night Blake wasn't there. I was still up, in the kitchen, when everything went aflame, all her framed magazine covers on the wall. I freaked out, throwing pans of water and managed to put it out.

There was glass and burnt paper and lumps of candle wax all across the living room floor. Fifteen minutes later we would've burnt to death. I ran upstairs and shook Amy awake.

'There was a fire!'

'Have you put it out?'

'Yeah, but we nearly died!'

'T, I'm *asleep*.'

Raye was there a lot. Like managers do, he brought round paperwork to sign. Once he left an old copy of *Music Week* lying around, which Amy would never have read. I picked it up and there was an article in it saying she'd sold four million albums. The thought went through my head for the first time, *Amy's gonna have a lot of money*. Another time, when Blake was there – two months on from the fireplace fire with smoke damage still up the walls – Raye brought pictures round for Amy to see of apartments to rent, very plush. Amy was stunned. They cost between £800 and £1,100 a week.

'Raye, are you 'avin' a bubble? Can I afford that?'

'Yeah, you can Ame.'

She had no idea about her money, Raye and Mitch were in control of her business already. She didn't look for new places to live herself. She wouldn't have wanted to move; it was suggested she move, implying she was a better person now. The one person who didn't seem surprised Amy could afford it was Blake. If they got married, he'd be a very rich man. How could he not think that? Anybody would've felt like that, if their partner was suddenly loaded. I don't think he was just a money-grabbing whore but he was a survivor, someone who'd had to hustle all his life to get by. So it was handy that the girl he liked being with, who worshipped the ground he walked on, was now so rich they could look after each other and have everything they wanted and needed. The dark side of course is that Blake was an addict. So he'd also be thinking, 'And I'll never have to worry about getting money for heroin and crack again.'

In May 2007, *Back to Black* entered the US Billboard charts and stayed there till the following March, when it peaked at number two. That's a colossal thing to happen to an artist from the UK. Not that Amy thought about it much, if at all. She did an interview with *Billboard* magazine when she was number two and the journalist was going on about boring business things, about markets and demographics. She was polite, she said she was grateful for the opportunities.

'But to be honest,' she said, 'I'm not the kind of person that will think about the demographic. I'm just the "turn".'

That was Amy all day long.

That May she was in America doing promo, with Blake. By now he had complete control over her life. He'd cut off all her friends. And some just couldn't cope with her new lifestyle with him. I hadn't seen Amy for weeks. Some of that was just what happens when someone falls in love. There was now tension between me and Blake. The message was clear: I don't want you around, I've had Amy all to myself, I can get her to do whatever I want, don't come near and fuck this up for me. That came from drugs.

I was in Sydney when Amy rang, where I was having a relationship with a bottle of vodka.

'Tyler, guess what? Me and Blake just got married!'

She was in Miami. I didn't know she was even *thinking* about getting married. She rang me minutes after they got married, I think because she felt bad. The people at Amy and

Blake's wedding were Blake's friends. Two of them, the witnesses. And Raye. There was no one else, not her dad, or her mum. I wasn't surprised they'd get married – Bonnie and Clyde against the world – but I thought at least she'd have a *do*. I thought at least I'd be there! But it was spur of the moment, both high as kites on drugs and booze. It would've felt romantic and ballsy and *fuck it*. Like Britney Spears in Vegas. I just said, 'mazel tov'.

Blake was her world, he was keeping her in his world and *only* his world. He was travelling everywhere with her, flying first class, an addict whose drugs were all paid for. Amy didn't care about money so she wouldn't have thought about a prenup or anything like that. If it crossed her mind that day that if they divorced he'd be entitled to half her money, or if she died he'd be entitled to *all* of it, she would've just shrugged. He was her man so he deserved it. She already looked after him and he knew she'd give him the blood out of her veins if he asked for it.

In terms of what actually went down around the marriage, I imagine Raye gave Mitch a call and said, 'Amy wants to get married,' and some paperwork was sent over pretty fast. That's only my assumption but there must have been *something* because Blake never did get any of Amy's money.

Mitch was now very involved in Amy's career. He was basically the second manager, alongside Raye, and they ran Amy's career between them. Mitch liked being in charge but he was protecting her too. He also liked a pound note and nothing would've happened without him having a say. If she'd died before they divorced, Blake would have been entitled to her estate, but it wouldn't have been right in anyone's mind to give Blake Amy's millions after what he put her through.

*

I never thought Amy would take heroin or crack because hard drugs just weren't her thing, like she'd always said. Blake was an addict but Amy was headstrong. Blake wasn't on heroin and crack twenty-four hours a day, either. It was something I was aware of in Jeffrey's Place; occasionally I'd see the foils and the crack pipes made of Lucozade bottles. I couldn't be certain she wasn't smoking those drugs at this point but I seriously doubted it. She was still healthy, even if she was getting thinner and thinner. I know in the early days of addiction you can still function, it doesn't destroy you overnight, but she didn't tell me about it and if she *was* doing it and she thought it was alright, I'd know about it.

Jeffrey's Place was now a shithole, barely liveable, so she moved for a while into the Kensington Hotel in west London. It was a luxury hotel apartment with its own living room and kitchen. She starting ringing me from there, many times over the course of a day. And the next day. Then I wouldn't hear for a day. She wasn't lucid. She sounded either slowed down or hyped up. She was hesitant and would only ring me when Blake left the room. We'd be mid-flow, talking, I'd hear the door go, then Blake's voice in the distance – 'Amy, what you doing?' – and she'd just hang up, without a word. She didn't want him to know she was talking to me or anyone else for that matter. I sensed sometimes she was frightened.

She started telling me what was going on.

'I think Blake's selling stories on me.'

'Well, that's not cool Ame, what d'you think about that?'

'I don't care, he's just trying to make his own money.'

She was kidding herself. She knew it was wrong but she was saving face. She didn't want to say 'My husband's an arsehole.' He didn't need money, everything would've been paid for. He was selling stories on Amy all the time, what they were up to, fly-on-the-wall stuff. He was talking to a tabloid journalist every day, then you'd read, 'a source said'. Amy was very slowly telling me that her life was fucked up.

I hadn't spoken to her for weeks until then and just assumed she was smashing it – she had the biggest selling album in the country that year, she was ridiculously famous, with loads of money *and* she got the guy she wanted. I was expecting her to tell me everything was mental and brilliant, about all the things she and Blake were up to. Instead she painted a picture: I'm stuck in this hotel. Can't go anywhere. Everywhere we go there's paparazzi. There's people following us. I can't handle it. I feel like a prisoner. *We can't do anything.*

I sensed the prisoner aspect also referred to Blake. There was no Amy anymore, no Blake anymore, only 'we'. Blake was in control of her life and management was in control of her career. I doubt Amy really wanted to move into a posh hotel in Kensington, it was management's decision: there were paparazzi everywhere now, so it was safer, there was security.

Amy would never say 'help me'. Those words would never come out of her mouth. *Never.* But she knew I would always help her and wouldn't judge her. Over the days on the phone, I heard her lighter spark way too much.

'What are you doing right now Amy?'

'Ah, y'know. I'm tootin' 'n' bootin'.'

I knew exactly what that meant. Crack and heroin. I was calm and sensible.

'OK Ame, well you know that shit can't go on forever, don't you?'

No response.

When Amy got back with Blake, I just wasn't around as much. I lost her to him. I wasn't worried at first – it was normal, my friend was in a relationship, I was doing my own thing. But now I'd come back and their world was very different. I thought, *Shit, look what's happened since I left, you're smoking heroin and crack and Blake's taken control of your life.*

Blake was the first person who gave Amy heroin. *Offered* her heroin. She made the decision to take it herself. To be with him and be on his level. She told me that years later. She just decided, well, if that's the thing that's stopping me from being with him then I'm gonna do it. She never saw it as a big deal. Heroin was everywhere in Camden. You could call it self-sacrifice but it's also just being madly in love. And doomed romance has a very seductive power.

In the Kensington Hotel, they were fighting. I didn't know at first. Drugs are bad enough, two people in a relationship on heroin and crack, in a room together for weeks, of course there's going to be fights. It stemmed from the drugs, it wasn't going on beforehand.

It was Amy's twenty-fourth birthday, 14 September 2007, and I went to the hotel to visit her. It was the first time I'd seen the paparazzi waiting for them outside, ready with the strobe light deluge that soon became a constant in our lives. Amy hated birthdays, she always said her idea of the perfect birthday was to be put under general anaesthetic all day until it was over. I was completely sober at the time, I'd temporarily sorted myself out, so in my head I had a role: I'm saving Amy.

I would encourage her to not be in this room all the time, just the two of them doing drugs. She'd been doing drugs with Blake in that room for two months solid by her birthday. Even she had to be bored of it by now. There had been times before when I'd encouraged them to go out: 'Why don't we go to the Hawley? You can bring your drugs Blake, let's just break out of this place.'

They didn't want to go.

In the apartment, he was always calling her into the bathroom, 'D'you wanna boot, Ame?' I thought, *Stop it, she's alright sitting there, don't encourage her, maybe she doesn't need it as much as you.* When I was there he'd text her from the bathroom, asking what she was doing. 'He texts me whenever I'm with someone else,' she told me, 'that's how he controls me.'

I sensed Amy wanted to go out. This time she used her birthday as an excuse. 'It's my birthday Blake, we have to go out.' Blake said OK.

The plan was to go to Jazz After Dark, the place where I introduced her to Phil for the 'Rehab' video – it's a shrine to Amy now. She'd been living in this hotel room, in her joggers and Blake's hoodie, and now she was excited, 'I'm gonna get myself dolled up!'

She always took ages to get ready but smoking drugs meant she was taking a hell of a lot longer. Blake was in the bathroom, bedroom, smoking drugs, doing his own thing. I sat there for four, five hours. I ordered a car, everyone was ready, Amy was all glammed up, Blake was dressed as well, cool. Out of nowhere, Blake didn't want to go. Me and Amy said we'd go anyway. She said, 'Give me a minute so I can say goodbye to Blake, go'n wait in the car.'

I waited ten minutes. I went back in and when Amy opened the door, her lip was bust. Split. Bloodied. What the fuck? I went to push through the door.

'No Tyler, just leave it.'

'What d'you mean leave it?!'

'T, I can handle myself.'

It was like she was saying this is bollocks but it just happens sometimes. I never want to get involved in other people's shit too much but I could've gone in, reared up, started on Blake; he would've had me in a fight and I wouldn't have cared. But I got two vibes from Amy: *Don't stir this up, this is our situation and you don't need to worry about it*. And, more typical in domestic abuse: *Don't start cos it'll get worse*. Which is the one I took away. I left and said, 'OK Amy. But ring me.'

I walked out but didn't get in the car. I just walked and walked. There'd been inklings before but now I knew: everything I'd thought might be happening in that room – control, abuse – it was all going on. I didn't do anything because she asked me not to and I trusted her instincts. I knew she could handle herself. I couldn't call the police, could I? Or, if I burst through the door, knocked Blake out, what difference would that have made? Would she have left him? Would she have said, 'Thank you T, you're my hero'? Of course not. She loved him. And as fucked up as it is, it came with the gangster's wife fantasy territory.

My life became about wanting to save Amy. I knew I'd be no use to her if I was a mess myself so that drove me on to sobriety. The thing that stopped me from dying many times was that I had to look after her. It was the same for her, with me. People could call it co-dependency but we kept each other alive. I threw myself back into her world because I felt I had no choice – we were soulmates. Those calls from the hotel were the beginning of Amy sending me an SOS. She was creating a safety net for herself through me. So what could I do? How could I not help her? And the only way I could really help was to be with her all the time, as much as I could. I knew that world would be bad for me but I loved her and I'd do anything for her. I thought about it very logically: *Alright Ame I hear you. I'm gonna end up in a mental hospital, but I'm going in.*

CHAPTER 15

It was the 21 September 2007 and Amy was duetting with Prince. Back in May, at the press conference to announce his twenty-one-night residency at the O2 Arena, Prince talked about 'Love Is a Losing Game' and how much he loved it. It would be a dream, he added, for Amy to sing it with him on his last night at the O2. Phil Griffin had started working with Prince, shooting his videos, filming his tours and they'd become close. So Prince asked Phil to arrange for it to happen, which he did.

Amy was made up at the idea, though it was only one week since her birthday when Blake had bust her lip. Phil rang me, worried. 'Is Amy alright, is she in a good place?' She was fine that day. He said, '*Please* make sure she comes, don't let me down,' and he also said, very specifically, Blake cannot come, do not create any scenario where Blake is there. I couldn't have stopped Blake from coming but I skewed it, told him it was work, it was professional. He was too interested in smoking drugs anyway.

Amy insisted I went with her. We got there, Phil had told Prince all about me and we were both introduced. Prince said to Amy, 'Shall we rehearse?' Amy said, 'Yeah, if Tyler can come with me, he's a singer too.' Typical Amy, she never left me out of anything.

We were in Prince's dressing room, which was the size of a house, with one whole side an enormous mirror, with a giant make-up table, expensive make-up on every surface, clothes on rails, clothes on the floor, everywhere. He was even tinier than you'd think – he and Amy were the same height! – and he looked like *Prince*, like an entity from out of this world, with glitter in his hair. He was wearing a dressing gown, like a smoking jacket, it was some shade of purple, it really was. He looked like Prince relaxing in his dressing room and he was *incredibly* nice, a gentle soul, it was all so comfortable. I felt like he understood Amy, he just got her. Not many people ever did, not straight away.

Prince sat down at his piano and they had a run-through, him singing most of 'Love Is a Losing Game', Amy mostly listening to him, even though for the actual performance he accompanied her on guitar. Then, and I'm sure he was just trying to please her, Prince said he wanted to sing with me too. We all sang 'Purple Rain'. It wasn't for very long – me, Amy and Prince singing together – but she made that happen for *me*. An amazing moment in my life. Even though I was nervous, thinking, 'I shouldn't even *be* here.'

Afterwards, we went into a private lounge area, Amy leaned over the bar, ordered us both soft drinks – she'd agreed she wouldn't drink that night – and we could see Naomi Campbell looking over. Then Amy whispered to me, 'Faye Dunaway's over there.' We'd been transported to a different dimension. Faye Dunaway, the actual Bonnie from the *Bonnie and Clyde* movie, looked so glamorous and beautiful. She introduced herself to Amy, 'Hi, my name's Faye.' Amy went all shy. 'Hi, I'm Amy.' Then out of nowhere, typical her, she said to Faye Dunaway, 'Tyler's mum's got better cheekbones than you.' She didn't say it in a bitchy way, she was blown away by the moment and what she was trying to say to Faye Dunaway was,

'You've got amazing cheekbones!' Faye Dunaway said, 'Thank you,' but she must've thought, *that's a bit weird*.

Amy would've smoked drugs that day at some point but she was fine, looking good, even if she was nervous. The way Prince always did things, he'd play two shows a night – the main show in the arena and then a smaller late night 'aftershow'. This comparatively intimate one was where Amy would perform. We were in the Indigo part of the O2, nearly 3,000 capacity and Prince's final performance in London. We were at the side of the stage when Amy started bottling it.

'I dunno if I can do it . . . I'll be able to do it if you don't go anywhere, just stand there.'

I could hear Prince's guitar backstage start the song. Amy started singing, then they were both on stage and she smashed it, the huge crowd cheering. *Fucking amazing*.

Phil told me afterwards he saw tears in Prince's eyes that night on stage. He told Phil many times Amy was the most important singer of her time, her emotional vulnerability and honesty moved him like no one else.

Something good like that only ever happened when Blake wasn't around. Right now, it was just me and Amy. I treasured the moment, enjoyed every single second till the end, my best friend singing with Prince as he played *her* song, that stunning song I heard her write on the kitchen floor eighteen months before. It was the first night in many months we'd had to ourselves and it was also a moment for her to recognize *herself*. And what she'd achieved. And because no one was around, she did. She'd normally be nonchalant – 'Yeah I sang with Prince, whatever' – and her collar would be up and she'd play it down, like insecure people do. I was the only person she didn't act cool with.

She came off stage and I was so excited. 'You just performed with Prince!'

She said, 'It's fucking mad!'

She never let people know that side of her, *never*. We might as well have been the two kids who went to Sylvia Young's that night. I was always trying to rip out with my *teeth* any moment of celebration, any momentary good feeling she might be having through everything that was happening. Because I could see it all just flying past her. And then Amy had some news.

'Blake's coming.'

Blake turned up. Prince, being the nicest man in the world, let Amy know Blake could use his dressing room too, she could do whatever she wanted in there, use his make-up, he wasn't using the room anymore. And now, with Blake there, the whole atmosphere changed. Blake was paranoid, itchy, going into Prince's toilet to do drugs. Everything switched to edgy. There was cash in the dressing room, just lying there, out in the open on the make-up table. No one was paying any attention to it. Amy was calm, everyone was drinking, there were other people in the room, Prince popped in, it was casual. We said our good-byes, left and me, Amy and Blake were driven back to the Kensington Hotel.

In the car, Blake made a joke about taking the money from the dressing room. It was hundreds of pounds. *He'd stolen Prince's money.* I was mortified. Amy brushed it off. I knew she knew it was wrong but in front of him she laughed about it, because she felt awkward. I knew she didn't think it was funny. It turned out Blake stole some of Prince's hairbrushes too, which Phil knew he was sentimental about.

The next morning, Phil rang me. Prince's security found out the money had been stolen and blamed Phil. They thought he'd taken it so they set on him, roughed him up and kicked him out. For some reason, Phil didn't have his pass with him and in those situations, you could be Whitney Houston's sister but if the guy who runs the door at Whitney Houston's show doesn't know that and you don't have a pass, you're a piece of shit. So Phil, instead of being the visual director of Prince's entire tour, was accused of being the guy who stole money out of Prince's dressing room, was beaten up and turfed out the O2. Phil, who had a good relationship with Prince, was devastated.

The following day, Amy got hold of Prince and apologized. She said she'd give him the money back. Prince said, 'I don't care about the money, it's just really not cool what happened with Phil.' So now it was Prince apologizing for *that*. I didn't find it funny at all. I didn't find it funny my mate had been beaten up either. I'm from nothing and for the first time I felt myself looking down on Blake thinking, that was really un-classy, mate. There was no talk that morning of how amazing last night had been, what it had been like for Amy to sing with one of the greatest artists of all time, he didn't even ask Amy how she felt about it. It was all about Blake stealing the money. I thought, *who are you, anyway? My friend is a ridiculously talented person who has these amazing opportunities, she loves you, and you're bringing your riffraff self into these magical moments you're privileged to even get near.* I wanted to say to her, 'Amy, who the fuck does your boyfriend think he is?' To which she would've probably replied, 'My husband.' There was always somebody trying to take it all away from her.

Phil told me even Prince could see that: he rang Phil on a few occasions afterwards asking if there was anything he could do to get her away from Blake, and all the madness surrounding her – he even offered to send a plane to spirit her away.

Amy's view of Blake was becoming seriously skewed. She was starting to see him as God. He was more important than everybody and everything. Even six months prior to this she would've been appalled – 'You've just nicked money off

Prince?!' But now, if she had to choose between fucking off Blake and fucking off Prince, Prince could've done one. And by this point, Blake was just a mess. A *mess*. And everywhere he went he created more and more mess.

CHAPTER 16

The Camden scene had started to spread out across London, especially east, around Hackney. A few people we knew were living in a gated redevelopment called Omega Works, in Hackney Wick, on the junction of the River Lea and Hertford Union Canal. It was new, modern, dominated by glass and some of the T4 crowd had apartments there. Amy's new hairdresser, Alex Foden, moved there and Catriona moved in with him, sharing the rent on a first-floor flat. She was a real character; Amy loved her stories about being out on the town, meeting geezers and she was now running Rokit, the vintage store in Camden. When she was homeless for a while she used to sleep in Rokit's storeroom.

Amy and Blake were back in Jeffrey's Place but he didn't have her captive as much, he'd just ring her every half hour. He was at the peak of his crack and heroin addiction, with a constant supply because money wasn't a problem, so he was on his own a lot. There comes a point in addiction where you end up in isolation, where your biggest relationship is with whatever you're addicted to. He was smoking three times the amount of drugs Amy was, so she was hanging out more with me, Cat and Alex in their apartment in Omega Works.

It was a big, square complex, four storeys high, very plush, overlooking a courtyard in the middle with glass walls everywhere. There were balconies running around the entire square and you could walk straight along to your neighbours' front doors. It was Phil who recommended Alex as Amy's hairdresser after they'd done a Timotei advert together. She went to see him and while he was giving me a bangin' haircut he had a spliff in his hand so they immediately had something in common: habitual weed smokers. He was a good-looking boy, well dressed and was becoming a big name hairdresser. Similarly to Blake, he didn't seem to have any connection to his family. He was a loner coming into this very appealing inner circle of Amy, me, Catriona, Chantelle and Naomi. We were a tight group who'd do anything for each other, this young bunch of fucked-up kids. And we *were* just kids, twenty-two, twenty-three. With everything we could ever want at our disposal.

Alex seemed to have no qualms about using his connection to Amy. He had Dermalogica skin products sent every week, mainly for himself, using her name. 'Hi, I'm Amy's hairdresser.' Every brand would send new products round, supposedly for her: hair, beauty, Fake Bake tan. She was a multi-millionaire, she didn't need a free box of Fake Bake, she could afford to buy a rocket to fly her nearer the sun to get a really good tan.

I sensed Alex had a child-like jealousy of mine and Amy's friendship and he wanted me out of the way. Amy couldn't see it in her crack psychosis. He was doing a lot of crack and heroin with Amy, drugs I never did, so to me it was his way of getting closer to her, the only thing he could have with her that I couldn't. He came to loathe me and I hated him.

I always chose to keep my enemies closer.

It was Alex who organized a night out in Harrods where they close the shop for you and everything's free. We could have anything we wanted. There was someone walking around with limitless champagne on a tray. There was Amy, me, Cat,

Alex and the Olsen twins were there too, the wholesome American teen stars who turned into wayward party girls. They were thin as Rizlas. At one point, Alex and Amy disappeared into an upstairs back room to smoke heroin in the gilded Harrods surroundings.

Amy chose a dozen Mulberry bags, for both of our mums and aunties, two grand each. They could never have afforded a Mulberry bag and she was very choosy about it. She chose cocktail dresses and about twenty pairs of Louboutins for her little size four feet. You just pointed stuff out and people put them into bags. I kept thinking about the irony, all this privilege given to people who could already afford it. I didn't want to take the piss and Amy was encouraging me to pick another nice bag for my mum. She picked out two jumpers for me, which really bothered Alex. He grabbed a laptop for himself. In the months to come, I'd stick a breadknife through that laptop.

Me and Amy were at Cat and Alex's in Omega Works one day, a standard day, as much as crackheads and alcoholics hanging out indoors can be defined as standard. All through Amy's addictions, I encouraged her to do normal shit, cook food, do the washing, tidy up, because normal is what was missing and what she so desperately craved. Today, like countless others, Amy was making meatballs. Making meatballs while smoking her crack pipe.

I once heard someone refer to cocaine as 'tomorrow's energy today'. From what I can tell, crack is more like 'this year's energy now'. As she stood at the stove cutting onions and rolling mince into perfect sized balls, she'd also randomly roll into cartwheels. *Cartwheels*. Right across the floor of this big, open-plan apartment, the living room and kitchen along one very long wall. Then she'd do handstands. Perfect handstands in between every tester taste of the sauce. She was good at it all, proper acrobatics. At the same time, she was singing beautifully, as ever, elated about cooking in the kitchen.

I'd never seen Amy that high. I was used to seeing Amy drunk, stoned, falling about. With crack and heroin it's not like being drunk. People on heroin and crack don't drink, they don't need to, she'd drink Lucozade and fizzy drinks, maybe have one alcoholic drink and it'd sit there for hours.

It sounds crazy but I loved seeing my girl happy like that; even when addiction is wreaking havoc in your life, there are moments of real happiness. The drugs were there for now and addiction was running its course, causing sorrow, pain and disturbing shit on a daily basis, but moments like that you relished, moments when you could lie to yourself, rare and fleeting moments when you pretend everything is normal. Everything is OK.

Blake rang. He was on loudspeaker on Amy's phone and he sounded totally paranoid. He was in Jeffrey's Place.

'I'm looking out the winda, there's people coming to get me.'

I didn't think anything was wrong other than the state of Blake's head. He kept ringing back every two minutes so Amy eventually said, 'Just come round to us, I'll get you a cab.'

He arrived outside the apartment, looking psychotic and dishevelled, like a hardened drug addict, basically. He came into the flat and started peering around the closed curtains on the glass wall overlooking the courtyard. Three minutes, later fifteen plain clothes police officers were suddenly inside the flat arresting him, right in front of us, doing the whole 'anything you say . . .' routine, clamping handcuffs on his wrists behind his back. We were sitting on the sofas with our plates of meatballs, forks in mid-air, looking at an actual police operation and there was heavy crack use going on in the flat that day, crack kept in Alex's bathroom. The *looks* between everyone. Alex pretended to casually saunter off to the bathroom and of course threw a load of crack down the toilet, I heard the flush. The police saw him get up and no one stopped him. You don't do that on a drugs bust. So there was a very clear sense that they weren't after drugs, they weren't after Amy. I always got the impression the police cared about Amy, that they didn't give a shit about the drugs. The whole world knew she was on drugs and the police turned a blind eye. I think the public loved her, felt sorry for her and saw Blake as the villain.

The police walked him out the front door, down the stairwell on the corner of the block and out into the courtyard. Amy ran onto the balcony outside and lost the plot, distraught, shouting, 'Don't take my Blake!' He was going through the courtyard, handcuffs behind his back, into the car and now Amy was screaming and crying. 'Blakey, my baby, don't worry!' She was threatening to launch herself off the balcony to get to him, I was holding her back and she was furious, punching me in the chest, kicking me, she even tried to *bite* me and I wouldn't let go, just wouldn't let her get down the stairs. She might have tried to beat up a policeman or throw something at them and then she'd be on a GBH charge. Eventually she gave in, collapsed into my arms, slid down my body and onto the floor. It was highly dramatic, but it was real.

Within five minutes of Blake being taken away, Mitch arrived. It could have been coincidence, or maybe someone told him the police turned up at the apartment, but I always felt that he had some involvement with the arrest. Why would Mitch suddenly be there? If he did get Blake arrested, it was a good move where he acted like a proper dad as far as I'm concerned.

Amy was shouting at her dad, 'I want Blake to have the best lawyer in the world, don't care what money it costs!'

'We will Ame, we'll do everything.' He didn't give a shit about Blake, obviously.

Raye was there within half an hour. They both talked to me on the balcony, saying there was a big tour coming up, she wouldn't do it alone so would I go with her? They were using me, manipulating me, but I didn't care, I saw it as an opportunity. There was a chance, now, of saving Amy. You couldn't get in between Amy and Blake and I wouldn't even have tried, she loved him so much. I looked at her through the glass, devastated, doing drugs with Alex.

Blake's mum and stepdad turned up at the flat along with one of his brothers. It was the first time I'd met her. She'd had a few drinks and I thought she was loud and foul-mouthed. My heart went out to Blake: this is your mum, you poor bastard. She had Blake's little brother with her, who was around fourteen, and it was like a weird family scenario which seemed fake to me. Amy bought into it. She was playing 'the wife', ordering food in, Kentucky Fried Chicken, making sure Blake's little brother had something to eat while they were all still doing crack.

Everyone in the 'family' was talking about how Amy would get Blake out of prison. Blake's mum was swearing at Mitch and Mitch was losing it.

'We're gonna spend a fortune trying to get your boy out of prison, why are you talking to me like that?'

Amy was in between them, arms out, trying to calm them down.

'Stop arguing, stop shouting, we're here for Blake!'

Then the teenage brother threw a punch at Mitch. There was screaming and shouting.

I thought *I'm off* and left.

*

119

On the balcony earlier, Raye and Mitch had made a suggestion: 'Why don't you and Amy get a place here? We'll see if there's an apartment available.'

Jeffrey's Place was now ruined anyway. Alex was here, Cat was here, I was usually here, it was the obvious thing to do, especially now Blake was gone, and probably for a long time. Amy came out onto the balcony. They were worried that this upcoming British tour, without Blake, wouldn't even happen. So they were reassuring her.

'Tyler will stay with you on the tour, Tyler will always be with you, you and Tyler are gonna get a flat here.'

They were doing everything they could and spending a lot of money to keep her together to go on tour. Who else would look after her and who could they trust? I know I made their lives easier. She wouldn't do certain things and they got me to get her to do them. I made her family's life easier, too. I heard them say it a million times. 'Don't worry, she's with Tyler, nothing bad will happen to her.'

CHAPTER 17

Amy used to say it a lot: 'The law don't apply to me.' She wasn't joking. It's not like she was up her own arse, in fact, she was the opposite. It was just *true*. She could get away with anything. Her and Alex got caught with weed at customs in Norway – it's very serious there and all that happened was that she had to pay a 500 Euro fine. If it was me? They'd probably put me in jail. Amy just paid up and was sent on her way, because she was 'Amy Winehouse'. The power that comes with being famous and having money is insane and she knew it.

There were times Amy deliberately smashed things in pubs – glasses, a table, mirrors, being rowdy – and there were never any repercussions. She was testing it, seeing how far she could go, because she was clever. We were in a bar once in Soho, central London, at the height of her fame, one of those nice bars with the wine glasses hanging down above the front of the bar. She reached up, swept her hand right along them, loads fell out and smashed on the floor. No one approached her and we walked out. I was horrified.

'Why did you do that?!'

'Because I'm making a point. The point is, why would they let me get away with that? How could they *let* me do that? Fame is bollocks. Fame is bullshit. Fame is ridiculous. I've just smashed a bar up and no one's gonna say anything.'

People heard about this kind of thing and assumed she was an arse. Sometimes she *was*. Because that's what drugs and alcohol do. But most of the time she wasn't, she was playing with fame. Sometimes one of the security boys would hand over money to a bar manager: 'Don't say anything, sorry it's all smashed up but this should pay to fix it.' Money got her out of so many situations.

There was a lawlessness in her that was always there but a lot of the time it was just funny. In 2007, the Sultan of Brunei's son Prince Azim was at a festival in London where Amy was playing. He was in his mid-twenties then, a renowned socialite, always around the music scene, hanging out with ridiculously famous people like Michael Jackson and Mariah Carey. He was also proper royalty, second in line to the throne of Brunei's absolute monarchy. The Sultan of Brunei is one of the richest men on the planet and Prince Azim himself was worth billions. He was there with his auntie and his PA, backstage in a marquee tent having some food – the only ones there – when hands outside the tent started splitting two sections of the canvas apart, ripping through the tape that was holding it together. It was Amy, she burst right through, turned to them and said, 'I've had enough of being out there, everybody's licking my arse, you'd think I was fucking royalty!' Azim thought this was hilarious. He invited her to come and eat with them – she was so thin then. Knowing Amy, she'd probably been on the other side of the tent doing an interview and thought 'Fuck this, I'm going through the wall!'

Years later, in 2012, Prince Azim became a good friend of mine and I couldn't believe it when he said he'd met Amy that day in the tent. He told me when she sat down with them she'd said, 'This is such a relief, you seem like normal people.' He didn't tell her anything about himself. He said he saw a lot of himself in Amy, in the sense they held very different positions of privilege in life but they came with the same price: they couldn't be truly free. Azim saw someone with a hard, protective outer shell who was vulnerable and delicate underneath, which he wasn't expecting. He was like that too, which made it all the more heartbreaking when he passed away in October 2020 at the age of thirty-eight.

Someone who definitely wasn't above the law was Blake. He'd been arrested in Omega Works in November 2007 for perverting the course of justice on a 2006 GBH charge. Blake and a friend had beaten a guy up, badly, in an altercation with a pub landlord, who needed plates put in his face to repair the damage, which included a broken cheekbone, nose and eye socket. There was one witness to the attack and Blake paid him off, £200,000, to either not turn up in court or lie. Amy must have paid for that because Blake didn't have that sort of money. I guess that meant she was an accessory even if she didn't know what the money was for. And she was above the law on that one, too. (Blake pleaded guilty to both charges in summer 2008 and was given a twenty-seven-month sentence.)

But after Blake's arrest in Omega Works, Amy had to be questioned about it and had a meeting with the police. She asked me to come with her. We picked the lawyer up on the way who briefed Amy in the car.

'I'll be honest, Amy, it's just a formality, they have to question you so go through the protocol; they're not interested in arresting you in any way so just say no comment, no comment, no comment.'

Amy was done up to the nines. She liked reality, loved anything in her actual life that wasn't about being a pop star. She was in her element. She couldn't *wait* to go to the police station and sit there and be questioned. Like a gangster's wife. Knowing she wouldn't be arrested.

She went into the police station at Old Street; I sat outside the pub next door and there were crowds of paparazzi and journalists there. One journalist came up to me: 'You do realize you could make an awful lot of money out of this situation?'

I threw my drink in their face.

Amy came out.

'How did it go?'

'It was *hilarious*. I just sat and went no comment, no comment, no comment. I think I'm gonna write a song called "No Comment".'

We went to Blake's initial court hearing on 23 November. It wasn't something I wanted to be involved in. Amy was brave and bolshy and ballsy but when push came to shove, she was a little girl and always wanted me to go with her. She'd give in and say, 'I'm nervous, will you come with me?' and give me thirty seconds to get ready.

The court was in East London, not far from Omega Works. We were in the back of the car, paparazzi following us in cars and on bikes so I was aware this was a very public situation. Amy had been in hair and make-up for three hours, I looked like a tramp and I knew we'd be on the telly. We pulled up at the court and there was more paparazzi, we walked into court through a curtain of flashing strobe lights.

I'd never been in a courtroom before. It was huge, like you see on TV, so it all felt like a film. Blake was standing in the dock. Me and Amy were standing in a glass box overlooking the whole court. I never saw Amy as anything other than Amy and I was starting to see how different she'd become in other people's eyes. It was like I'd turned up with Princess Diana. That was the day Blake was remanded in custody and sent to Pentonville prison, awaiting the trial next year. He'd be in Pentonville for months.

Amy started crying and screaming, pressing her hands up against the glass; it was so dramatic and it was heart-breaking, she'd never thought for a second he might actually be put away. Standing beside her, watching her, with her hands, face and beehive pressed up against the glass, despite all the Blake-induced chaos, broke my heart too. Tears were streaming down her face, she was shouting, 'Blakey don't worry, I'll get you out!'

I looked around at everyone in that courtroom and no one, *no one* was looking at Blake. Every single person was looking at Amy, watching her behind the glass. It really *was* like being in a film. Everything about it was unreal. Blake's in handcuffs, he's going to prison; Amy's all glammed up, she's a superstar. I was standing next to this *character*, that's how it felt. Watching everybody watching her having a breakdown. I'd see that again and again – how your life, no matter what you're going through, no matter how real it is for you, no matter how devastated you are, no matter how heartbroken you feel, this is *entertainment*, for everybody else. That much was very, *very* clear.

With Blake in Pentonville prison Amy's addictions spiralled. She became a force all of her own, putting his addictions to shame. She went to the next level, that was her nature. The self-destruct button she did better than anybody else. She wasn't the kind of person who, when Blake was taken away from her, would say, 'Oh, I tried to get through it sober but it all got too much for me.' No. Amy made a decision. 'I'm gonna *destroy myself*.'

I knew what she was thinking. It was so fucked up it was almost funny: *Oh, you think you're gonna save me now? Come on everyone, yeah, the destructive force in my life has gone, well I'll show you how much you can save me, I'm gonna fucking do myself in 20 billion times worse. I'm gonna smoke as many drugs as I want and not give a shit if I die tomorrow cos I don't have my Blake and my life isn't worth living so come on try and save me now.* The full Shangri-Las song, basically. She made it clear to me: she wanted me around, she wanted my support, but *do not get in my way.*

We went back to Jeffrey's Place after the hearing and she shut herself away in the bathroom. I wasn't worried she was gonna hurt herself or kill herself but I sat downstairs, heard the lighter going and I knew she was *gone.* Things had already escalated but I knew in my heart: this is the next dimension.

I had my own coping mechanism. I poured myself an extra-large Jack Daniel's with fizzy codeine and sat there on the sofa thinking: *I don't know how we got here, how you've ended up one of the most famous people in the world, your husband's just gone to prison, now you're on crack and heroin, I'm basically looking after you and too frightened to leave you on your own, but here we are. And now we're going on a massive UK tour.*

CHAPTER 18

Winter 2007 and Amy hadn't performed for months. She hadn't really done anything for months, she was too immersed in the Blake drama. But I felt hopeful about things. About experiencing Amy as a performer again, a singer again. Maybe it would be like it was when we used to tour together.

I couldn't have been more naive.

We were all leaving together from Omega Works – me, Amy, Alex the hairdresser, Naomi the stylist – getting a flight from London City Airport to Scotland. I checked through my bags and found a bundle of hair extensions. I looked closer and wedged into the middle of the extensions were rolled up rocks of crack. The only explanation I had was that Alex had put them there as he would have wanted a ready supply of the stuff for him and Amy. If I'd been caught at customs, they would've put me in *prison*. I confronted Alex.

'You see them hair extensions with crack in them? They're in your bag now mate and you can do what the fuck you want with them.'

Maybe it wasn't him but he didn't deny it and just looked stunned. I didn't say anything to Amy. He was her official hairdresser and all I cared about was looking after her because she wasn't capable of looking after herself.

Going through customs, I realized there was actually nothing to worry about anyway. When Amy went to an airport, there were barely even passport checks; it was 'you're Amy Winehouse, zoom through'. We were on a commercial flight. Amy was at the window, I was in the middle, Naomi on the aisle. Amy got up, hiked herself over me and Naomi like a lad, vest on, tattoos out, off to the toilet. Two minutes later, I smelt the smell and thought, *Oh no, you're absolutely kidding me.* I'm very familiar with the smell of crack and heroin. Vile, disgusting, smells like shit and sugar. Naomi laughed. Even I had to laugh, thinking, *Oh Amy, only you, darlin', would do this.* The smell of crack, sweet and fizzy, was seeping out from the toilet, under the door, you could *see* smoke inching down the aisle. Everybody was looking around, sniffing: is the plane on fire?! The pilot himself came over the tannoy, like it was entertainment: 'Ladies and gentlemen, can someone kindly tell our famous friend to stop smoking in the toilet?' I thought, *She's not having a fag, mate!* Everyone laughed. I got up, went to the toilet, Amy opened the door and she was laughing too, stinking of crack.

When we landed there were no repercussions, no smoking fine, no police apprehension. She was still above the law.

Amy was playing Glasgow Barrowlands, the famous venue with the sprung dancefloor. We always stayed in decent hotels but the one near Glasgow was a grand, Scottish country manor where toffs probably stayed to go hunting. Amy walked in and loved it. 'This is alright, innit!?'

It was the first tour when she was 'Amy Winehouse', a household name. It was a completely new experience, where the crowds were five times bigger. In the dressing room it wasn't like when we were listening to Minnie Riperton and having a glass of whisky. A pool table had been drafted in, with everyone putting their *per diems* together on the baize to pay for cocaine.

The Barrowlands crowd was full on. Just before Amy got on stage, she froze.

'T, I can't do this, will you do what you used to do and stand at the side of the stage?'

I stood there and watched. And she did what she did every night on that tour, she cried and talked about Blake, tears trickling down her face.

'I'm sorry I'm not on the best form, my Blakey's in prison.'

On every stage, she said, 'My Blake incarcerated', like he was a man done wrong, even though he was on remand for nearly beating someone to death. She was still so skewed in her thinking. She threw the mic stand, it landed in the wings near me, she ran off stage, I ran round and she threw herself into my arms, crying. She went back on stage, finished the show, which didn't get any better. We went back to the stately manor.

Everybody had rooms but we all piled onto Amy's aristocratic four poster bed. Amy smoked some heroin. The others fell asleep and I was still awake, watching Amy over by the window, now chatting with Raye. I lay there, for hours, distraught, thinking *this is seriously fucked up*.

Island released 'Love Is a Losing Game' while she was on this tour. We'd tried to make the video weeks ago, before Blake was put away. A huge, elaborate set was hired at Pinewood Studios, a street had been built, there were plans for fake rain. As usual, it was all on me to try to get Amy there. Not Raye, Mitch or anyone at Island. Amy had stayed with Blake the night before; I got there in the morning, there were a hundred people waiting for her and Phil Griffin was frantic. 'Please, *please* Tyler, you're the only person who can get her here.' Everyone always thought they were getting me to manipulate her but I always just told her the truth. I rang her.

'Ame, the set looks amazing, there's a hundred people here, it's Phil directing, I think the video's gonna be brilliant but everyone's doing my head in so if you're not coming tell *me* at least so I can fuck off.'

She turned to Blake. 'Blake, it's the video shoot today, it's Phil directing, d'you wanna go?'

He shouted at her. 'No Ame, fuck that, we ain't going!'

'T, we ain't coming darlin'.'

He had that level of control.

Me and Phil had to make the video for 'Love Is a Losing Game'. We had editing equipment installed in a spare hotel room and put the montage of images and performances together. We wanted Amy to be involved. She did come in once. She said, 'I don't care, you and Phil do it, you know what I like,' walked out the door, swung the door back open and said, 'Make sure you put in loads of Blake!' And that's why he's in it.

The commercial flight when Amy smoked crack in the toilet was the last commercial flight she took on tour: after that it was private jets. She was too well known to have the public see her pull a stunt like that again. To make the process smoother and to reassure Amy about continuing the tour Raye was telling her, 'Look, we're gonna make it easier, no more going through airports, we're gonna hire private'. Amy thought it was absurd. 'What, private jets?!' I felt that even more so, because who was I that I could fly on private jets all of a sudden? We were in this privileged bubble but we were still just two best mates, like we always were.

There were two tour managers, one was called Curly, lovely fella, Scottish, a real father figure. He was a recovered addict, been sober for years and management drafted him in on purpose – if anyone could deal with this level of stupidness it was him. He knew the craic, he knew I wasn't a waster, wasn't a leech and he knew my role was to look after Amy. I talked to him a lot about her problems and he taught me a lot about heroin, about addiction and illness. He suggested a heroin replacement tablet called Subutex and knew where he could get some without a prescription. Amy agreed to take it, to stay on a level for the tour without going through full withdrawal.

She was on Subutex one night when she had a bath, like the old days. We got in bed and she put on *Cry Baby*, the Johnny Depp film, which she loved; she drew the *Cry Baby* tear on her face many times. She was a bit upset, talking about Blake.

'Me and Blake used to watch this film, Johnny Depp reminds me of my Blakey.'

I hadn't had Amy on my own for a good week properly, for a chat. I was lying next to her and had one of those moments, got a bit emo. Amy had just taken her Subutex.

'I'm so proud of you Amy, for trying to beat this heroin addiction, you've *realized*,' I said. I was so happy and proud.

She jumped out of the bed. 'Tyler, are you fucking off yer head?! What, does everyone think they're gonna get me sober? I'm only doing it cos it's what they've told me to do, but I've only gotta take these tablets while we're on this tour and when we get back to London I swear I'm gonna get tooted and booted off my fucking nut, cos I miss my Blake.'

She might as well have added, 'So stop crying, stop thinking this is the beginning of me getting better because it fucking ain't. This is the beginning of me getting *a lot worse*.'

She wasn't angry at me. She was just *angry*. She crushed my optimism but I loved that about her too. She'd bring me back to reality – *get that fairy tale bollocks out of your head*. It wasn't long before everyone was crushing those Subutex tablets up and snorting them as lines.

I'd managed to stay sober-ish for months by now, through the Kensington Hotel weeks, her birthday bust-up with Blake, the Prince situation, and now I was starting to unravel. I knew going on tour with Amy wouldn't do me any good addiction-wise, the timing was terrible, but I was here for a reason: to take care of her. I had responsibilities, which also meant pressure. Seeing how her own addictions had escalated, so fast, since Blake went down, made me edgy too. It made me feel like I needed 'help' from my own supposedly trusty stabilizers, to get me through every day. I just couldn't tolerate this sober. I started to fuck myself up again, for her, but that's what friends do.

My drinking slipped back. I started doing a lot of cocaine as part of my role was to stay awake and keep an eye on Amy in the night. Most people on the tour knew about the drugs, that's how things are in the music industry. I was on a mission. In hindsight, I was also fuelling my own addictions but I absolutely believed it was the right thing to do. Another part of my role was to make sure there was no drug paraphernalia left in any hotel rooms before we checked out. I was the 'responsible' one.

Amy was playing London and we were staying in the K West Hotel, which everyone called The K Hole. We were always there for parties, for Kelly Osbourne's birthday, it was the new place to be in London. Amy had already told me, 'I'm gonna *destroy* myself in London.' The gig was in Brixton in two days' time and we had a party in the K Hole that lasted two days. Loads of people turned up. Including Pete Doherty.

We knew Pete from the Camden scene but he still unnerved

me. He looked like the living dead, a zombie, with a big dressing on the side of his face like you'd get in hospital for wounds. He was in the room injecting heroin in front of everyone, I'd never seen that before, I definitely felt like I was in *Trainspotting* now. Amy being around him disturbed me, I was scared she'd start injecting herself, which she never did. She always smoked.

Pete was on a sofa doing this blood painting of Amy and Blake, embracing. It was beautifully done, Amy's arms around Blake and Blake's hands behind his back, in handcuffs. She was high on heroin, without crack, and she was very chilled. He was sitting there injecting, taking the needle out of his arm and using the blood to do the painting. He asked Amy for some of her blood, being all artistic and meaningful. She had self-harm marks and most of the time they were fresh so she scratched a wound, he took a few drops and painted them in.

Mitch arrived. He'd known Amy was doing drugs for a long time by now, it was public knowledge, but she'd always made a point of not doing them in front of her dad, had the decency to go off to some other room. I personally never heard him say anything to her directly but he would usually say something directly to the people around her when they were doing drugs. It was like he always needed someone else to blame for Amy's addictions. Now Blake was out of the picture, here was this full-blown heroin addict with a huge plaster on his face and blood everywhere. Mitch caused a massive scene, bawling at Amy.

'What the fuck are you doing hanging around with him?! Aren't you gonna try an' get better?!'

'Dad, don't embarrass me!'

Mitch just left.

There was a party in Amy's room that night, about thirty people, everybody drinking, taking drugs, ordering room service. At one point she left the room, I went looking for her and found her in some couple's room, doing coke with them while they were asking her if she was gonna have kids. I got her back to her own room and felt responsible. She'd been talking to strangers, they could've filmed her. But that was typical Amy, leaving her own party to go and sit with a couple of randoms.

Eventually it was only me and Amy left. The room was destroyed – drink, drugs and food on every surface. Amy was constantly, relentlessly smoking crack, just like she said she would. The room was dark, the light of daybreak creeping through the window and her eyes were half closed, like a cat's, the way crack addicts' eyes always go. I had nightmares about those cat's eyes for years. I was thinking: *This isn't my friend, this isn't right.*

I fell asleep on the sofa, woke up, saw a bowl of cold sausage and mash and projectile vomited. I'd felt iffy all night. I'd had this feeling once before on tour where I'd felt iffy, this feeling of something travelling up my veins, like I was actually gonna die, in a room full of heroin smoke. I couldn't stand up properly. I'd said to Curly, 'Is there any way heroin could be in my system?' He just laughed. 'Of course you can get the passive effects.' I was horrified. 'Jesus Christ I'm on heroin!' Now it was happening again, the passive effects of crack.

I was in the bathroom for an hour, lying on the floor, head over the toilet, Amy rubbing my back. 'I'm so sorry, I can't believe I've done this to you!' She meant it too. 'I don't care about harming myself,' she'd always say, 'but I'm not gonna harm someone I love.'

Nick Shymansky came to the Brixton show. We were all backstage – me, Alex, Naomi, Cat – Amy was off her face. I was doing loads of coke, drinking. I was on painkillers. It had all affected me, the craziness, the cat's eyes – I was losing the plot. So when Nick came in, it was like the *actually* responsible one had turned up. He took me into a room.

'Tyler, you don't look right mate, what are you doing?'

'I'm helping Amy.'

'How are you helping Amy? You're on coke!'

'Yeah, but they give me that cos she stays awake for three days on crack so I need it to stay awake and keep an eye on her.'

He knew I'd lost the plot.

'You need to get away from all this. Otherwise, you'll both be found dead in a hotel room.' He said it wasn't too late for me. 'I know you're trying to help Amy, I know they're using you to help Amy, but going on tour with Amy is not actually a replacement for you doing it yourself. You're only twenty-four. You could still have a deal if you wanted one. If you get your-self together, you can still have a stab at life.'

I cried. Everything had been a hundred miles an hour and suddenly a real person came in and I stopped. I broke down and put my arms around him. I was lost. And when you're lost, it's easier to concentrate your mind on something other than your own problems. And I'd definitely put my mind on *something*.

Amy played Bournemouth. After the gig, we were in a hotel room with some local girls who were trying to be normal with Amy. 'I like your make-up!' Amy had started writing me notes when she didn't want us talking in front of everybody. She handed me one that said: 'Why d'you keep running in circles?' She could see I was a broken man. I never slept. She took me aside.

'Are you alright?'

'No, I don't wanna drink anymore, I don't wanna do coke anymore, I want you to get better.'

I was crying again. She got me my Night Nurse, told me not to worry, to go to sleep, in that mothering way she still had. I hadn't slept for so long. I thought, I'll sleep now and tomorrow is another day.

I woke up and Amy was gone. I freaked out. Curly came in.

'Don't worry, she's in London. We need to take you home, the tour's been cancelled.'

She'd just gone *fuck it* and got in the car with the two Bournemouth girls who gave her a lift straight back to London. I could see Curly was pleased: enough madness. Maybe she was trying to spare me more madness too.

We had a tour bus and he walked me to it; Alex was there, I could smell the crack. Curly sat me down. He told me Amy wasn't well, she needed help, she needed to go to a psychiatric unit, in a hospital. I didn't want to believe it. He said she was a heroin addict, a crack addict, she had bulimia, she was a self-harmer. I sat there sobbing. And sobbing and sobbing. No one had ever said these things to me out loud before, ever. He said if these things didn't get sorted out, Amy would die. His words fell on me like bricks. He also said, 'But people do get better.' I got up, went to the fridge, got a bottle of Jack Daniel's – far easier to swallow than the words I'd just heard – and kept drinking and drinking and drinking until I passed out in a bunk.

It was the beginning of people not being able to deal with Amy. People around her thought she was a nightmare. They gave up on her. Sometimes she *was* a nightmare. Her problems were far too big for any one person to deal with. For any one person to help with. But I didn't know that then. I was still a kid.

The bus took me home to my Amy.

CHAPTER 19

Straight after the cancelled UK tour, we were due to move into our apartment in Omega Works. After Amy had bolted back to London, she had checked into a hotel, so I went round to pick her up. She was still so exhausted from the madness of that tour that I had to carry her through the glass front door of Omega Works in my arms. She was unconscious and so thin she was practically weightless. It felt surreal, walking into this stunning modern apartment while the friend you love so much is half dead in your arms. I laid her down on a sofa in this huge living room and thought: *It's a new place, it's a new beginning.*

Our apartment was on the ground floor *and* the first floor, a massive space two storeys high with balconies on both floors, in the opposite corner to Alex and Cat's flat. We could go out onto the balcony on the first floor and walk straight along, all the way round to Alex's. It was almost laughably luxurious. We had glass walls everywhere too, one half of the ground floor went all the way up to a ceiling 20 to 30 feet high; the other half went up to the second floor, a mezzanine, with a spiral staircase in the middle. Amy's bedroom was on the mezzanine, all glass, with black curtains. If you looked up and the curtains weren't shut you could see into her bedroom. There was a dining table that turned into a pool table. There was a *hammock*.

Raye came round and tried to get Amy out of bed to deal with the cancelled tour.

'Ame, you have to come and see the lawyer, there's a meeting, otherwise we're not gonna get the insurance for the tour.'

'Raye, I'm asleep.'

'It's gonna cost us hundreds of thousands of pounds.'

As usual, he turned to me. 'Tyler, please try and get her up.'

I said, 'She doesn't wanna get up.' I'd rather she had the sleep anyway, that seemed more important to me at the time.

She told him, 'I don't give a fuck about the money.'

Raye left. I imagine the money was lost. I never asked.

The key to the front door was lost within three days. Because we weren't sensible, we didn't sort out a replacement. We'd go in and out of a downstairs window. Paparazzi were now living outside the apartment, just two at first, and they'd get shots of Amy climbing out the window, on sleeping tablets, having just woken up, distraught, thin, squinting in all the flashing lights.

Sometimes we'd use the paparazzi; they were now part of our lives. The complex was in the middle of an industrial estate, the nearest shop a petrol station half an hour's walk away. So in the middle of the night, if the drink had run out, the paps gave us a lift.

'Could you take us to the off licence?'

'Alright, hop in.'

Amy would always lose everything, especially her phone. We were looking for her phone one day, hours and hours of 'where's my phone?' Then we could hear it ringing somewhere really near. She burst out laughing, shouted 'Hold up!', put her hand into her beehive and pulled out the ringing phone. I was pissing myself. She wore her beehive indoors as well as outdoors now, usually one of those big ones Alex attached, so she'd keep things in there so she didn't lose them. She hid drug wraps in there too.

Her beehive was now a work of art. In the early touring days of *Back to Black* she'd send herself up, she knew the beehive was just as famous as she was and sometimes, when the gig was over, she'd have fans backstage. There'd usually be little girls there who loved Amy, with their mums, and sometimes we'd take one girl and her mum into the dressing room and Amy and Alex would beehive the little girl up. One time this tiny girl's beehive was *massive* and I was sitting there laughing thinking, 'What's going on?!'

We'd occasionally go out with Russell Brand – he always called her 'Winehouse' – and whenever she saw him she'd put a Barbie doll in her beehive. Russell was a good laugh, incredibly bright and they just got on – they were like two lads together out on the town. Other nights weren't so funny. She was also an acquaintance of Mos Def and we were all in a hotel room together one night. Amy kept popping off to the bathroom to smoke drugs. She would never do that shit in front of him but of course he knew. He was concerned and had a word.

'Amy, that shit's no good, y'know?'

She idolized him. She knew it wasn't cool.

'Mos, I know that, man.'

It was a sad moment for all of us.

Friends came round to Omega Works. We saw Grimmy a lot, Adele sometimes – she was a massive fan of Amy and they met through work. Amy didn't like an awful lot of new artists but she thought Adele was the nuts; she could sing and her character was right up Amy's street. We had a few good parties around then, everyone there just jamming, singing, playing guitar, having a drink. Adele with her can of cider.

Mostly though it was just our inner circle, drinking, me doing cocaine, Amy and Alex smoking crack. It became normalized. I'd numb myself to it all with alcohol, watch it all from a sofa thinking, why is everyone sitting indoors drinking and eating Haribo sweets and smoking crack *all the time*? How has this become our life? Doctors were now permanently on call and put Amy back on antidepressants.

One night when we were both fucked up, Amy got up from a sofa, went over to her laptop and put on a slow song, a jazz standard, 'The Nearness of You'. She came over to me on another sofa, took me by the hand and pulled me up into her arms. She wanted us to slow dance, it was her way of stopping the madness, a moment of normality. A simple dance, such a beautiful thing to do.

So much of Amy's life was now run for her: everything to do with work, money, food shopping, where she lived, even *how* she lived, which meant how she accessed drugs. She wasn't visiting some dealer, buying crack and heroin and being followed there and back by the paparazzi living outside. It had to be delivered, or a dealer came round, and that had to be organized. It had to be paid for, money transferred to dealers, and that had to be organized for her. She wouldn't have known how to do it.

In the middle of the chaos, there was one positive new force in Amy's life, Dionne, who would become her goddaughter, the twelve-year-old daughter of her friend Julie. She was a talented singer, loved music and Amy formed a real bond with her. Occasionally Dionne came round and before she did, Amy would always sober up and get herself together to look after her. She wanted to be responsible for her and she was good at it. Dionne had come to see Amy back in the K Hole, when Pete Doherty did the blood painting and no one did any drugs around her while she was there. Amy started putting her hair up in a beehive and everything looked almost normal. It was still fucked up in a way, a twelve-year-old girl in any of these environments, but Amy would never do anything in front of Dionne, and neither would I nor anyone else.

Amy kept missing visits to see Blake in Pentonville. I didn't care if Amy saw Blake or not, he was not a concern of mine, I was trying to save her. But I'd use an upcoming visit to get her head together, encourage her to get a night's sleep, eat some food. And she'd still miss the visit. It had a devastating effect on both her psyche and her addiction. He was supposedly the love of her life; she was the gangster's wife and she couldn't get it together to see her gangster husband behind bars. Every five minutes she'd be back on the crack.

I tried to get her ready in a designated amount of time. The car sat outside, waiting, for four, five hours while she did her hair, make-up, clothes, trying to look nice. Nine times out of ten she wasn't ready in time and the car left. She'd say the night before, 'Please make sure I'm up, don't let me miss it!' I'd give her Valium, she'd sleep, I'd get her up. I would be sitting downstairs, ready, while she ran in and out, smoking crack, getting ready, until it was too late. When she missed the visit she would destroy herself, cut herself, smash something, do even more drugs, *give up* on herself. Missing those prison visits played a huge role in Amy getting worse. Her addiction became bigger than anything else in her life.

Blake rang me from prison. 'Why didn't she get here?' Sober Blake, not the Blake who went off in handcuffs. 'Please mate, make sure she gets here.' It was all on me, again. His whole world was Amy, no one else cared about him.

There were a few times when she finally got in the car, running late, all dolled up. I made sure there were no drugs on her – I was nervous, she was going into a prison and you couldn't take her word for anything. But when we got to the gates they wouldn't let her in. Too late.

The odd time the visit *did* happen she'd come out on a high. And of course with addiction, you use when you feel like shit and you use when you feel great, a reason to celebrate.

But when she didn't make it, she'd go upstairs to her glass-walled bedroom, slam the door, there'd be tears and within half an hour she'd cut her arms to ribbons.

A decision was made to try to get her old friend Juliette involved in Amy's life again. Juliette had stayed away but they'd never had any argument. There was a call from either Raye or Mitch, days after the end of the cancelled tour, and Juliette came round to Omega Works. She was waiting for Amy to appear, saying to me, 'What's going on? I can't be involved in this.' A doctor turned up, went up to Amy's room and gave her antidepressants.

Amy eventually came down, eating ice cream out of a pot, even though she didn't eat much, and was weirdly ecstatic: '*Oh my God*, have you tasted this? The most amazing ice cream in the world . . .' All I'd seen Amy do for the past few days was smoke heroin and crack and cry all day.

Juliette said, 'I think you wanna watch your dosage of them tablets.'

I felt sad. I hadn't seen Amy happy for so long and this was such a *fake* happy, whatever it was they'd given her. Juliette just wanted to leave. I went upstairs and Juliette followed, there was still a lot of love between us. She was worried about me.

'But how are *you* doing, Tyler? You're gonna end up in a mental institution, you're gonna have a *breakdown*.'

No one had said that to me before.

'I know I am. But what can I do? I can't leave her. I can't leave her with arseholes like Alex. I've got no choice.'

I started crying. She hugged me. Amy came into the room. For her, given all the madness she'd just been through – Blake in prison, the tour, the self-destruct button – all of a sudden there's her two childhood friends embracing on the bed and I'm crying. It burst her fake happy bubble.

'Tyler what's wrong, why are you crying?' She put her arm around me and kept saying, 'What's wrong?'

I didn't want to say anything, didn't want to upset her. I was rocking back and forth and then I just lost it. *Lost it.*

'You!' I was really shouting. 'YOU! *You're* what's wrong! I don't know what to do! You're gonna fucking *die.*'

She just stood there. Like I'd scared her. It was one of only two, three times I ever shouted at Amy like that. I saw the switch in her eyes, *bang.* She walked straight out of the room. The whole length of the upstairs hallway was lined with glass wardrobes. All I could hear was *Smash! Smash! Smash! Smash! Smash! Smash! Smash! Smash!* Until she'd smashed every single one of them. I sat on the bed listening to this terrifying noise and just *screamed.* Juliette ran downstairs. I got up, walked downstairs, climbed through the window and sat outside shaking and smoking. The paparazzi were sitting in their cars. One of them came out.

'You alright mate?'

I was crying my eyes out, couldn't hold the words in: 'No, my best friend's a heroin and crack addict and I dunno what to do, *I dunno what to do.*'

Juliette came out and said she'd stay with Amy that night, to give me a break. My aunty Sharon lived ten minutes away and Juliette said she'd drive me. Before I left I bandaged Amy up. She was covered in lacerations and grazes. Her arms, her hands were bleeding but not gushing, not bleeding from a main artery which *could've* happened. Self-harm was now another

143

serious problem, one I was almost used to. I had her doctors' numbers and I spoke to them a lot. I was responsible for tablets like Valium, and I'd started to build up a cache of bandages and prescription cream for self-harm. It's what happens when you're dealing with addiction: you're living with it, prepared, with a bunch of pharmaceutical tools. I bandaged her up in silence. There was nothing to talk about. I was numb.

I got to Aunty Sharon's, shaking. She gave me vodka, I took Night Nurse and went to sleep in the safety of my family knowing Juliette was with Amy. Next morning, after a good night's sleep, I got up, Aunty Sharon made me a sausage sandwich and I was ready to go back and sort it out. I threw myself straight back in again. That's what I did, over and over and over. When you're looking after someone who's that unwell you start to become unwell yourself. You lose yourself. But you don't give up. I didn't care what it was doing to me. *You don't give up*. And I never *did* give up.

I started to try to take control in any way I could. Amy had a dealer friend who would come round. If there were four balls of crack wrapped in clingfilm, I'd take them out, break bits off and reshape them into four smaller balls. Amy always knew how many balls were coming but she was out of her mind so you could lose some and she wouldn't know. I just kept telling myself: *this will end*.

Alex's addiction was becoming worse and worse. I wouldn't see him for days and I'd wonder if he was dead. I'd go along the balcony and look through his window, check he was still alive and he'd be pale as a ghost on Xanax. If you've been smoking crack for five days on no sleep and no food you need to go to sleep for two days solid. You wake up from that and you're white, drawn, deathly. I'd check Cat was OK too, and she was, despite living with that kind of chaos.

Management started talking about a trip away, to the Caribbean island of Mustique, just me and Amy. We'd been invited to stay at Bryan Adams' house on the beach – the eighties Canadian rock dude who was now a big-name photographer. For months we hadn't seen daylight. Our plush apartment was now a crack den. We needed to fly towards the sun.

CHAPTER 20

Raye had a working relationship with Bryan Adams so, knowing Bryan had this beautiful beach house in Mustique, he pulled some strings and orchestrated a trip, just after Christmas 2007. Mustique is a private island where millionaires and billionaires own homes, people like the fashion giant Tommy Hilfiger. You can't go there without permission and the whole island is on account, you just sign for everything you need and it goes on a pre-existing, approved account. I didn't even know who was paying for it – whether it was Amy, Island or free on Bryan Adams but we were known around the island as Bryan's guests. It's like the whole island is a hotel and instead of saying 'I'm in room 759' we'd say, 'we're at Bryan's'. There would be no crack and no heroin on Mustique, maybe a bit of weed. It was Raye's way of trying to help Amy, sending her on holiday for a bit of respite, but what she really needed was rehab.

The night before, I didn't sleep as usual and packed Amy's bags: shorts, vests, shirts, dresses, joggers, ballet pumps, bikinis. Her doctor knew she was going away and had given me the usual tools: antidepressants, sleeping pills, bandages, wound cream, codeine-based painkillers, withdrawal tablets, plenty of Valium. Mitch came round and gave me her company credit card, even though you didn't really buy anything on the island.

It geared me up, knowing I was in charge. Amy, being addicted to drugs, didn't want to go, said she'd rather stay at home.

Mitch was furious: 'You ain't even seen the pictures, it's luxury, out of this world, you don't wanna go and it's a twenty-five grand holiday? If you don't wanna go, *I'll* go.'

'Go on then, Dad, *you* go.'

I could see what she was thinking: *You love all this shit, don't you, Dad? Can you not see the state of me right now? The turmoil I'm in? How I don't need any stupid luxury twenty-five grand holiday I couldn't give ten fucks about?*

By then, Mitch had his own record deal and was touring. She'd say to me she'd reached the stage where she was the parent and he was the kid. She felt he should've been dragging her by her hair out of that flat, getting her help. But that wasn't in his character. Amy was very aware of that.

Curly took us to the airport in a cab, Amy half asleep, going through the motions. He checked us in, gave me our passports, tickets and patted me on the back. 'Good luck.' We flew first class, which was a luxury lost on two broken-down kids like us. At least Amy could get a good sleep, in one of those massive booths with chairs that flatten out into a proper bed. I gave her the prescribed Valium she needed, she slept and I thought about the opportunity ahead of us: she couldn't get hold of drugs, maybe this could lead to rehab. There was a *chance*.

We got to Barbados and were fast-tracked through a packed border control. People were standing in lines from all over the world, passports in hands, just staring at Amy. It was like she was Whitney Houston. I could hear them, 'Uh! It's Amy Winehouse!' She walked through, calm, like she was used to everyone staring. It was me that wasn't used to it. It was the first time I realized, properly realized, how famous Amy had become: in one year she'd gone from a left-field jazz singer in Camden

Town to an actual global star. We'd lived in a bubble for so long, through all the drug dramas and turmoil, I'd almost forgotten there was an outside world, forgotten there were millions of people who knew about her, who loved her music, who were in awe of her. We were 4,000 miles away from home and I saw it on the faces of all these people from all over the world.

We were met outside in the scorching heat, 'This way Miss Winehouse!' – she always hated all that – and went through to the Mustique terminal, which was like a bike shed. I got out my bottle of JD and relaxed. It was just us, like we'd gone back two years to the days we'd always travel together.

The pilot picked us up and took us to a tiny, four-seater propeller plane, and we flew over the perfect turquoise ocean, the pilot pointing out there were schools of sharks down there. We were laughing, thinking we might never make it to Mustique, flying over shark-infested waters in a tin can. We landed on the tiny runway of this beautiful, typical Caribbean island, the airport a shack with a straw roof. A jeep pulled up, it was Bryan Adams on his own, introducing himself and slinging our bags in the back. He drove us to his house and we were in paradise: palm trees, powder white sand, aquamarine ocean and no one.

The house was stunning: wooden, situated where the island tapers into a narrow strip so the design was long, lengthways, with beach on both sides. He showed us round. Every room had huge wooden shutters which opened onto the beach. With the bedroom shutters open, you'd be sleeping with the ocean ten feet from the edge of your bed. I could see Bryan was in on the situation with Amy. He wasn't surprised when there was no 'this place is beautiful!' from her. She was polite but she was jet-lagged and said she just needed to go to sleep. He took her to her room, she got in bed – I doubt she even *saw* the ocean in front of her – and fell asleep. Bryan suggested a walk, to a clifftop nearby called Lookout Point. We climbed to the top and could see a Caribbean storm brewing on the horizon. He asked for the latest update.

'OK, what's the situation with Amy, how bad are things?'

I felt like I'd arrived at rehab already. Whoever had reached out first, Raye or Bryan, there was obviously a plan: she can come here and recover. Then he was asking me about *my* life. I never had moments like this. The last one had been with Curly the tour manager. I got upset, sitting on this mountain overlooking the ocean with the red sky and the storm in the distance. I broke down, telling him how bad it really was and he put his arm around me like a big brother. I had a bottle of Caribbean rum in my hand. Drink was the first thing I looked for in my room, panicking – *where's the drink, is there drink in the room?* There was, a large bottle of 60 per cent overproof Caribbean rum that tasted like pure cane sugar.

I felt safe. I was in this beautiful place, with this stranger I'd only heard of before cos my mum really liked that song 'Everything I fucking Do, I Do It for You'. And he was *sound*. A lovely man, caring, with such a big heart. For the first time in a long time it felt like there was an adult around. Someone who recognized that we were kids. And we were fucked up. His message was clear: who knows what'll happen, but welcome to my sanctuary, away from the madness you've just described. See how things go, anything you need, I'll help you. *Welcome.*

It was night-time in the Caribbean, I'd had a good few rums, I was relaxed. I had my own room but I was looking after Amy so I lay down next to her, with her head cradled in the pillow next to me. I had one of my moments. I was hopeful. *It's just me and my girl, we're safe, she's fast asleep, no harm can come to her and there's no one else here to ruin it.* It felt like *this* was the new beginning. Everything was going to be alright.

There were other people staying at the house, all lovely, responsible adults. Vicky Russell, a stylist, Ken Russell's daughter. I was in a film of his when I was a boy, a little part, I told her, 'Your dad directed me a film when I was about seven!' A guy called Harvey, a video director, super gay, super eccentric, and Val, an Oscar-winning make-up artist. The first few days, Amy got on board with them as well. They felt sorry for Amy and felt sorry for me. They saw me with all this responsibility, saw me outside sometimes having a fag with my head in my hands. But they were all looking out for us. Harvey would encourage us into all manner of 'photo shoot' stupidness. He'd cajole both of us into wearing eyeliner, he called it 'kittening up'. He'd appear out of nowhere with his camera and announce: 'Come on you two, we're kittening now, just for ten minutes!' I wish we'd spent a lot more time there with all of them.

There was a big dining room table and people in the house could eat together. Bryan is vegan and there'd usually be pumpkin soup, food we weren't interested in. We were always polite, while thinking, *where can we get some meat?!* The island only had a few restaurants and Vicky told us about a place called Basil's Bar, by the beach, serving food, burgers. There were buggies at Bryan's, like golf buggies, and I drove Amy there, even though I can't drive. Vicky joined us. Amy was hyper, the amount of food she was eating was insane. We must've ordered seven, eight meals, burgers, chicken, it was a running joke at the table, 'We need meat, we're down at Bryan's!' The staff were laughing. Then she'd go to the bathroom. Come back. Eat loads more. Go to the bathroom. About five times, again and again. Vicky said, 'Is she alright?' It was obvious: bulimia was now *another* serious problem.

Amy went back to her room. Soon afterwards, Bryan came into mine.

'Tyler, can you smell that? I think she's using, I can't have that sort of thing happening here.'

He was cool about it and I was horrified. She'd managed to smuggle something onto the flight, stuck the drugs *somewhere*. He told me to be careful.

'When you get back to Barbados airport, make sure there's absolutely nothing anywhere, they won't care she's Amy Winehouse, you're not in England anymore, they'll stick the pair of you in jail and throw away the keys.'

I was *terrified*. Amy came out of her room really high. Like she was when she was doing cartwheels making meatballs. I sensed it was heroin *and* crack. Everyone was sitting around the dining table, it was so awkward. Amy's eyes were rolling in her head as she played her guitar. I persuaded her to go back to her room, I didn't want people seeing my friend like this. She said, 'Let's go out.' We got in the buggy, drove around and found a West Indian bashment rave in a sweaty den. We ended up in a house party, a locals' place, reggae and bashment music blaring out. All the staff on the island must have been there and Amy loved it: 'Yeah, real people!' After all that concern at lunchtime, I thought, *She's high now but this will end so just enjoy it while she's happy.* We were dancing, no one cared she was 'Amy Winehouse', she was normal and she loved it.

The following day, the drugs ran out. In hindsight, I realized she'd wanted to go out the night before to see if she could find more drugs and she couldn't. She started going through withdrawal. Everyone was aware of it. Now Raye was on Bryan's phone and the phone was handed to me. Raye spelled it out.

'Look, this is gonna be really hard for you, she's gonna be

sick, *really sick,* throwing up, she'll probably defecate, but don't worry, there are doctors on the island.'

So much for my moment of optimism. I was scared. I sat down with Amy.

'T, I'm going through withdrawal.'

'Tell me what to do.'

'Just try and keep me asleep, I'll sleep as much as I can, I've been through this before . . . and get me loads of sweets.'

People coming off heroin want sugar.

The first night I gave her Valium and pulled a chair to the end of her bed, knowing I wasn't going to move. She was rolling around, shaking, like I'd do with the alcohol DTs. I looked out at the beautiful ocean, crying, thinking how naive I'd been. I thought I was prepared for this and I wasn't. In the morning I thought, *Right, how do I help, get her through? She needs sustenance, she needs to eat.* I went into the kitchen, Bryan has staff, women; they were highly religious and told me, 'We're praying for you and your friend.' I thought, *Forget talking to me about God, where's the blender?!* I got it out and used what was at my disposal: bananas, maple-sweet Jemima syrup, Night Nurse, rum, crushed ice.

I'm not a doctor. I should never have been given this kind of responsibility – Amy needed serious medical help. I was trying to make her something that would knock her out. She kept taking it. 'That's lovely, keep it coming.' She called it Sleepy Juice. She'd wake up, I'd be on the end of the bed. 'T, make me more Sleepy Juice.' I kept making it. One time she sat up.

'T, you really love me don't you? You're the only real friend I've got.'

'Of course I love you. I'm here, I'm gonna keep on looking after you, I'm gonna make you the drink and you'll get through this and you'll be alright.'

The withdrawal got progressively worse. I thought, *Am I giving her too much?* I couldn't bear to see her in pain. She kept asking for more Valium, begging me, half an hour after the last one. I didn't have a clue what was too much. That's why I thought the drink was a better idea, what was a bit of rum and banana? I didn't know what I was doing. She threw everything up, writhing, moaning. There were points where I got her out of bed to hose her down outside with Bryan's rainwater hose, to keep her clean, comfortable. This couldn't go on, she needed professional help.

I went to find Bryan and told him, 'Call a doctor.'

A doctor came round and put her on a drip. He asked what I'd been giving her, looked at the Valium packet and said the dose wouldn't even touch the sides. He gave her much stronger Valium, painkillers, electrolytes, whatever, and it calmed her down. It destroyed me, thinking Amy was basically in hospital here. I'd get used to that in the future but I wasn't used to it then.

I'd spoken to Bryan about my mum and he said I should ring her. I was upset on the phone, telling her that Amy was on a drip, I thought she was going to die. I asked my mum to come out to help me, she said she would and Bryan said he'd organize it. Everything in this surreal paradise was suddenly very real. Bryan spoke to my mum. The adults were here. I felt protected.

Bryan took me back up to the clifftop and told me Eric Clapton owned a rehab on the island, would Amy think about going there? I didn't think she would. He looked at the bottle of rum clenched in my hand. 'Maybe you should go too, Tyler.'

I knew I needed to. I'd been upset in front of him before and this time I fell into his arms, crying, and he instinctively knew what to say to an addict: 'It's beautiful there and they'll look after you.' I told him I couldn't afford anything like that. He smiled, maybe at my naivety, and said he was sure Amy would pay for me to go to rehab.

I started feeling hopeful again. Maybe we'd both go to rehab. My mum would come over in a few days, she and Amy were so close, maybe it could really happen, at last?

The next morning, I wasn't thinking about me anymore – as far as I was concerned, Bryan had got me in a moment of weakness. *I'm* not an addict, Amy is.

Ally Hilfiger came round, Tommy Hilfiger's daughter. She knew a lot about psychological trauma after living through a childhood with undiagnosed Lyme Disease, the symptoms had sent her crazy, and she kept saying, 'If this isn't sorted out, Amy will die.' She came to see me a lot and was very supportive, telling me how she knew of a rehab place Amy should go to. She said, 'You can use my dad's plane.' As the days were going by, Amy was getting better but I also knew she was still militantly anti-rehab. Ally invited me over to their family house where there was a get-together. 'And we've plenty of meat!' I was wary of leaving Amy but she was asleep and the others in the house assured me they'd keep an eye on her.

Dinner at the Hilfiger's mansion was very civilized, everyone was seated outside on the beach eating steaks they'd had specially flown in. Mick Jagger was there with one of his daughters and Bob Geldof's daughter, Peaches. People were asking about Amy. I tried to hold everything in but I got upset again. It was Mick Jagger who comforted me.

'Don't worry man, she'll be alright, people in that world go through this sort of thing.'

All I knew was he was a rock star who'd been through everything, who knew all about drugs and fame. He was saying to me, in a wise way, calm down, this is normal, Amy's a rock star too and this is part of the process. He spelled it out: when all of a sudden, out of nowhere, you're the most famous rock star in the world, everyone goes through what Amy's going through. Of course she's on heroin, of course she's all these things, she'll come out the other side and there's nothing to worry about. I thought, *You've probably sniffed heroin off a supermodel's arse and here you are in the Caribbean, eating steak in a millionaire's beachside mansion. So that's where Amy will be one day too, sitting on an island looking back, 'I remember when . . .'* I held onto that.

More days passed. Amy was becoming lucid, all I had to do was keep her here a few days longer and then we'd have the rehab talk. Raye was now ringing Bryan about it. Everyone was enthusiastic.

Amy was able to get out of bed one night, for an hour, her strength was coming back. There were sofas outside her bedroom, on the beach, and we lay down on one of them underneath the stars. The worst of withdrawal was over and she had some weed – had probably asked a pool boy for it – and it took me back years, seeing Amy roll a spliff. It was another moment. All my life I'd been very anti smoking weed and it always did Amy's head in. She'd always say, when we were younger, 'One day, you and me, we'll have a spliff together, just the once.' So now she said, 'This is it!'

I went to the fridge, I'd had enough of the diesel rum so I got these little civilized beers out and we lay down on the sofa smoking this spliff. I'd never smoked a spliff before. I felt really, *really* chilled out. And now I felt even *more* hopeful. We were having a proper chat.

'Ain't life mad, Ame?'

'T, what the fuck are we doing here? Lying under the stars with the ocean there. Look at them three stars, in a constellation.'

It was Orion's Belt. To this day, whenever I can see the stars, I always see *those* three stars. And I always say to myself, *Look, there's Amy*. It was warm, the ocean was right there and it was pure bliss. Just me and her. We cuddled up together and fell asleep, under the stars, with the ocean lapping and the sound of the chirping crickets.

The next morning, Amy woke up and she'd gone from being calm and relieved that she wasn't in agony anymore to basically saying, 'Fuck this shit.' It was like she'd come round from unconsciousness. 'What am I doing here, where am I?' She was weak physically but she was back on her feet. And agitated.

'T? I wanna go home. Ring Raye, tell him we're *going home . . .*'

I was devastated, I hadn't even mentioned rehab yet. I came up with excuses – we can't get flights, it's New Year's Eve. The only thing I could think to pull out of my arse was my birthday.

'Can we just stay here for my birthday, the fifth of January?'

It was like I'd got her: *Shit, I can't ruin his birthday*.

A day passed and she came back with an idea. 'T, I don't wanna ruin your birthday, so I tell you what we'll do, I'll get you a villa, I'll fly your mum out, whoever you want, you stay there for a couple of weeks, have a big birthday, but I'm gonna go home, cos I need to see my Blake.'

Suddenly Blake was part of going home. Before, Blake was starting to barely *exist*.

'Ame, I would never let you do that, fly people out and pay for villas. It's *me* you're talking to!'

She was now so deluded, so used to people taking advantage of her, wanting her for her fame or her money, that she thought she could buy *me*. I was offended.

'Yes, I'm that kind of a wanker, that's me all day long Ame. I've laid with you and rubbed your back and made those drinks and cleaned you for the last week and now I'll go and stay in a lovely villa and sit in a hot tub and you can go home by yourself and rot. As if! I'm going home with *you*.'

All hope of Amy going to rehab was gone. Everyone accepted it was just too soon.

Flights were booked. There was a PA who'd obviously never met Amy saying, 'But we can't get first class, we can only get business.' As if Amy cared! She would've paddled back in a *dinghy*. But she did end up ruining my birthday – that was the day we flew home.

On 5 January 2008, my twenty-sixth birthday, we weren't flying till late afternoon and everyone in the house brought in a chocolate birthday cake and sang happy birthday. There was a look in Bryan's eyes which said, 'I'm sending these two kids back to hell.' Amy was getting stronger and wanted to do something fun for my birthday. I suggested the ocean. It had been right outside our rooms but we hadn't set foot in it. Not *once*. Bryan drove us in his jeep round the cliffs and Amy asked if she could drive, even though she couldn't drive. He let her have a go and she loved it, she was in control, in the driving seat for once, literally and metaphorically. She relished the freedom, was *possessed* by the freedom, driving like a maniac on steroids, off the bends, tyres screeching. Bryan kept grabbing the steering wheel to get us back on the road, shouting, 'Amy, we'll go off the cliff!' She was pissing herself laughing and she looked so free. Bryan was laughing too. Meanwhile, I was in the back seat shitting myself.

We got to a glorious beach and walked into the sea up to our waists. I tried to persuade her, one last time.

'Are you sure you wanna go? Will we stay?'

'Drop it T, we're leaving.'

*

We were driven home to Omega Works and Amy couldn't *wait* to get back indoors. We had new front door keys by then and we'd forgotten them. It was morning, after this long flight, after this long time in Mustique, where nothing had worked out, and now the door was locked. Amy was freaking out. I gave her Valium but she started punching the back of the car, shouting, 'I'm gonna smash the door in!' I rang round everyone I could think of, no keys. We were in the car for an hour and a half, Amy losing the plot. I thought, *Fuck it,* I've got no choice. I asked the driver if he had a crowbar, *anything*. He got a crowbar out of his boot. I got out the car, took the crowbar up to the front door, which was all made of glass, and smashed the whole thing in. I pulled all the shards out the way and pointed into the house, fuming.

'Go on, Ame!'

She walked through the space where the door had been.

'Cheers T.'

She'd been aggravated on the flight, aggravated in the car and walked upstairs in this terrible mood. Minutes later, she came back down and she was calm, lovely – 'Alright Tyler?' – as if nothing had happened. She started singing and doing the washing up. I thought, those are some *powerful drugs*. I walked through the hole where the door used to be and sat outside smoking a fag, thinking how fucked up drug addiction is. How drugs rule your life and your mood even after two weeks of not taking any. How Amy would never have gone through withdrawal on Mustique if there were any drugs there, she would've burned down the island to get to them. How, if I hadn't smashed in our front door with a crowbar, she would've thrown herself through the door. I *know* she would, she would've headbutted the glass and I'd now be taking her to hospital.

I felt helpless. I was running out of ideas.

CHAPTER 21

The tabloids ran stories on our trip to Mustique. The paps took pictures at the airport on the way home, on the way to smashing our front door in, the only time we looked decent – Amy's signing autographs, me looking really brown. The reports said Amy had left Blake in prison and 'gone on a romantic holiday with *George*' – the Sony A&R guy she was with for a while, who she wrote 'Me and Mr Jones' about. Who is also a black man. I was captioned 'George'. I don't know how they get away with it, I really don't.

Back in Omega Works, everything carried on just like it was before Mustique, now with extra randoms turning up. We were still fully nocturnal and known for being chaotic, which attracted wrong 'uns. The third bedroom had been turned into a studio where empty spirit bottles were always kicking around. There was speed-tidying whenever Raye or Mitch came round, which wasn't that often.

There hadn't been any work for Amy since the UK tour was cancelled. From a public perspective, it looked like her music career had just ended. But in our heads, this was the bohemian way, excess was just part of being creative, with a 'fuck you' attitude. There'd be a guitar out, me and Amy would have pens and paper out, always writing. She'd be on crack and I'd be on Valium and booze, encouraging each other in being fucked up *artists*. Which is all bollocks. Amy believed it so much she convinced me of it and I absolutely fell for it. It was better than thinking *we're just fucked up*. I was drinking all the time, it kept me steady, a functioning alcoholic. We wrote a song together called 'Mr Jack' about a bottle of Jack Daniel's. I'd never *not* have a bottle of Jack Daniel's clutched to me. I'd go to sleep hugging a bottle of JD.

There was a lot of crack psychosis behaviour. I'd lie awake for four nights in a row sometimes, keeping an eye on Amy. She'd get all her hairbrushes, hairpins and headbands and lay them out on the table in coordinated colours. She'd put all her pink jumpers there, all the red dresses there, or, at three in the morning, 'Let's paint this entire room black . . .' She was constantly painting the walls. Amy would be the chief decorator and there'd be five randoms with paint pots and brushes painting the walls with her through the night, their project for three hours. At least it stopped her doing drugs constantly. Meanwhile, I was doing the usual routine, trying to keep things supposedly normal, throwing away portions of crack, cleaning the toilet. This was our life.

Friends came by occasionally, sometimes Grimmy or Kelly Osbourne. She came over with a pug once so we had this little doggy running around. We were all sitting round the dining table, I had a JD and fizzy codeine and the dog jumped onto the table and started lapping it up, out of my glass. Without a word of a lie, the dog took a lit fag out of the ashtray and started running around the flat, the fag in its mouth. Kelly was pissing herself; we were all shouting, 'Fucking hell, you can tell that dog's an Osbourne!'

It was late January 2008, three weeks after Mustique and it felt like a distant memory. I was depressed the trip hadn't worked and I was stick thin by now, borderline anorexic. Alex was still around. The day after we got back from Mustique, he was taunting me, watching Amy smoking crack saying, 'Well done, you did a really good job there, getting Amy into rehab.' Hitting people just isn't in me but I punched him in the face for that. Then I put the breadknife through his free Harrods laptop.

He didn't retaliate. As an addict, he was just pleased Amy hadn't gone into rehab and left him to do drugs on his own.

Amy decided to dye her hair blonde – a terrible idea, it made her look extra thin, extra ill. Of course, Alex went along with it, smoking crack with her while dyeing her hair. A few days later, I woke up late at night and she wasn't there. That never happened. I freaked out and started ringing Alex, Cat, Kelly. The big hole where the glass front door used to be was now boarded up and we'd nailed stuff to the door frame so it couldn't be opened, making the door redundant. So we still used the window next to it as the front door. I climbed through the window, looked out in the courtyard and the electric gates swung open. A pick-up truck drove in with a big trailer on the back filled with people. Who's in the middle of this bunch of pikeys? Amy, all hyped and happy.

'I just popped out! These lot are coming round . . .'

They all came in through the window.

I was pleased she was back but who were these randoms? They were mostly fellas in Adidas tracksuits and baseball caps. I sensed they weren't really our people – they could be dodgy, dangerous. Amy had picked them up in a pub, a whole crew. 'Come back to mine!'

Amy was upstairs when I spotted two of them going up there as well. Randoms didn't go upstairs. I went up and they were in my room, sitting on my bed, intimidating me, they could've beaten ten tons of shite out of me, stabbed me. I went in to Amy.

'There's two fellas on my bed.'

'Oh, don't worry, they're Blake's friends.'

I thought *fuck that,* this is where I live! I went in, I was nice.

'Sorry fellas, this is my room, can you go downstairs where the party is and not be in my room?'

They just looked at me, didn't move. I noticed one of them had a camera on a chain round his neck. It was tiny, but I could see a lens. I went in to Amy, told her she should get them out and she wouldn't listen, 'They're sound, they're Blake's mates.' I wasn't sticking around with this lot. My bedroom window led out onto the first floor balcony and right next door was another mate of ours. I climbed out the window and went there for the night. And that's when the video was filmed of Amy smoking crack.

We talked about it years later. Amy's view was that Blake organized it. In the same way he sold stories, maybe he needed the money. But she couldn't prove it. Raye came round and threw a copy of the *Sun* onto the dining room pool table. Amy was front page news: 'Winehouse World Exclusive. Amy on Crack. Nosedive to Oblivion.' There was a link to the video and Raye played it to her on his phone.

'Oh that's nice, innit, someone's done that to me, in my own room, fucking wrong 'uns . . .'

I had my head in my hands. 'I *told* you Amy.'

Raye looked at me. 'Told her what?'

'I told her someone had a camera.'

All I heard Raye say was, 'Look, you lot need to be more careful.'

He said to Amy, 'You're gonna have to talk to the police, you've crossed the line.'

It was scary. I thought, *Am I gonna have to talk to the police as well?* I didn't but I didn't know that then. Raye told us to sort ourselves out; we'd have to get up early tomorrow. We both went upstairs. I was in my room with my bottle of JD when Amy came in, sat on the end of my bed. She said something she'd never said before.

'T, why are you drinking so much?'

'What d'you mean? I'm not drinking any more than I usually do. I just wanna go to sleep, babe.'

She told me to take some Valium. I told *her* to take some Valium. We both took Valium and I went to sleep.

I woke up in bed next morning feeling a tapping on my shoulder.

'Ken, Ken . . .'

My *mother?* I opened my eyes and my mum was there with my stepdad Danny, there were empty bottles everywhere, empty packets of Valium and tablets and stupidness, the world I deliberately shielded my parents from. I was amazed she wasn't screaming at me, or my stepdad wasn't punching me in the head. She was calm.

'Ken, come on boy, we're going home now . . .'

'What d'you mean?'

Danny's standing there. 'We're *going home.*'

Now I understood: I didn't have a choice, I was being interventioned out of the situation. I was scared and angry: was I about to be carted off to rehab? I walked into Amy's room, she was there smoking crack. I was livid. I wanted to *kill* Amy.

'What is my mum doing here? What the *fuck* have you let my mum and dad in here for?!'

She shrugged. 'I dunno, they just turned up . . .'

We all went downstairs. Raye was there, Mitch was there, Alex was there, a make-up artist was there. Amy very rarely had a make-up artist, she normally did her own. Alex got his pastes out and started dyeing Amy's hair black again, she was being glammed up so she didn't look like the person in the crack video. And she didn't. It was a stunt. Three hours later, she was immaculate, with perfect skin, make-up hiding the impetigo from smoking drugs. I was stalling and stalling, I didn't wanna leave and Danny was seething, watching all this happen. Amy was sitting there, hair in rollers, dye and hair extensions everywhere, Lucozade bottles with the foils everywhere, smoking crack. For once, right in front of her dad. She obviously just didn't care anymore. And Mitch didn't know how to deal with her. All we heard him say was, 'Ame, we need to get ready, come on!'

My mum took me aside.

'We've got to go *now*, Danny can't stand there any longer watching this.'

We left. I got in the back of the car, extricated out of my bubble. My mum turned to me. 'D'you know why I'm here, boy?'

'No, I don't, Mum.'

She started crying. 'That's what I love about our Amy, she rang me.'

I thought, *Amy, you cunt! How could you do me like that?!*

She carried on. 'As fucked up as she is, and she needs help, she knows when there's something wrong with you, so she rang me last night, crying about *you*. Ken, she told me to come and get you.'

I broke down in the car. Her words hit me like a bullet in the heart. Of course there was something wrong with me, living through all this madness. It was only three weeks after Mustique. I was *completely lost*. But Amy, in the midst of her own chaos, wanted to spare me this new situation with the police. She knew I was scared. She was also worried about my drinking, thinking about saving *me*, even with a crack pipe in her hand, when she needed saving even more. She broke my heart that day. It's not that I didn't know she loved me but I didn't know she'd even noticed I was so lost. But I knew I couldn't leave her. I had to go back. I begged my mum to let me go back.

'*Please*, I can't leave her, you don't realize, I stay up with her, I make sure she's *breathing*.'

Danny was horrified. 'Well, what's her dad doing then?!'

My mum was furious. 'We need to get Amy, put her in the back of Danny's van, take her away with us and look after her.'

I think Mitch was worried that if he did something like that

Amy would completely cut him off and he'd have no clue what was going on in her life. That's the problem with being rich and famous when you're an addict. Maybe if this had happened seven years earlier Mitch would've been able to do a lot more. Mum calmed down, she understood my situation.

'I know I can't keep you at home boy, you'll just break out. I know how much you love each other, you've been like this since you were kids. So if she needs you to look after her . . .'

There were caveats.

'If I ring you, at any time, answer the phone. If I say I wanna see you, I wanna *see* you. So I know you're alive, boy.'

Danny added, speaking for them both: 'And if you touch them drugs, I swear I will kick your head in.'

Danny and Mitch were clearly different characters. Danny was talking, specifically, about heroin and crack, which I'd never done and knew I'd never do. It was the only thing my parents seriously worried about. Whenever I saw them I was scrutinized, I could see them trying to detect if I was on heroin especially, because the minute that happened I wouldn't have been allowed to go any-where, I'd have been in the back of the van, locked in a room. I could've been the most famous boy in the world and there wouldn't have been a manager, or a label, or a deal, or any amount of money that was due on the next tour, that would've stopped my parents from trying to save me. Who knows if it would've worked, or if I'd have done just as I wanted like Amy. I know many people have never understood why Mitch didn't just lock Amy away somewhere – but I'm not sure she'd ever have let him do it.

I stayed at my mum's and got a good night's sleep. She made me a sausage sandwich in the morning and I was ready to go, again. When I got back, nothing had come of Amy's meeting with the police. There was just more 'no comment'. Days later, we heard the news about the Grammys.

CHAPTER 22

If Amy didn't get herself together for the Grammys, look clean, *be* clean, she wouldn't win any Grammys. The message from the Grammys board was clear: you're nominated for six Grammys, not many people get nominated for so many, we want you to be this year's poster girl for the Grammys, so can you please not be the crack addict in the video? Amy wasn't allowed into America: she couldn't get a visa because of her drug use. So there was a set-up: we'll film her Grammys in London, at the Ravenscourt Theatre in Hammersmith, and live broadcast her performance. *If*, by then, she's a shiny happy person.

She agreed to go to hospital for two weeks beforehand, the Capio Nightingale Hospital. She'd still never been to rehab, would still never go, so it wasn't presented to her as rehab, it was presented to her as creating an illusion. It wasn't about not being an addict anymore – as soon as the Grammys were over, she could do whatever she wanted.

Amy went along with it, created the illusion, doing in hospital what she'd usually be doing in hospital in the future, relaxing and medically withdrawing. She wasn't suffering, probably on Subutex, staying steady.

The day of the Grammys was the day Amy came out of hospital. We went straight to a hotel in Hammersmith and she was in the bath when Raye rang. As always, if Amy's in the bath I'm sitting on the toilet, washing her hair. She was looking so well, so replenished, raw and natural. She finished the call.

'Guess what Tyler? I've won a Grammy! I'm a Grammy award-winning artist!'

They'd officially let her know about one. She didn't even say which one. It didn't matter: she'd *done it*. She was covered in soap and bubbles, I was dressed in my shirt and I threw my arms into the water and picked her up out of the bath, my arms right round her. I kissed her all over her face, 'You've won a fucking Grammy!'

She played it down – 'Calm down Tyler!' – but she was happy in that moment, a massive smile on her face, bubbles everywhere. *Amy won a Grammy*.

She was so glamorous that day in her classy black dress, a gold rose pinned by her best big beehive, healthy, sober and beautiful. And yet backstage at the Ravenscroft Theatre, people were scared of her, because the headlines were always scary. In the crack video she *looked* scary. In the dressing room, no one wanted to disturb her so no one approached her. Darcus from Island was the only one who chanced it, even though Amy never respected him musically. On the first tour we did together, back when I had my nose fixed, she said on stage, 'I wanna thank Darcus for doing my hair.' He used to be a hairdresser. She was taking the piss because she didn't take him seriously. Amy was a nerd who knew music inside out, every Cole Porter song, every Gershwin song, and Darcus didn't have a clue. Nick took Amy to Darcus at Island and Darcus got all the applause, but it was all Nick.

Backstage, Darcus said to her, 'Let me know if there's anything I can do for you Amy,' and she belittled him in front of everyone.

'Yeah Darcus, there is something you can do for me. Sign Tyler.'

I just *died*. He'd *dropped* me. Everyone heard it and laughed.

We spent most of our time behind a red velvet theatre curtain between backstage and the stage itself, just the two of us. I kept telling her how proud I was of her, how she deserved every single one of her Grammys, how, despite all her problems personally, musically she was the shit. And no one could ever take that away from her. I was proud of her for putting herself through what it took to get clean, so she could be here, bearing in mind how bad things had been for so long. She jolted me back to reality.

'T, I didn't go to rehab, the label said I just had to go to hospital for the Grammys. As soon as this show is over, I'm gonna get straight back on it.'

I was upset, deflated, but I also wanted to headbutt her. *You idiot*. You're clean, sober. And you still haven't got the clarity to at least *attempt* to stay sober.

The Grammys was all a pretence. It was meant to be a celebration of her life: Nick invited Juliette and her other old friend Lauren, the bloke who taught her to play guitar was there, her mum and dad were there, her aunties, sitting in a fake audience of record company executives. Amy didn't mix with any of them. The highlight for her was seeing her band again, who she hadn't seen in so long. Every now and then the curtain would open and she'd do her performance or receive an award and sit back down saying, 'When is this shit gonna be over? I just wanna do drugs.' She won a then record-breaking five Grammys.

Everybody was celebrating, except her. I understood that the label deserved it, they'd worked their arse off for this. Charlie the plugger, Shane the PR, everybody was having the night of their lives, drinking champagne – fair enough. Amy was lonely and depressed. She wasn't allowed one drink. The curtain represented the divide between two completely different worlds. She accepted there was a show to perform but she was so over singing those songs. She was the monkey holding it together to perform and win all these awards for everyone else.

The famous 'uh!' moment of surprise – her mouth open when she wins Record of the Year for 'Rehab', announced by Tony Bennett in LA – I think that was acting. That wasn't a typical Amy reaction. That was the part of her that was putting on a show. All the hugging of her dad and mum on stage, it was all for them. In my mind, I could still see her in the bath, in that beautiful moment, holding her tiny body all covered in soap suds, going all over my shirt. Everything else was bullshit.

As if Amy's world wasn't collapsing enough, the night before the Grammys, Camden had been on fire, an inferno breaking out across Camden Market and setting the Hawley Arms alight. It was almost burnt to the ground, the inside was gutted. When Amy won the Grammy for 'Rehab', the last thing she said in her speech was, 'This is for London! Cos Camden Town *ain't* burning down!'

We all went back to the hotel afterwards, Amy sitting on the floor of her room, talking to Raye, completely off her head. Raye was telling her that, now she'd won five Grammys, she was gonna sell four million more albums. He told her, 'You can have anything you want now.' Amy said, 'I want a record label. And I wanna sign Tyler.' That's how her Lioness Records label came about. I told I didn't want her to sign me, it wasn't a good look. And at that time, being an artist again was just not on my agenda. Being there for Amy was my only agenda.

There was a desire in Amy that night to just run away. When there was just us left, with security outside the door, she actually thought she *could*.

'T, let's go, let's just pack our bags, get away from here, I dunno where, just *go*, I don't want anything to do with this world anymore.'

I went along with it. She'd been away from home for two weeks so she had all the stuff she might need. I packed her bags, her little Fred Perry holdalls – she never had a suitcase – packed my own stuff. She looked out the door: 'Fuck, security are there!' It was the beginning of her *always* wanting to run away. From her life. That's why we moved so many times. But you can't run away from yourself.

I'd had the opportunity that night, behind the curtain, to ask her what hospital had really done for her. It was the first time she'd gone into a place like that.

'So how was it? Are you OK? Was it hard? Did you speak to someone?'

She kept saying she only got clean for the Grammys, but that wasn't my question. She was sober and she hadn't been sober in so long.

'But how do you *feel*?'

'I'm bored.'

'No, how d'you feel *on the inside,* you're *clean*, you look amazing, your body's clean. It can't have been easy and now that you're *here,* don't you at least consider *not* going back there?'

'T, it was basically a five-star hotel with pharmaceutical drugs.'

'Why don't you stop taking drugs right now? Why don't we do this together?'

'No, I'm going out tonight and I'm gonna get on it.'

I was now pissed off.

'So what are you saying? Cos you know you can't do this forever.'

We were back to what I'd said when her and Blake were holed up together in the Kensington Hotel. What she said next floored me.

'It's only crack that's dangerous anyway. CEOs of companies, entrepreneurs, people who run empires do heroin, the trick is to do it in moderation. '

This was told to her by someone she trusted, it was maybe his attempt at damage control, but it was infuriating. I thought, *What a fucking idiot.* This was music to the ears of an addict, the last thing she needed to hear. I'd wanted to know, for my own peace of mind, if she still wanted to do drugs. Are you finished? Are you not finished? You look finished! Oh, you're not finished. So we'll just carry on then. It was more than obvious that winning five Grammys couldn't make her happy, but what could? She gave me her reason for doing drugs and drinking a million times: life was boring without them. But life had been interesting to her without drugs *before* and it could be again, I *knew* it. For now, we were stuck. But not even just stuck.

It was about to get *a lot worse*.

CHAPTER 23

Omega Works was destroyed. Being a rented property, it cost hundreds of thousands of pounds to put that place back together. Every wall was painted a different colour, much of it black, with patches of purple, green, orange, no distinct lines – unsurprisingly, those crack psychosis decorating jobs weren't done well! The hammock was wrecked. The pool table, which had never been turned back into a dining table, was a stained, alcohol-drenched, cigarette-burnt, crack-bottle burnt, piece of no-longer green felt. It had gone from a huge, stunning, state-of-the-art contemporary apartment to looking like a nineties rave had gone on for months in an industrial factory squat. It was a scenario which became a running theme: hell in paradise. When you're an addict, no matter where you go, no matter how beautiful anywhere is, within weeks you will destroy it. Because the problem is in you.

Amy wanted to move back to Camden. She rented a two-bedroom flat in Prowse Place, round the corner from Jeffrey's Place, which she still owned (and Mitch still owns today) and where Amy's stylist Naomi was now living. Prowse Place was over three floors, compact but beautiful: my bedroom was on the ground floor at the back, there was a long corridor, stairs straight up to the first floor, open-plan living room and kitchen on the front side, so you could see the paparazzi outside the window. There were now more paps than ever living outside in cars. To the right of the front door was a garage with a pool table. Amy's room on the third floor overlooked the living room, another mezzanine like Omega Works, with a freestanding glass staircase going down. I spent most of my time on the sofa in the living room underneath Amy's room, doing cocaine, listening to her lighter firing onto her crack pipe. So much for the advice to stay away from crack.

My cocaine use was out of control, five grams a day. I hid it from everyone. Amy didn't know. I wasn't even high, it just kept me alert. When you're always sipping neat vodka, now up to three bottles a day, it just levels everything out. I could stay awake to keep an eye on Amy for days. It was all normal to me, little lines of coke, little sips of alcohol, constantly. My pockets were lined with Haribo sweets and little wraps of coke. Buying coke was easy, I knew a dealer who lived two minutes away and there was never any less than three grams in my pocket or less than half a bottle of spirit in my Fred Perry bag. Sometimes I'd think, I'm so drunk how am I still standing? I'd go to pick up a cup and miss it, and yet never feel drunk. Because drunk was normal. And sober was chaos. Sober was panic attacks.

I could afford my addictions. I signed a publishing deal, somehow, with Global around this time. A hundred-grand publishing deal under the pretence of the bohemian songwriter bollocks. I was known as Amy's best friend, I spent time with Mark Ronson, it was a no-brainier for Global. There had been *some* writing. I wrote a song called 'Loser' and every lyric was about drinking your last drop of shame. I played the 'Mr Jack' song I wrote with Amy to Mark Ronson; we were scheduled to go into the studio and I wasn't capable. No music came of the deal but it would pay for me to go to rehab.

One night one of my cousins rang, he was in Camden with his mates and Amy, being the way she was about my family, invited them all round even though everything was chaos. There were fifteen, twenty people in the flat, it was getting raucous, when Amy stopped the music, put on a slow jazz song and did what she'd done back in Omega Works. She took me by the hand, put her arms around me and we slow danced in front of everybody. It was something we did when the time was right from then on, a moment of calm in the madness, her way of connecting back to me. A definitive moment for us forever.

Prowse Place was where we first had live-in security, twenty-four hours a day, Andrew and Neville, who we called 'the boys'. Security weren't there to protect Amy from other people, they were there to protect Amy from herself. One of them would sit in the downstairs toilet, watching who came in and out, like a bouncer in a club. Behind my bedroom there was a tiny garden, no grass, just paving stones and a wall. This was the wall Amy's drugs would be thrown over. It had all been worked out. Amy never had any physical money, she didn't even have a bank card or a credit card – she didn't need them, everything in her life was paid for on account. Every Monday morning Mitch would come round with cash in a brown envelope for the boys and that paid for any incidentals. Amy would say to me, 'I feel like a mug when I've got no money in my pocket' so I'd get money out of a cash point with my card, give her £200 and she'd be ecstatic, it was such a novelty for her. It made her feel in control, normal, when not much else did. Someone else was still doing bank transfers to pay the drug dealers, or the dealers would come round, introduced to the boys as Amy's 'friends'.

There was a drum kit at the bottom of the glass stairs, Amy asked for it. Whatever she asked for, it turned up. She used to joke about it.

'If I asked for the blood of a small African virgin child they'd probably bring it round.'

A vintage jukebox arrived in a big lorry, full of 1950s and 60s seven-inch singles. Raye told her it was from Blake, but I think it was from management, an attempt to cheer her up, even though she hardly mentioned Blake anymore. It was so big she put it in the garage next to her pool table. Whenever anyone walked into the garage, she'd say, 'D'you see my jukebox? My Blakey got me that.' I didn't say anything, I couldn't bear to break her heart.

We still had our 'bohemian' mentality but Amy was becoming increasingly frustrated, aggressive even, less in a state to write poetry, more bang drums all night long, which added to the madness. She became a very good drummer.

After the Grammys, the volume had been turned up on her stardom. Every tabloid in the country wanted to write about her every day. They all wanted new pictures, new stories. Six paparazzi were permanently outside, waiting: open the front door and there'd be strobe lights flashing in your face like sheet lightning. The Hawley was still being refurbished after the fire but she knew she couldn't just go to the Camden pubs anymore, like a normal person, without them following her. Which made the volume go up on her addiction, too.

Amy became batshit crazy, living at one hundred miles an hour. I started to see a nasty side. She was never nasty to me but sometimes she wasn't that nice – most addicts aren't. She was an addict before but she was still lovely. I'd seen her agitated plenty of times, like when she was screaming about smashing the front door in with the crowbar, but she was becoming the Amy that people were scared of. On drugs she could be intimidating. She didn't have a lot of patience for people coming up to her, treating her like *the famous person*.

Now, there were charges made against her for things she'd done in public. That was the difference in Amy now. She was lashing out – at the world, at what fame had done to her and at the fans who were a by-product of that fame.

At some point, someone in the Hawley claimed she assaulted them. In the normal world, when someone had a drunken or druggy scuffle, you wouldn't hear anything about it. If you're in the public eye, people go to the papers, go to a lawyer. Amy wasn't violent by nature, she'd never just lay into someone, but if someone was doing her head in or wouldn't give her space after she'd asked for it politely, she'd tell them about it. If they persisted she'd throw them up against the wall, 'Get the fuck away from me!' She felt harassed, people wouldn't let up, even when it was obvious she didn't want to be approached, or was clearly in a bad mood, or in the middle of a conversation, or even an argument. People couldn't help themselves, it was like they felt they owned her because she was famous. They'd come right up to her and say, 'Oh Amy I can see you're not happy, but can I please have a picture?'

I still believed the real Amy underneath it all would *wake up*. This wasn't her. She was becoming more and more isolated.

Alex hadn't been Amy's hairdresser since the end of Omega Works, he was a serious crack addict and management removed him. In Prowse Place, he tried to get back into the circle and it bugged everyone how Amy didn't really know what he was like. Especially our buddy Chantelle, who'd seen it all since the old Camden days. He came over once, was outside ringing Amy's phone. I wasn't there that day but Chantelle was. Amy saw him from the kitchen window, said, 'Oh for fuck's sake, it's Alex,' but went to let him in anyway.

Chantelle couldn't take it anymore. She said, 'Amy, do not let that scumbag into this house, no one's ever wanted to tell you but let me tell you what he did to Tyler . . .' She told Amy about all the shit that I'd put up with from him, including my suspicions about the crack I found in her hair extensions.

Amy stood there listening and kind of snarling, saying, 'Did he, did he now?' He was still outside shouting 'Amy!' up at the window. Amy turned to Chantelle, said, 'Hang on, I've just gotta do something,' walked into the kitchen, grabbed a bottle of vodka, casually opened the kitchen window, shouted, 'Alex, one second, just stay there!' She leaned out the window and slung the vodka bottle at his head. And *got him*. She actually dusted her hands and said, 'Well, that's the end of him, then.'

I'd started to feel sorry for him by that time, he was such a mess. And so did Amy, eventually: when he finally went to rehab, she paid for it.

It seemed as if Mitch and Raye couldn't cope with Amy in person anymore. And that's why the decision was made by management to introduce staff. It was a bit like rich, middle-class parents who can't handle their naughty children getting a nanny in. Several nannies. In Amy's case, this meant not only the boys but a personal assistant. She didn't need a PA, she was barely doing any work, maybe the odd appearance or festival.

She felt more and more like a prisoner. The windows in Prowse Place were misted up with spray so the paparazzi couldn't take pictures of the inside. The more her addictions escalated, the more she wasn't supposed to go out, wasn't *allowed* to go out, in case she was photographed in a state in public. If she tried to go out, the boys were told to ring Raye. Fame, to her, equalled a total lack of freedom, of independence, of being her own person. And she resented it. Amy had needed those things from a young age, maybe even more than most. She'd had them for a brief few years and achieved so much with them, and now there was a fortress being built up around her like she was a teenager again. Instead of the stern stepdad and straightlaced mum, there were strangers, with instructions to tell her what she should and shouldn't be doing, like a child. At the same time the boys were becoming more like family than hired security, looking out for Amy like she was their little sister. But maybe it wasn't so surprising: Prowse Place was becoming more and more like a kids' playground.

There were childlike novelty objects all over the flat. Haribo had heard about Amy's Haribo habit and were now delivering free sweets directly to us. We had a special little plastic stand-up Haribo table with three legs, like a five-year-old would have. The tabletop was a round container full of Haribo sweets, which any crack addict would love. There was a proper candy-floss machine, which became a cocaine candy-floss machine, people sprinkling cocaine into the machine when it was whipping up the sugar. I ate plenty of it and don't remember getting high off it – it was decadent, cartoon ridiculousness. It stood beside the sink in the kitchen where the window looked down onto the paps. We had a Slush Puppy machine, for making really strong cherry slush puppy margaritas when people came round.

Amy was childlike now in many ways. She'd sit in my lap and suck her thumb; that had never happened before. There were times in Prowse Place where I'd scarper – not for long, just a day – and when I came back, she'd run to me like a kid would when their dad came home from work, jump up and put her legs around me. How could I not want to look after her?

Jodie Harsh was becoming a big drag queen on the scene and Amy befriended her. I remember her as a boy, with a skinhead and a tracksuit, he always looked like he'd headbutt you. Amy would watch Jodie take her make-up off, turn back into a boy and be fascinated, 'You're so good with make-up contouring, *how*?!'

Amy and Jodie would walk outside the front door, Jodie in full drag queen gear, Amy with her biggest beehive, carrying trays with little cups and saucers of tea for the paparazzi. Amy would make them bacon sandwiches in the morning and scold them, 'You ain't got nothing better to do? No homes to go to?! Go home and see your wives!' It was all silly games, something to do. She would open the front door at two o'clock in the morning wearing a headscarf; the tabloids said she looked like Hilda Ogden from *Coronation Street*. Or she'd open the door with a Hoover, in her pink marigolds, or be putting the bin bags out. She was like that all the time, there was always stupidness. She'd put a bowl of fake fruit in her beehive, for a laugh. The paparazzi *loved* her; she was a gift from heaven.

Dionne came round one afternoon and Amy played a game with her, with the paparazzi. Amy wanted to get out, go to the Hawley, said the three of us should go. She had Dionne put on a little pair of runners, Amy had on her ballet slippers and we all stood at the front door. Dionne was so excited; all the paparazzi were outside.

Amy opened the door, the cameras started to flash and she slammed the door shut again. 'Dionne, we're gonna have to run.'

Dionne was all wide-eyed. 'I'm up for it!'

Amy looked at me, looked at Dionne, 'Ready?' She opened the door and we *legged* it. I got hit in the side of the head by one of the cameras, was lagging behind, Amy was holding Dionne's hand and the pair of them were pelting along the road for a good five, ten minutes, paps chasing, and Dionne absolutely loved it.

The silly stuff kept us sane. Crack addiction isn't fun. Amy's lungs got so bad she had emphysema. She still had impetigo and bad skin bothered her; she used to say, 'Don't worry you won't catch anything.' As if I cared. I used to suck cocaine out of Amy's nose. She hardly ever did coke, why would she when she was smoking crack? But if she did and we were going out, or coming back in, with the paps always at the door, and I saw a lump of cocaine hanging out her nose I'd say, 'Wipe your nose.' She'd then attempt to sort it out and if it was still there three seconds away from pulling up outside the flat, I'd just . . . suck it out of her nose!

'Thanks, T.'

After a succession of PAs she didn't like, Amy finally found Jevan, who was sound. He'd known Amy previously and took everything with a pinch of salt. It used to piss Mitch off that Amy was paying him, even though a PA wasn't even her idea.

'What does he *do*?' Mitch would scoff. 'He comes round 'ere every now and again for thirty grand a year?!'

One of his jobs was to feed the cats. Amy had wanted cats, so cats came, at least eight of them. One litter tray was in the living room but the room they liked best was my bedroom, so that's where the rest of the litter trays were. I always hated cats. I lay in that room many times withdrawing from alcohol, sick as a dog, sweating, shaking, the smell of cat shite all around me. Occasionally I'd lean my head off the edge of the bed to vomit into the over-flowing litter trays, hallucinating, with the cats' meowing chorus all around me. That room was hell on earth.

I woke up early one morning and Amy and Pete Doherty were singing to me and playing with baby mice. All I could smell was cat shit. And vodka. Pete uploaded videos online and they were all over the tabloids, the two of them off their heads with a box of baby mice, talking bollocks. They said one of them looked like the dude from Razorlight and Amy was using another one of them to send messages to Blake. This wasn't the Amy I knew.

I stayed away from her when she was batshit crazy like that. I'd drink just to pass out in my bedroom for ten hours. I'd lie in that bed, sick, withdrawing, wondering what the fuck my life was all about. Amy would notice and look after me again. She'd be on the end of my bed playing guitar and singing like she used to when we were kids – the Beatles' 'I'm Only Sleeping' and Carole King's 'So Far Away'. She knew it comforted me like Valium comforted me. Sometimes, after we'd been awake for days, just me and her, all the randoms gone, the best moment for me was when Amy finally fell asleep. I'd lie next to my girl and feel so calm. Her behaviour was like 50 billion fireworks going off at once but when she was asleep, she looked like the Amy I used to know. Just Amy again. Like when a dad says his daughter's a nightmare and then goes on about how beautiful she is when she's asleep.

A girl called Neon became part of our craziness, an artist signed to Mike Skinner's label, The Beats. She was tough, tattooed, really cool and wouldn't take any of Amy's shit. They were pals and for a time were actual girlfriends, even though I don't think Amy was in any way bisexual. Shit just happens. I was exhausted, in turmoil, and Neon was fresh, young, just come onto the scene, she wasn't damaged, insane or addicted and she'd want to go to parties. I definitely didn't. Amy would go out with Neon and it was healthier than Amy sitting upstairs on her own with her crack pipe Lucozade bottle. I'd stay in and have some peace. Neon had a really good friend called Violetta and her and Amy really hit it off too, she was only nineteen, nothing to do with the music industry and still lived at home. She was fearless and didn't take any of Amy's shit either, wasn't impressed with her fame or any of it. I think Amy saw the freedom in her she didn't have for herself. Having these two around was good for Amy: they wanted nothing from her but friendship.

Blake had faded away, disappeared. She'd stopped talking about him altogether, she was just so *gone* by now, nothing else existed but her addiction.

She was hospitalized many times. There was one incident back in 2007. The tabloids went big on it, saying she'd overdosed with a list of drugs – ketamine, ecstasy, crack. It wasn't even a memorable incident, these things happened. But it was only in Prowse Place when I started to get The Fear. That the worst would actually happen.

She was always doing crack when she was upstairs in her room. I'd lie on the sofa and call up sometimes, to the mezzanine.

'Alright Ame?'

'Yeah.'

I'd hear her cough – the emphysema – and she'd talk while holding the smoke in tight, cough again and let the smoke out bit by bit. It drove me mad. I was on the sofa when I heard what sounded like choking. Proper choking. Then a bit of retching and vomiting.

'Ame? You alright?' Nothing. I shouted. 'Ame! Amy, you alright?'

Nothing. *Fuck.* I ran upstairs, into her room and she was lying on her back, flat down. She had sick on either side of her face. I leapt onto the bed, shaking her, shouting her name. She wasn't breathing at all.

I freaked out. I shoved my fingers into her mouth, down her throat, nothing came up. I lifted her upright. 'Wake up, wake up, *wake up!*' She still wasn't breathing. I got behind her, to put her in the Heimlich. I was still screaming her name, sobbing, pulling her upwards, trying to get her body to physically reject whatever was in there, throwing her around this bed, shouting 'No!'

I was desperate, I rammed my fists from behind into her stomach, almost punching her in the stomach, losing it, crying. I thought, *That's it, she's dead.*

I kept going and kept going and eventually a noise, 'ack-ack-ack!' and a massive breath, 'huuuuuuuuh!' She was breathing again, *breathing,* with her eyes open. I was stunned, in shock, and I laid her back down on the bed. She looked right at me.

'Tyler, you alright? You look like you've seen a ghost.'

I sat on the bed beside her, shaking, grabbed a bottle of JD, took a swig and lit a fag. I couldn't believe what had just happened. I'd just saved her life. She didn't have a clue what was going on and she needed to know.

'You just nearly died!'

'Well, it's a shame I didn't.'

She didn't mean it, she was playing the hard nut, like 'whatever'. I was angry, upset, I got up, walked out, went halfway down the stairs and just stopped, sat down and started sobbing. Amy heard me, she got up and came down.

'Tyler, what's wrong?'

'You nearly died, you *nearly died*, you don't realize what's happening, you're gonna have to stop this shit, it can't go on, I was holding you, you weren't breathing . . .'

I never normally let go like that, I always held it together. I kept going.

'I know you don't wanna go to rehab but will you at *least* see a therapist, will you do something? You have to *promise* me.'

She hugged me. 'T, I'm not going anywhere.'

I heard that all the time. Then she *did* promise me.

'I'll do something, I will, I *promise*, I will, I will, I will, I will.'

I didn't tell anyone about it, I was too scared. The next day I just carried on. Amy carried on. I thought, like I always thought. 'This will end, let's just ride this out and *it will end.*'

For months now, there had been work opportunities put in her diary and they always got pulled. Most things didn't matter. But an offer came in that *did* matter: the James Bond theme. It was the 2008 Bond film, *Quantum of Solace*, the second one to star Daniel Craig. Amy was made up about it and Mark Ronson would produce. *Of course* they picked her, that year she was the biggest artist in the world. The fourteen-year-old me at Sylvia Young's, the seventeen-year-old me that begged Amy to make her first demo tape, was ecstatic. I thought, this has to happen, I can't let this *not* happen, I have to help Amy make this fucking happen.

I was certain. *It's going to be brilliant.*

CHAPTER 24

The residential Doghouse Studio, two miles from Henley on the banks of the river Thames, is like a scene from *Midsomer Murders*: set in leafy English countryside, quaint, picturesque, calm. It was April 2008 and for the next couple of months, other than the odd week back in Prowse Place, this was Amy's home for the writing of the Bond theme with her *Back to Black* musical soulmate. Mark Ronson knew the score: he absolutely loved Amy but accepted she was a drug addict, accepted dealers would turn up in this tranquil paradise. But as long as at some point, at three in the morning, or whenever she got up in the afternoon, whatever stupidness had gone on, if she managed to squeeze out one hour of creativity and a Bond theme actually happened, he could cope.

The studio complex had a big main house which we never went into and a little cottage where we all lived: Amy, Mark, me and any visitors. There was a kitchen and lounge downstairs, with a spiral staircase in the corner leading up to a floor of bedrooms. I looked at that spiral staircase and thought: *Why do we always have the most precarious staircases wherever we go?* They were precarious enough for sober, together people! Outside there was a big wooden pub-style table, a beautiful lawn, bikes for use anytime, the river right next to the cottage garden. It was late spring, it felt like summer and coming out first thing in the morning or watching the sunset was bliss. There were also paparazzi on the other side of the river, hiding in the bushes.

It was a rock star's hideaway so the owner Barrie Barlow, the drummer from Jethro Tull, did what he could to keep paparazzi out: there were video production 'blue' screens positioned as barriers throughout the grounds – enormous pieces of plastic hung over silver poles, fifteen feet tall, thirty feet wide. There wasn't a hedge, a wall, a gate, or any open space which wasn't blocked off, so no one could see inside. A perfect media blackout fortress. I didn't see it myself but we heard, over the next few weeks, that Barlow turned the garden hose on paps he caught hiding in the bushes.

Given what had just happened in Prowse Place, the OD scare when Amy choked on her vomit and I thought she was dead, I upped my game. Her addictions were still escalating, she was in permanent chaos and this was the time in Amy's life when it wouldn't have surprised me *whatsoever* if she died. At any given moment. So my mission was simple: keep her alive. That was my mantra. It was more important than ever to lie beside her every night, awake, making sure she was breathing.

Mark Ronson powered on with the music. He'd be in the studio trying to create beats and moods, trying to encourage Amy. It wasn't working. I'd sit at the mixing desk with Mark and Amy was so high on heroin, eyes rolling in her head, she couldn't even hold the guitar in her hand, just falling asleep on the sofa. Mark's face said it all: what am I supposed to do with this?

At times we'd all jam together – me, Amy, Ronson and our friend Neon who came to visit. Mark even said to me, in desperation, 'Amy doesn't wanna do anything, she doesn't wanna write – what if we all write something together, then she might write something with you?' I just laughed. 'I can't write the Bond theme, that's not what they're after!' He said it didn't matter, if a file left this studio with music written and a vocal from Amy, whatever it was, it would be used.

Dealers turned up. I was pissed off that someone had organized it. One dealer I'd seen many times before arrived in a new £150,000 car, dressed in expensive clothes looking like a businessman, obviously prospering. While Amy was a next-level mess. Her self-harm was also escalating; I could see the fresh marks. I'd walk down to the river whenever Amy had cut herself again just to sit down and think and talk to myself: 'Don't have a breakdown, smoke a fag, keep yourself together, have a sip of Jack Daniel's, keep Amy alive.' Then I'd see a little head pop up from the other side of the river, in the bushes. *Click! Click! Click!*

I'd try to create normality, like I usually did. Here, first thing in the morning, I'd get on one of the bikes to the nearest town fifteen minutes away and buy all the breakfast, making sure everyone ate. On the way back, there'd be two giant carrier bags on either side of the handles, all the breakfast and all the alcohol for everybody, two bottles of vodka either side trying to keep balanced, but I always kept falling over.

Amy had a new, temporary PA by now, another Alex, Alex Haines. Management hired him and he was far too inexperienced to be in a world like that. He was a lovely young guy from the countryside who'd never done drugs in his life, wasn't even a drinker. I felt massively sorry for him; he arrived a bright-eyed innocent, had a fling with Amy and our world chewed him up and spat him out. He ended up living with Alex Foden, the poor bastard, and sold a story on Amy. That wasn't the lovely young guy we met.

One day Amy announced, 'Peter's coming.' Pete Doherty

turned up with Mick from Babyshambles. The *Trainspotting* vibe was back. I bailed out, went elsewhere in the complex.

Next morning, I got up, made a cup of tea, splashed some JD in it, went outside to the table for a fag, creating my morning normality. Mick appeared and sat down. I'd never met him before. He was terrifying, he looked *dead*. I thought, *I don't even wanna talk to you, you're off your face*, and went off to the bathroom for a wash. I was wearing shorts, t-shirt and no shoes and I stepped on a heroin needle. It pierced my skin. I kicked it away, walked out into the hallway, wiping my foot, going to get a plaster. I saw Mark and told him.

'This is ridiculous, I've just stepped on a needle, they're on the bathroom floor, I could have AIDS, hepatitis, all sorts.'

Mark said, 'Man, I've had enough.'

Mark is a professional. He'd been trying to do his job with all these randoms creating havoc. He'd been patient; there were times he didn't want to be around any of us and had gone off to the local pub for lunch, waiting. But now he was leaving.

'It ain't gonna happen,' he told me, walking away with his bags. 'Look after her, T.'

The Bond theme was cancelled but Island still thought new music of some kind could happen, so they drafted in Salaam Remi. He was in the studio with a band, working out ideas. Salaam is a lovely guy, another responsible adult, and now the same things were happening again: me, Amy, Neon and Salaam all jamming and Amy slurring on heroin. She'd then do crack to liven herself up, become so scatty she'd go up and down the stairs for no reason and eventually just disappear. This went on for days.

I was in the garden when I saw Neon one day, stumbling by the river, drunk, trying to get into a wooden boat. I legged it over the grass and saw her go under. It wasn't for long but she must've swallowed water and now she was just lying on the grass. I thought, *Is she gone?!* I put my mouth on her mouth, blew air in and the water popped out. She looked up at me, smiling and laughing. I was shocked. *Not again*. Life was just like that now.

Amy's self-harm was now so bad she needed proper medical attention. I called Raye.

'We need a doctor, it's ridiculous down here, she's cutting herself to shreds.'

Other than our early days at Henley, Raye hadn't come down at all so now he arranged for a psychiatric nurse to live in the main house that we never went in. Every morning this nurse would come along to our cottage wooden table, me and Neon would be sitting there – Amy wasn't even up yet – and she'd say, 'Good morning guys,' like we were about to have group therapy. She'd quiz us daily, whenever she got the chance, about our feelings and our mental state, pausing mid-sentence to write the analysis down in her notepad. It made sense to send a psychiatric nurse but we really needed a *nurse*, someone to resuscitate us if need be, to bandage people up – a first aid nurse not a therapist. She was shocked by the chaos and told us straight: 'You all need serious psychiatric help. You all need rehab. Why isn't somebody intervening? I'm appalled this behaviour is being allowed to continue!'

Through all the madness, Amy could still be funny. She was amazing at accents and in the middle of the night she'd teeter round the beds in her high heels pretending to be this Polish nurse character, wearing an apron from the kitchen, handing Valium out to everyone.

'Darling! It's *bedtime* darling, you need your medication . . .'

I'd piss myself laughing. And put my Valium under my pillow, staying awake.

*

Another beautiful morning at the wooden table, cup of JD tea, fag, my daily moment of sanity. Out of nowhere I heard this smashing, wailing and screaming from upstairs, it was terrifying, piercing. I ran into the living room and Amy was staggering down the spiral staircase, screaming, falling into the sides. She had a light blue vest on and she was covered, from her shoulders down to her wrists, on both arms, in blood. *Saturated* in blood. There were cuts on her chest, blood all over her vest. I couldn't even speak, I thought, *Jesus fucking Christ what's happened?!* and legged it halfway up the stairs to where she'd fallen down. I'd seen Amy cut herself plenty of times but it never resulted in gushing blood like this, it was like she'd cut her wrists. She was off her face, high on heroin, she could barely stand up. I half-carried her down the stairs and into the hallway. 'It's alright darlin', it's alright darlin' . . .'

Neon was standing there just staring so I mouthed to her, 'Go and get the bandages and creams!' We were sitting on the hallway floor, Amy in my arms and I was wiping her with tissue, looking for serious cuts. Neon was helping me, wetting tea towels in the kitchen, while Amy wailed and cried. It was obvious: she'd been upstairs and totally lost the plot, smashed the bathroom to pieces, smashed the mirror into shards and just went for herself. Everywhere. Like a frenzy. She'd freaked herself out, really scared herself this time. When she came down the stairs it was like a real-life horror movie, a slasher movie, in vivid colour. It was *horror.*

I got her bandaged up, calmed her down and helped her into the kitchen, told her we'd have a cup of tea. I didn't want to call the psychiatric nurse. I didn't want anyone on the outside seeing Amy like this. She wasn't bleeding anymore. I sat up on the kitchen worktop and she was standing next to the kettle. I was still calm but this was the moment to tell her.

'Amy, this can't carry on, you can't do this to yourself any-more, you're gonna *really* hurt yourself. What were you thinking?'

She seemed like she was holding it together, just listening, was OK with what I was saying and didn't say a word. Suddenly she just grabbed the kettle, swung round and threw it straight at me, and it hit me, on the side of my body. It *stung*. I was shocked, Amy *never* hurt me, she'd never done anything like that to me before.

'What did you throw a kettle at me for? That fucking hurt!'

Something inside her went 'bang!', like it did when she smashed the wardrobes up in Omega Works. She started screaming right in my face.

'Hurt? *Hurt?!* What do you know about hurt? What do you know about pain?! What does anyone know about pain! I'm so fucking hurt! I'm fucking dying! My *Blakey* . . .'

She was still screaming when she swung her arm across a stack of plates on the worktop, which all tumbled and crashed onto the floor. She went for the cutlery drawer, opened it – it was all happening so fast – pulled out the biggest kitchen knife she could see and held her other arm out like she was about to stab herself in the wrist – there was no doubt about it.

'Amy! No!'

I leapt off the worktop, kicked the knife out of her hand and rugby tackled her to the floor. She was punching me and kick-ing me but I couldn't let her go, she was going to kill herself right in front of me: *I could not let her go.* She was struggling and struggling – considering everything she still had a lot of strength. In this tiny kitchen space, with all this lunacy and horror, welded to someone who'd completely lost their mind covered in bandages and blood, I was terrified. I reached over, grabbed the knife on the floor and slung it out the door as far as I could. I was still convinced she was going to stab herself or stab *me* so I grabbed her again, *enveloped* her. She was struggling again, we were wrestling on the floor and finally the fight started ebbing away, out of her body, I could feel it, she was slumping back in my arms. She stopped screaming and started crying and crying and *crying*. She'd finally let go, sobbing and sobbing on my shoulder.

'I'm sorry Tyler, I'm so sorry Tyler, I'm *sorry* . . .'

And then she said the words I'd never heard her say before. *Never*.

'Help me. Help me, Tyler. I dunno what to do. Help me. Help me. *Help me*.'

I was sobbing too, loosening my grip, knowing the demon had gone and she was Amy again. I looked at her and she was vulnerable and human, like she always used to be. Like she was when she wrote her music on the kitchen floor. I thought, *There you are*. You. *You're still that little girl, my little sister, my Amy, you're still here and you need help and we'll get you help. You've finally realized it. Instead of all this bravado.*

I knew this wasn't about Blake, it was so much bigger than that. Blake was clearly not the problem. Blake being around was the problem and now Blake *not* being around was the problem so . . . what then? She knew it herself. There was a bottle of JD on the floor in the corner I could reach, so I stretched over Amy, grabbed it and took a swig. My heart-rate calmed and I wrapped my arms around her, kissed the top of her head: 'Shh, shhh, it's alright darlin', it's alright.' Seeing her this broken killed me, tears were rolling down my face. I just sat there, thinking, *How the fuck did we get here? How did this happen? What can I do? How can I make all this stop?* It felt like the tipping point for both of us.

Neon was standing in the hallway and I told her to get the

nurse. I gave Amy Valium, asked the nurse to stay with her, went outside and I rang Raye. I explained what had happened and told him this couldn't go on.

'I can't do this anymore, *we* can't do this anymore, this needs to be the end of all this shit. You need to ring Mitch and tell her family.'

'Don't worry, we'll come down.'

The seriousness of it was understood, loud and clear. I walked back in; Amy was asleep, the nurse next to her. I thought, *Amy's alright, the nurse is alright, Neon's alright.* I grabbed the bottle of JD, walked into the garden and lay down on the grass. I wanted out of all this. I glugged and glugged and glugged and glugged and passed out.

I came round, still on the grass, the sun was setting and everybody was there. Mitch. Janis. Raye. Aunty Mel. I'd been lying there all day without a top on and I'd been bitten to pieces, gnat bites all over me. No one had come to wake me up. I went over. Most of the times I saw Janis her MS was bad and you felt she never really fully knew what was going on with Amy or was in any position to do anything about it. I went over, gave her a kiss and she talked about normal nonsense. She was a beautiful person in her way and she just wasn't well. I walked behind some bushes and vomited violently, from the alcohol and the shock.

There was a real sense of *this is the end*. It was surreal – this sunny May evening, all the family there, sitting on little benches round the garden. Aunty Mel had brought all this salt beef and Jewish food. Amy was up by now and was holding onto Raye, her thin, bandaged arms around this massive man – she was a third of his size, about six stone at this point – crying on his shoulder. I saw Raye was crying too.

I thought about her standing in that bathroom. I know her

and what she would've been thinking. 'What's wrong, what's wrong? Me. *Me. I'm* what's wrong. My self, my body, my brain, I am the problem. So, if the problem is in me, I'll destroy myself. I'll cut me. End me.'

I didn't leave Henley with Amy, she was with her family now. I left in a car by myself, going down the A40 to my mum's, not back to Prowse Place. When I called my mum to tell her what had happened, I felt relieved. *Relieved.* I'd been so worried and I wasn't worried anymore. Amy needed help and she'd finally asked for it. I wasn't capable of what was needed now. I wasn't a doctor or a nurse or a psychiatrist. I couldn't save Amy. Not on my own.

In that car going down the A40, I knew it was time for me to help myself, too. I just kept on thinking, *It's over, it's over, it's over.*

And it *was* over.

CHAPTER 25

Amy had smashed full pelt into the wall. With serious addiction you have to hit the wall. Because if there's one more mile on this crazy road you're travelling on at 150 miles an hour, you'll take it. She went to hospital, it wasn't a rehab, a place like the Capio Nightingale Clinic she stayed in for the Grammys. She didn't make that decision herself, she was too messed up to decide anything. She just knew she needed help, she'd finally asked for help, so she was taken with no arguments.

Over summer 2008 she'd go in and out of hospital getting to grips, finally, with her crack and heroin addictions, physically, psychologically, emotionally. Amy going through the process of giving up drugs happened because there was nowhere else to go: after Henley she just knew it was over. *But.* Even though her problems were still severe, even though she was obviously still vulnerable, management went ahead with her Glastonbury 2008 Pyramid Stage performance just a few weeks later. It would've been in the schedule for months. That was the performance where Amy went into the crowd, some dude grabbed her breast, people booed her when she mentioned Blake and she elbowed a fan in the face, threw punches into the crowd. The headlines went around the world. I know I was there and I don't remember any of it. I don't remember even *being* at Glastonbury that year because I was hitting the wall myself.

After Henley, I went back to my mum's. She was in Spain, so I was alone for three solid weeks. I rang the boys, they told me Amy was in hospital so now that I wasn't looking after Amy and no one was looking after me, I went for it. I drank to seek unconsciousness. I'd wake up in bed cuddling a bottle of vodka, start drinking again, take a few tablets. I didn't just have an alcohol and drugs problem, I was having a full blown nervous breakdown. I knew I'd have to sort myself out eventually, but I didn't have to stop drinking today. But I *would* stop, soon.

Every morning, when I came back from the shop with a bottle of vodka or two – I wasn't hoarding because, of course, I was going to stop – I'd pour a glass of neat vodka and stick a straw in it, shaking so much I couldn't hold it still. Then I'd have whatever shite microwaveable meal I'd bought and drink until I was unconscious. Being conscious was unbearable.

It dawned on me: *I'm going to die.* It wasn't that thought that concerned me, it was that my mum would find me dead. I rang Nick Shymansky. He was at an Arsenal football match, I could hear the crowd. 'Nick, I need to go to rehab.' It was the first time I'd ever said it out loud. He was calm. 'OK man, don't panic, I'll sort it out, leave the door open.' I went back to sleep.

He organized a rehab in Hastings for drugs and alcohol addiction and a woman called Ally and a guy called Sayed turned up. I got in the car and we drove two hours to Hastings, after I'd stopped for a bottle of vodka first. I wasn't bothered about going to rehab, I felt like I was doing the right thing. I was on my way to some nice spa in the countryside, they'd give me loads of drugs, the most powerful sleeping tablets, and in a couple of weeks I'd be fine. That's what I knew from Amy's world. I felt *good*, music was playing in the car, I was joking with Ally and Sayed – they told me they used to be addicts themselves – feeling sociable after being isolated for so long, smoking out the window, nibbling bits of Valium. I drank the whole bottle of vodka and passed out.

Outside the rehab it took them two hours to wake me up. The building itself looked like a stately home and inside it was like a hostel. It definitely wasn't some lovely spa in the countryside. Ally told me she needed to check through my bags and the panic hit me. Were they about to take my Valium? My dopamine-infused tablets? It was worse than that: this particular rehab has a core belief in no drugs for anything: no sleeping tablets, no withdrawal meds, you can't have a paracetamol for a headache. A doctor's assessment decides whether you're able to handle this level of cold turkey. You're offered a *massage* to get to sleep. They give you vitamins and Calmag, calcium and magnesium, which makes you shit yourself. I was terrified. Then I passed out.

Around midday next day, I was taken outside into the gardens. I could barely stand and Ally and Sayed walked me round like I was an invalid. The next three days were nothing but sweating, vomiting, shaking, hallucinating and hearing things: absolute hell. I didn't know where I was. I was agitated, started throwing things, shouting at people, punching people, breaking down in tears. I punched Sayed many times and he took it, as part of his job. I was coming off not only booze but Valium, benzoates, codeine, everything. I'd be shouting, 'Get me out of here, I don't wanna be awake!' and they'd hold me until I fell down on my knees. I launched the massage table at the wall and it hit Sayed, went to punch him again, burst into tears and he said, 'Tyler, give in man, you're gonna be alright, I know it's hard, I've been there mate.' I was crying and crying. He said, 'You've got a lot of problems, if I had to give you a number out of ten, as an addict, you're a nine.' I said, 'At least I ain't a ten.' He said, 'Ten is dead. But don't worry, I'm here for you.'

Sayed became my friend. We drank mint tea together under the stars, made with mint he'd grown himself in the garden. I gave in and accepted it. But not for long. Days later, I kicked off again, wanting to leave. They sent in a French-Canadian woman; she was posh, she'd never been an addict and she was a bitch to me. She said, 'Well, d'you think you're ready to go? *Do* you?' She was trying to psychologically break me down and I knew it, so it wasn't going to work. I lost it. Smashed up tables, chairs, hurled cups at walls, smashed everything in the room except the windows. She just left and Sayed came in. Nick was on his phone, he passed it to me.

'What are you doing man, you can't leave?!'

'Nick, I can't do it, it's too fucking hard!'

'But you don't have a choice, Tyler, you need help!'

'But I feel a bit better to be honest, you know I still have the publishing deal, I'm supposed to be in the studio.'

I was still signed to Global, still living off their deal, and all I'd been doing was drinking myself unconscious.

'I can get back to my life, I can turn it around.'

'You just wanna drink! Can't you see that?!'

'I don't! After what I've been through in the last week? I don't wanna ever drink again! I just wanna *go home*. I can't stay here, it's too hard, this is just too hard for me.'

I absolutely believed if I just went home I could stay sober. I left, got to Liverpool Street train station and rang my mum. She was back from Spain and she was furious, told me there was vodka and drugs all over the house, said she didn't want to see me and hung up. Years later she told me there were thirty-seven empty bottles of vodka in her house.

I was lost, again. Not even my *mum* wanted anything to do

with me. I'd already started staying in hotels when my drinking was seriously bad. I was so ashamed of myself I'd hide away and obliterate myself, smoke by the window and wonder what the hell happened to my life. I'd drink the mini-bar dry, then order six hot toddies from room service. Managers would come to the door, wondering if I was alright. Eventually they'd kick me out, they thought I was about to top myself. Paying hotel bills is what I did with my new publishing advance.

Days were blurring together, events were like snatches of dreams. Me and Amy were still living in Prowse Place, on and off, between hospitals and hotels, on our separate paths, but intertwined as ever. That August she also had to play two legs of V Festival, she was in hospital getting clean before that, so she asked me to look after the cats. My only memory is of freaking out when the cats jumped up on the kitchen table, paws padding straight into my piles of cocaine. Everything became blurrier: I went to one of the V Festival shows, drove a golf buggy around, Lily Allen sat on my lap sucking her thumb. Another night I was in Adele's flat in Notting Hill probably being really annoying: I loved her cover of 'To Make You Feel My Love' and begged her and begged her to play it on her piano, which she did. There were flashes of seeing Pete Doherty. There were flashes of an incident where someone gave Amy a dodgy pill, not intentionally, Mitch got wind of it and rushed her to hospital. I wasn't even there at the time. There was still so much chaos and I wasn't capable of doing what I'd been doing before, being the friend to her I had been, because I needed help myself. I was running *to* Amy, and then running away from Amy, back and forth, trying and struggling. Because I could not cope anymore: the responsibility had finally gotten the better of me. The boys, though, were always there and I'd talk to them wherever I was, wherever she was, so I knew she was alright, or *becoming* alright.

Then I was somehow sober again, living in a hotel in Liverpool Street, sitting smoking by the window, looking for answers I could never find.

In early September Mark Ronson was having a birthday party in Jazz After Dark and that night, after a good spell of sobriety, I just decided I was going to drink. I thought: I just can and I'll be alright. I wasn't even feeling anxious, that's how insane alcoholism is. Everyone knew I'd been to rehab, everyone knew I needed to be sober so I did it privately, slipped into a little bar by myself, had a shot and walked back into the party without a drink in my hand. Soon enough I was doing lines of coke, shitloads of shots and still managing to hide it from everyone. Adele was there and she just knew. In a room full of people rambling on about how proud they were of me for abstaining, she could see I wasn't sober. She said, 'I don't know why no one else can see it, but I can and you need to stop all this, Tyler, it's no good for you.' She was still so young and so wise already.

Over the next few weeks I went in and out of sobriety. I'd talk to my mum on the phone but she still wouldn't see me. She said, 'Whatever happened to my boy who was gonna make me proud?' It killed me, it was tough love, a dagger in my heart. Chantelle was my angel then. Since Henley, she'd stayed with me in hotels, looking after me – sometimes I didn't even know she was there and she was making sure I didn't choke on my vomit, making sure I kept breathing. She was everything to me that I was to Amy. We were in a hotel when she suggested I ring my dad. He was very unwell with severe depression but his missus Helen is a spiritual healer. She specializes in meditation, acupuncture, physiotherapy and she also helps addicts. The time when I got beaten up it was Helen who fixed my back.

I stayed with them for three weeks. I had a plan in my head: if I can get myself sober I can go back to rehab without going through withdrawal and I'll be able to do their programme. Helen helped me: she lit joss sticks, made me drink potions. I'd wake up and be drenched in sweat, expelling all the drink and drugs, me and the bed soaked in pints of water. I meditated and ran in the forest, vomiting during the run, getting the toxins out.

The damage already done to my head was apparent. I'd hear voices taunting me, telling me I was going to die, drink myself to death, and there was nothing I could do about it. I would constantly see an old man over by a tree in the garden, I was terrified. Helen told me he was a bad entity, a bad spirit. He looked like an old Scottish homeless alcoholic. At night, as soon I closed my eyes, he was *there*, like he was lying on top of me, staring into my eyes, taunting me, breathing on me. I believe in entities and I believe that when you're weak they'll attach them-selves to you. So it helped me, knowing that if I got stronger, these entities would leave me. Helen told me I'd had entities before. She told me Amy had *five* entities.

Sometimes when the old man was there, I'd find myself walking round to the off licence and just having one drink. Not to get drunk. I'd buy myself a miniature. And then go back and buy myself a bottle. My dad realized what was going on and had a go. I sobered up again, spoke to my mum, told her I was going back to rehab. This time she stayed on the phone.

'I haven't given up on you,' she told me. 'You are my son, I would die for you, I'd do anything for you, you're doing well, get yourself into that rehab and it'll be the making of you.'

I got off the phone and stayed sober. I thought, my mum loves me again, I'm alright again, everything's going to be alright and I'll be able to look after Amy again. I rang Mitch and he told me she'd been in hospital and now she was in St Lucia, an island in the middle of the Caribbean Sea. I had no idea. After the horrors of Henley, after the Glastonbury altercation, after V, she'd had no work commitments so now, finally, she could fully recover, thousands of miles away from the headlines in the UK. This was the green light I needed: Amy wasn't just being looked after, she wasn't even in the country, so now I could go to rehab, and when I came out I'd go to her. I rang and set a date.

The night before I stayed at my mum's. It was a big deal, like I was going off to travel the world. We were lying on my bed and she told me, 'You're stronger than you think, this will make a man out of you.' It was beautiful. I went to bed.

Sayed was picking me up at five in the afternoon. After being so positive the night before, now my mum was saying how pleased she was I was going because she'd suffered so much. She said, 'It's been so hard for me.' It touched a nerve. It was the kind of thing I'd see happen in Amy. It was almost like the moment in Henley after she threw the kettle at me.

I said, 'Hard for you? This isn't happening to *you*. This is happening to *me*!' Danny was there as well. I said, 'You're my parents, you raised me! If I'm like this, it's *your* fucking fault!'

Danny looked like he was about to punch me. I'd gone over my upbringing in my head a lot, hoping to find some trauma, some abuse, anything to explain why I was like I was, and there was nothing. It was just me and my chemical make-up. I'm naturally just a fucked-up person. Maybe I was just scared that day. Maybe I was looking for an excuse. I grabbed my bag and walked out the door. It was mid-afternoon. I looked back over my shoulder and they were both staring at me, fear all over their faces. I got to the end of the road and rang Sayed.

'I know you're picking me up in two hours, I've just had an argument, I'm going straight to the shop for a bottle of brandy, there's a ditch at the end of the road, behind a bench. I'll be in it.'

I bought the brandy, went to the field, got in the ditch, drank my brandy and fell asleep. Sayed found me. Next morning I woke up in rehab again.

I had to go through withdrawal all over again. Not as bad, but still terrible: the voices, the hallucinations, the old man was there. I came out of it, started the programme and stayed there for three months. This wasn't the Priory, it didn't cost two hundred grand, it was like student halls. I shared a room with two other boys. There were loads of boys there just out of prison. It was brutal, no one was lighting scented candles. That's probably why it worked.

Every day I sat in the sauna, sweating out toxins. There was endless therapy. You're shouting at walls, telling walls how you feel, throwing things, having confrontations with strangers who are right in your face, saying the most terrible things about you, and you have to tell them all your insecurities and not make eye contact – all mind games, exercises and techniques. It teaches you how to confront yourself and deal with yourself and deal with anything. How to not be affected by things, how to separate your mind from your body. Ultimately it just keeps you busy. All your problems are still there but you're slowly coming back to earth. They said that when I first came in I had a scarf wrapped up to my eyes, a hat on, wouldn't look at anyone and now I was talking to everyone.

That thirteen-year-old boy who won a scholarship, who was ambitious, who had letters from exam boards saying I was in the top one hundred achievers in the country, who took his exams early, that boy was gone. That boy had got himself into a situation where he'd travelled the world, got a record deal and then all his dreams were shattered and everything was fucked. And then Amy was fucked. Now, in rehab, I just got up every day, had breakfast and did the schedule. I was good at it, I got into it. It was like I was turning myself back into the boy I used to be. And when things were at their toughest, when I felt like giving up, the thought of Amy, of knowing unless I was sober I couldn't help her anyway, pulled me through. I was getting sober for her as much as for myself.

Every weekend you could make calls and every weekend I spoke to Amy in St Lucia. Every single time she asked me where I was. She had no short-term memory whatsoever, everything was about *now*: there was no tomorrow and there was no before. I told her every week, 'I'm in rehab' and every week she said, 'Oh my God! Who's put you in rehab?! I'm gonna get you out!' I could hear her saying to the boys, Neville and Andrew, who already knew, because they'd heard it the week before, 'Tyler's in rehab, we need to go and get him! Tyler, I'll send a plane! Come to St Lucia!'

And every week I said the same thing: 'No Ame, I want to be here, my head's getting better, I'm not drinking.'

'Oh, OK.'

She was still so anti-rehab, to her it was like I'd been kidnapped and put in prison. I missed Amy so much. I'd never been away from her as long as this. I'd been through this intense journey on my own, had a new perspective – a stone cold sober one. I finally knew addiction is a disease where the only cure is abstinence. And that's what I wanted.

People think you go to rehab and it fixes you. It doesn't. It's the beginning of a very long journey. You don't come out *reborn*. You come out dull and deflated like a shrivelled up balloon. You also have a real appreciation of feeling slightly normal. Of being slightly in control of your anxiety instead of thinking, *I feel panicky, better drink some vodka.* Those things don't leave you. They haven't left me now. You learn coping mechanisms. I never had and I never do have cravings for alcohol or codeine or Valium, but when stressful things happen I have to go for a long walk. It takes time.

In rehab, my mum and Danny visited me every week and brought me a McDonald's. When I came out they picked me up and Mum was so happy, so proud of me. 'It's so great to have you back.' Meaning: it's great to have *you* back. I'd been someone different for so long.

I was scared as well: can I pull this off? You have to learn how to do everything in life again, sober. What really strikes you is how normal everything is. You realize how *dull* normal life actually is. Drink and drugs give you a lot of pleasure before they fuck you up. It's like someone turned the dial down on the lights in life, and the speed of life and the colour of life. I don't know how people do it. Even though I *am* doing it. But you start to experience highs again. Natural highs.

In the years that followed, my friends were still on the path of excess but I'd still go out with them. I'd still go to house parties 'til four in the morning. I was never concerned at three in the morning when people were racking up lines of coke that I'd want to do one. They couldn't have paid me to. When people asked, I'd say I was allergic to alcohol. Because I am. I became a serious Red Bull addict. I realized how boring it all was, the drama, the drunk people. But at least I had a focus straight away, of getting back to taking care of Amy. If I hadn't had that focus maybe I would've relapsed again. But I wanted to be sober *so badly*. It's like Russell Brand says – who's a genius in addiction theory – the only decision you have to make is not to have the first drink. Simple. After that point it's no longer within your control. One drink, you're already gone. He says it's like handing your keys to the lunatic.

In rehab you're encouraged to stay away from what we'd now call triggering environments. You're told you can't be friends with the people you used to do these things with. I never bought into it. Amy was my soulmate and I wasn't going to lose her. It's not like we'd relied on each other to feed our addictions anyway.

Against everyone's advice, I was ready to get on a flight to St Lucia.

CHAPTER 26

I was picked up at St Lucia airport and driven for two and a half hours; it's a big island. It was a few weeks after my rehab and I hadn't seen Amy for months. But I had clarity and peace of mind on everything that had happened over the last year and a half. I pulled up at this huge villa and met the person looking after it.

'Welcome,' she said, 'let me know if there's anything you need.'

'Where's Amy?'

She was on the beach, seconds away, down a little road, which opened out onto the main beach, a big eating area and a bar. I walked down and looked around the cove – we were circled by mountains. There was Amy, surrounded by a crew of children.

For years I knew that when people thought about 'Amy Winehouse' they thought about this character, with the beehive. I was presented with someone I hadn't seen for years. Amy in little shorts, bikini bra, barefoot, but the biggest thing – and I'd never seen this before, she always had thick, long, brunette hair halfway down her back – was a curly, dark scraggy bob. *No beehive.* She looked just like Janis. I'd never even *thought* that before. The character was gone. She looked free.

She stared at me, stunned, frozen against the backdrop of the turquoise sea. She knew I was coming but she'd obviously forgotten. I heard her speak.

'Is that my Tyler?'

She burst into tears, ran towards me, jumped into my arms, put her little legs around my waist and I just held her for what felt like forever. I'd missed her so much. She touched my face. 'Am I dreaming?!' It was beautiful, just me and her and nothing else, no stupidness, no paparazzi, just Amy in her bare feet, no make-up, no eyeliner. But I could see how fragile she was.

She grabbed me by the hand, took me round the resort and introduced me to everyone. 'This is my boy!'

This was the girl who always wanted to be normal, to be friends with people, have a cup of tea with the neighbours, and she'd made pals with everyone. There was a place down the road called Marjorie's Bar where the locals went, nothing like our posh expensive resort. Every morning, Amy got up and walked straight out of the resort to Marjorie's. She took me down there, like a proud mother showing off her son. I met Aunty Marjorie who ran the bar and looked after the orphan children, about fourteen of them, mostly under twelve years old. One older girl, maybe fifteen, was staring at me and Amy laughed. 'I know, he's gorgeous, innee?!' I met the St Lucian boys who were only seventeen or eighteen who ran all the sports activities Amy had gotten into, like horse riding.

We didn't talk about Henley, her hospital, my rehab – nothing except now. She was too fragile: *Let's not rock the boat*. I also registered she had a Caribbean accent; she was talking like a local girl. That's how she was speaking to 'the boys', her security guys Andrew and Neville, who were also here, and they *do* have Caribbean accents, they'd talk to each other in patois. Just like Blake's cockney rhyming slang, Amy had picked it all up, but this went deeper, it was like she didn't really know who she was anymore. Her identity, I'd find out later, was lost.

It was clear that drink was now a thing. She wasn't necking

bottles of neat vodka like I'd been – that was a level she'd *never* been at – but she was clearly on holiday. Her breakfast, usually eggs, always came with a Bloody Mary. At nine in the morning. That wasn't ridiculous, people on holiday do that all the time. She'd drink in the afternoon, maybe pass out for three hours, get up and start again. It was obvious: she'd replaced drugs with alcohol.

The stereotypical story of the crack and heroin addict is they hit rock bottom, decide to rebuild their life, go to rehab in a temple in the mountains and emerge reborn. That didn't happen to Amy. She went through the drug withdrawal process in hospital, successfully, came out and was told she was going to St Lucia for a year. She had nothing to do with that decision either. She was here for several reasons: to be sheltered from her crazy world, recover from drugs, be in the sunshine – all with a view to writing her next album.

Tax was also a factor. After the Grammys, Raye told Amy she should think about going away soon as there were gonna be some big tax bills. Every major pop star in history has done it: if you spend however many months of the year out of the country there's substantial tax relief, sometimes *no* tax. It was a ruse all paid for by Island Records, with the ultimate impetus, understandably, of writing a new album. It was eighteen months since *Back to Black* came out and the music industry was now obsessed with 'retro' sounding female artists, whether the short-lived Duffy or the incoming phenomenon of Adele. And there *were* attempts at music: occasionally Amy was in the studio here with Salaam Remi.

St Lucia was a ruse on another level, too: they had to place her in a location where there weren't any drugs. I've been told this is what happened with the Happy Mondays back in the early nineties, when Factory Records sent them to Barbados to get Shaun Ryder off heroin and attempt to write a new album. He got himself an even worse crack addiction instead. But there was no crack on St Lucia. Or heroin. There was plenty of alcohol though.

Amy's villa had five bedrooms, with rooms for Andrew and Neville, who were constantly with her now. It was such a relief: other people were watching her, not just me. They were becoming even more like family now. I only thought about it much later but those boys were pretty much our age. I'd assumed they were grown-arse men in their thirties. They were ex-marines, trained to hurt people and I felt like their little brother. They properly looked out for me as well. The villa was cleaned daily, the rooms had little balconies, there was a swimming pool out the back. Everything was civilized.

Violetta was here too, the new friend she'd made through Neon back in Prowse Place and, even though she was so young, she was the stabilizing one. When Amy was drinking a margarita on the beach and wanted to do shots at the bar, Violetta would have a word. 'No Amy, you don't need shots, you've got your margarita, it's one in the afternoon mate.' Amy listened to her.

I could understand Amy wanting to drink. I thought, *Well, you've been smoking crack for eighteen months, you've become stupidly famous, you've been in this destructive relationship, you've cut yourself to pieces, you probably don't even remember getting married, now you're going through a divorce. If you need a few drinks to get through the day, you crack on darlin'.*

Divorce proceedings were happening when she was in St Lucia and she never even mentioned it. We didn't have a single conversation about Blake. I'm not sure the divorce was all that much to do with Amy. Her dad probably said you need to get divorced; he might even have told Blake to file for adultery, anything to get him out of her life. There were reports in the tabloids about a £250,000 divorce settlement and maybe that was true but I never knew anything about it. Amy wouldn't have deliberately kept that from me but it's not the kind of thing she would've said either. Because she didn't give a shit about money. She might have known nothing about it. Or it might have been mentioned to her and she said 'whatever'. But I reckon Mitch did a deal with Blake that bought him off. And I wouldn't have blamed him, the way things had become. Amy wouldn't have appreciated him having that level of control over her life but she wasn't present enough to have any control over anything herself.

Amy was a very damaged person in St Lucia, genuinely lost, she barely knew who she was anymore or half of what she'd been through. That damage was written all over her face; it still haunted her but she was trying to move through it and move on. Really trying. I was so proud of her for that. She was still erratic though, even without drugs. The second she woke up it was *bang!* like a firework, off round the resort, the beach, her little bare feet stomping everywhere, visiting this one, that one, until she'd exhausted herself or passed out with drinking over many hours. She wasn't Caribbean chilled, it was like she was still on the run, moving all the time, still running away from herself.

There was also a normal side I hadn't seen for years. When I first got there Amy opened my suitcase, which of course my mum had packed – I was still a kid till I was twenty-nine. I had my new little shorts, Fred Perrys, polo shirts. Amy took out all the freshly folded and ironed clothes and lined them up in the wardrobe. A few days later, she came in and started rooting through my wardrobe saying, 'Them boys ain't got anything.' She'd brought in one of the horse riding boys, he went for a shower and she took out all my clothes, looking for what would look nice on him. She did him up to the nines in Calvin Klein pants and Fred Perrys and he was made up. I was more than happy to give them away, I could always get more.

Amy didn't mix with the people in the resort, she mixed with the black people and the locals, always going to Marjorie's Bar where the orphans were. She was like the Pied Piper, little kids around her all the time, hanging off her heels. She taught them the arm moves she used to do on stage with her backing singers, like The Supremes, one arm out at a time. All the kids would be in a row, Amy in the middle directing them, going 'one . . . two . . . a bit more attitude!' They *loved* it. She did everything for these kids and got into trouble for it. She took them into the Kids' Club in the resort, where mummy and daddy would send their posh kids while they were in the spa covered in lotus oil. She took the orphans up to the buffet, which was free for guests, so as far as Amy was concerned they should stock up, they were hungry. Amy would get a look from the guy serving eggs and say, 'I'm paying for it!' thinking, *if that's all you care about I'll pay ten times over so these kids can have some boiled eggs.* The woman in charge had enough one day and turfed them all out. Amy kicked off big time. In front of all the kids, she screamed, 'You're all fucking cunts! You only wanna look after the spoilt rich white kids! Fuck you!' She slammed the door of the Kids' Club so hard the whole hut shook. I had my head down trying not to laugh. *Get in!* I thought, *That's my girl.*

Amy would sit and talk to Aunty Marjorie for hours, with a cocktail, about serious things. Aunty Marjorie had an awareness of who she was and all the shit she'd been through. She would ask her about Blake, about drugs, and Amy would talk openly, like she did with my mum.

She was rehabilitating herself. Part of that was horse riding along the beach, wind in her hair. There was a new side to her emerging, of dedication to physical fitness. Every day we'd drive to a resort nearby which had a circus-style outdoor fitness gym with a trapeze and all sorts. I'd sit on the beach, iced coffee in hand, watching Amy walk the tightrope. An actual tightrope! Tied between poles, about four feet off the ground, with crash mats underneath. She could do acrobatics, she'd do the splits and backflips, bending herself this way and that way. It was mind-blowing, she had skills! But then Amy never did things by half. She was good at everything she tried to do. We always had a home with a gym from then on. It was like she was building herself back up after the biggest comedown of her life, after this two-year crazy 'dream' where she became a superstar, whose last clear memories were writing *Back to Black* and making the video for 'Rehab'. It was like she'd woken up, finally. But it was also like she didn't know who she was anymore. She was look-ing for a new identity.

At night sometimes, after a day of her running around, steadily drinking, exhausted, we'd listen to the Soweto Kinch album, like we used to years before in Jeffrey's Place. We talked about things we'd never talk about when Amy was sober. She said to me, 'I don't know who I am anymore, I haven't got a Danny who the fuck I am, what happened?'

She'd turn questions back on me. I asked her, 'Are you happy, Ame?' and she replied, 'Are you?'

I stayed silent and then she said, 'Well, there you go then.'

Then I said, 'But I'll tell you one thing, I don't wanna drink anymore.'

She didn't say anything to that.

I encouraged her to relax, go to the spa, have a massage, detoxify. Every time we went to the spa, she cleaned it out of every exfoliating product and cream she could, she'd say, 'This is on the record label, it's all on Darcus.' But she was never happy there because there was no chance of her getting a drink.

We were there, mud all over our faces, smelling of rotten egg and I could tell she'd rather be at the beach with a margarita.

There was silly stuff too. One night, she and Violetta were drunk and decided to put on face masks. 'Halo' by Beyoncé had just come out. The pair of them were jumping up and down on the bed, mud masks on, singing 'Halo' and changing the lyrics to 'I can see your dildo!', pissing themselves laughing like kids.

There was one little orphan girl who was always with her, like she was her daughter, around six or seven, tall, very skinny; Amy wasn't much taller. They'd meet at Marjorie's Bar every morning, spend all day together until Amy took her back. She loved Amy and Amy loved her – another thing getting Amy through the day. People say it's a tragedy Amy never wrote another album but the real tragedy is she never became a mother. I will always believe that. Looking after this girl was a coping mechanism – having responsibility, being around innocence and naivety, the antithesis of everything Amy had been through. And she made sure she never got drunk in front of her.

One day Amy came to me in tears, inconsolable, heartbroken. The little girl had said to Amy, 'Aunty Marjorie said you're gonna take me home to England, you're gonna adopt me and look after me.' Amy knew that wasn't possible. She was sobbing her heart out, 'I can't do that, can I? I feel terrible, she's got no mum.' I don't know if Aunty Marjorie really said that, or if the little girl made it up. But Amy was crushed.

Juliette and Lauren had been out too, before I got there, arranged by management, trying to rekindle past connections. Amy said it hadn't gone well: 'T, I don't even know why they were here, we've got nothing in common anymore, I don't know them anymore, I've had two albums out, been all around the world, I've been married *and* divorced since I've seen 'em f'fuck's sake. I think I just annoyed them, but they got a free holiday out of it.'

Whatever their reasons for going out there – maybe hoping to find that friendship again – Amy was cutthroat like that.

Mitch, who had a TV deal by now, turned up in the hope Amy would be in shot at some stage for a documentary that was being made. Amy didn't really want him there. They argued; he was trying to get her to sign autographs for fans who were out there on holiday and she wasn't up for it, not on camera. 'I've got no make-up on, my hair's all over the place . . .' He'd turned up looking like a superstar.

Mitch wasn't ever a horrible, malicious man. Amy loved her dad and he loved her, but I felt his love of the fame, glitz and glamour had a detrimental effect on her. He liked money, he liked being flashy, he liked being in charge and in control. He loved all the attention that came with Amy's success – but she hated it, especially the fame. I'm not sure someone like Mitch could understand that. He was so caught up in her success I felt like he didn't see his daughter for who she was anymore, and maybe not even himself; it was like he was a character in his own way, 'Amy Winehouse's Dad'. He wasn't the down-to-earth black cab driver I knew as a teenager anymore, the one who would've put his foot down and told Amy no when she needed to hear it.

I don't think he knew how to confront Amy's addictions and issues, he just didn't know what to do about them.

Mitch was a celebrity in his own right now and was used to the perks that fame brings. I'd wanted to pay for my own flight to St Lucia, which I could afford, and he said, like he always said, 'We'll get that.' It was never '*I'll* get that', even though he had a record deal, a TV show and was touring the world, all off the back of his daughter's success. It was a working-class thing to say, too, 'We'll get that, son,' and in back of my mind

I'd think, *No, you won't be getting it Mitch – Amy's getting it.* It wasn't his money and it did my head in for years.

Amy's world had become his world. I think, ultimately, Mitch was a London cabbie who couldn't believe his luck. It didn't mean he didn't love her, he did. But Amy would get frustrated with him; he loved all the glamour so much. It upset her but he was her dad. And when Mitch left St Lucia, he left her disturbed.

I was there for five weeks, enough time to see she was prone to breakdowns, everything she'd been through was made so much worse by drinking too much. Some nights she got angry, smashing cocktail glasses. One night she had *way* too much to drink. The villa had a big open-plan living room, with a staircase split either side up to the bedrooms. I was sitting in the living room when I heard Amy screaming. Usually I'd go straight up there but I was fresh out of rehab, I was fragile myself and didn't react. I felt useless, just sitting there, but I knew I couldn't handle it. It got worse, I could hear it all, she was punching the walls, smashing stuff up, probably punching herself in the face – she'd do that a lot, too. I couldn't ignore it. I ran upstairs and she'd cut her arms up again, smashed plates and bowls. I bandaged her up, gave her Valium, tried to calm her down. 'Ame, chill out, you're just drunk.' I didn't want to make a big deal out of it.

I went downstairs and it had just done me in. Seeing her self-harm in all its glory again, having to deal with it again. I hadn't experienced anything like that for months. In my post-addiction, post-mental breakdown, only recently recovered head, something flipped. Once I knew Amy was alright, she was with Violetta and the boys, I thought, *I can't stay here, I need to get out, go somewhere, do something different.* I walked out of the villa.

I was about to hand the keys to the lunatic.

CHAPTER 27

A crew of British Airways staff was staying on the island in their own villa near ours, they were our age and we'd become pals. They were having a party, I could hear it. So I turned up at theirs.

I was chilling on the sun lounger out the back by the pool, sipping my Diet Coke, so relieved to be away from Amy's breakdown, knowing she was safe with the boys. There was a bottle of rum on the table and I kept looking at it. I felt so good because I'd gone without alcohol for so long. I thought, *You know what, I don't want to get drunk, I don't need to destroy myself. But I'm just gonna have one drink. I can have* one *drink, surely?* I just wanted a moment of peace, in amongst all this chaos that had been building up, where Amy was a little bit more drunk every day. And living here, I couldn't get away from it.

One fucking drink. How bad could it be? I poured a neat rum, cautious, I had no intention of getting drunk. I knew what alcohol did, I knew it would relax me and then I would go back to the villa and go to sleep. I sipped the rum on the sun lounger. Three seconds later I felt the burn in my stomach, I felt it go through my veins, aaaaaah, it calmed me right down. It was so strong, like I'd just injected vodka. The warmth, the familiarity, it was like finally coming home after months away at sea. The trauma I'd just witnessed evaporated into thin air. I thought, *This is the stuff, what have I been thinking, getting up every day and dealing with my own anxiety? When I could have this feeling? I'm alright now!* I thought, *Nothing's that bad, Amy's gonna be alright, I'll get back to the villa, go to sleep, happy days.*

I got back, I wasn't drunk. Amy was asleep, I went to bed. I couldn't sleep, the guilt for drinking was creeping in. I had another thought: *I just need one more drink to help me doze off. Just one more drink. A good night's sleep and I'll be fine by morning, tomorrow is another day.* I knew where there was a bottle of 80 per cent proof rum, the same stuff we had in Mustique. I padded downstairs to get it and I don't remember anything else. I just drank from the bottle in my bedroom until I was unconscious, drinking to forget I was drinking. I've a vague memory of waking up next morning and getting myself a Diet Coke, of wanting Amy and Violetta to just go out so I could get to the bar and put a shot of vodka in it. What followed lasted eight days. I only have flashbacks of those days.

I stayed away from people. I immediately went back to my old habits. I had two bottles of rum hidden behind a bush near the pool. I had a bottle hidden in my suitcase in my room. I had a bottle hidden behind the bleach in a kitchen cupboard. I spent most of the week passed out, only awake for three or four hours on any given day. It was like Amy always used to say: 'Tyler drinks until ambulance.'

I was told much later how the boys removed the bottle I was clutching in the middle of the night. How I woke up one morning in Neville's bed, the poor bastard was making sure I was still breathing. I have vague memories of going to Marjorie's Bar in the dead of night. It was locked. I broke in, smashed the doors open, stepped over the bar, grabbed a bottle and took it back. I did the same thing in our resort bar. It was dangerous, especially at Marjorie's – the locals would've known who I was but if some random St Lucian man saw some white dude in the middle of night breaking in I would've had my head kicked in.

I recognized at some point I was in a bad way. I called the girl in charge of the villa from my bed; she knew I was a recovering alcoholic. 'I've relapsed, I need to see a doctor.' I saw a doctor and asked for Valium – so then I was on Valium, drinking 80 per cent proof rum and not eating. Somehow, I went to the airport, I must've rung and booked a flight. I walked up the steps of the plane feeling edgy, sat in my seat and reality hit me. I jolted out of an actual blackout: the last thing I remembered was being in bed in the villa. I panicked: *I've relapsed, I'm on a plane, I'm blind drunk, I can't go back to London like this, my mum will kill me! Get me off the plane, how did I even get here?!*

I stood up and shouted 'I need to get off the plane!'

An air stewardess said, 'You need to sit down, sir.'

I was insistent: 'NO, you need to let me off!'

I was escorted by security to customs then put in an airport cell – a tiny little room with a desk and an official asking questions. Everyone on the island knew there was a celebrity staying there and I was trying to explain that I had to get back to her – Amy, Amy Winehouse the singer, I need a car, could they contact the resort?

'Which resort?'

'I don't know!'

I finally got out. They gave me my case and there was a minibus cab waiting. The driver *knew*: 'I know where she is, we all know where she is . . .'

Yes! I got loads of cash out, I must've given him about a grand. 'Mate, please, *please* just take me there and can we stop somewhere? I need a drink.' We pulled up at a petrol station where I could buy some alcohol. It was night time, I was in this minibus with this class St Lucian dude, he was smoking, I was smoking and we were both sipping rum. Yes! I'm going home! I even asked him if there was anywhere I could get any coke. Thankfully there wasn't. I got in and collapsed in bed.

It might have been days later when I heard the slap of Amy's bare feet coming up to my bedroom door. She walked straight in and started shouting. I was scared. I knew I'd fucked up, it was like my *mum* was in the room.

'You're drinking again! D'you want me to ring your mum? Shall I start smoking crack again? Will I just start smoking crack again, Tyler?!'

She made me feel *terrible*. Pulled the moral high ground on *me*. This had happened a few times that week she told me afterwards – I didn't remember. I hadn't had a drink for about thirteen hours, I was shaking and what she said winded me. I went to get up and I could not put my juddering legs on the floor, I couldn't stand. The boys carried me downstairs and I slipped into a violent seizure, right there on the living room floor. With that level of alcoholism, if you don't have a drink you'll have a seizure. I'd had this before, spasms, a fit. Amy was trying to make sure I didn't swallow my tongue. Someone called an ambulance. Amy was in tears; Andrew, Neville and the resort girl were all disturbed. Neville had been in the army, in the Iraq war. He told me afterwards he'd seen people go through traumatic events but he'd never seen anyone have a seizure as bad as that.

The ambulance was going to take too long so they put me in the car, the boys in the front, speeding. I was in the back with Amy, who was crying, rubbing my hair. 'You're gonna be alright, baby boy.'

I was wailing, crying, I just *knew* I was about to die. I was lying with my head on her lap looking out the window at the sky, knowing this was the last time I'd *ever* see the sky. Still shaking and jolting, all I could think was, *I'm not gonna be able to help Amy anymore, I'm never gonna see my mum again, all she's gonna hear is I relapsed and died.*

The boys carried me into A&E. I was fired onto a bed, needles and drips put in everywhere, my arms hooked up to every machine. They cut my clothes off me with scissors, down to my pants. There were four nurses, working at speed. I blacked out.

I woke up next day in this dazzling white room. I was freezing. I could hear nurses' voices. I'm alive! This old, *old* man came in, the head of the hospital, shining a torch in my eyes. He got me to look out the window at the palm trees, register where I was, in this tiny hospital in the Caribbean. I couldn't believe I was still *here.* He was very kind. 'You're gonna be alright.'

I was aware this was a private hospital, Amy had been here already, the staff knew her well. I knew they'd give me anything I wanted and I begged them not to give me any drugs. I knew I'd never touch anything, *anything*, ever again. The old man looked at me as if to say *oh please,* you've no idea what we had to give you to keep you alive. I was wearing a gown, I didn't even have pants on anymore, my arse was exposed. He sat down, told me I'd had the worst seizure even *he'd* ever seen.

'I don't wanna scare you but you shouldn't be alive, with the levels of alcohol. You're a very lucky boy. And your friend loves you very much.'

Amy had probably been screaming at him, 'Do whatever the fuck you have to do to keep him alive! I don't care what it costs!'

*

The next day, Amy came and gave me a big hug, reassured me, told me they'd look after me in here. I found out later I drank between fifteen and twenty bottles of that rum that week, that they knew of. After she left, I was so paranoid with alcohol withdrawal I was convinced I could hear her talking to Violetta outside. I could hear Amy's voice, really calm.

'Violetta, it's too late for him, he can't pull it off, he's never gonna be able to be sober, it's not fair on his mum, on everyone. He's my friend and I love him so I'm gonna kill him.'

This was real to me. I had The Fear, the most real hallucinations I've ever had. I fully believed it and understood her rationale. Of course. She's doing me and my mum a favour. I freaked out: *I'm about to die, Amy's going to kill me.* I ripped every single piece of beeping equipment and the needles and lines all out of myself. With blood going all over my gown, my arse is out, I bolted into the bathroom, locked myself in and pushed a chair up against the door.

I heard 'Amy' walk away. I opened the door, terrified. The senior doctor came in. I made him take me around the whole hospital to find her. He told me I was hallucinating; I was shouting, 'Don't lie to me, everyone's on her side, get me out, she's told you to keep me here!' He said he'd give me something. 'Oh no, you'll give me a weird injection!' He opened every cupboard, every toilet, doors to patients' rooms, until eventually I was convinced it wasn't real and she wasn't going to kill me.

The next day, Amy and the boys came to get me. I was sitting on a bench outside the hospital, chain smoking. Amy came over and I was *still* scared. My body jumped so much I fell off the bench onto the ground. I was babbling at her, 'Ame! You were outside saying you were gonna kill me for my mum . . .' She was pissing herself laughing and I was still nervous – it wasn't funny yet. She was as calm as I'd seen her in ages, she'd obviously found the stash of Valium I'd got from the doctor. But I could see it in her face that what happened to me had spooked her, even though she'd kind of caused it. In some ways it sorted her out; she was forced to realize there was other shit happening and she wasn't the only person in the universe.

We went back to the villa. I knew the next few days of withdrawal would be hard. At night I heard 'Amy' smashing stuff up, screaming, and it was all in my head. I closed my eyes and could see my mum and my friends all turning into skeletons, degrading, dying. I couldn't be on my own and as soon as the sun came up I'd walk on the beach with Andrew and Neville. And I knew, as soon as I was better, I would leave St Lucia. I also knew I would never, *ever* drink again.

And I never did drink again.

I don't know how it's been possible, and if I could tell people how that works then I'd be a multimillionaire. Maybe it's just self-preservation. The life force. Something in human nature from the dawn of time that strives to keep us alive. Whatever it is I'm so grateful, still, to be sober.

Amy saved my life. Had I not been her friend and not been rushed so fast to a private, expensive hospital, I probably wouldn't be here. I had all those thoughts even at the time. It cost money, to save my life. And Amy paid for it. *And I think that's OK.*

Raye came over to St Lucia to check on things. He said the same thing I'd been told in rehab: when people move away from addiction, they can't stay friends with the same people. I sensed this was the outcome he would've wanted.

'No,' I said. 'I'll work it out. I fucked up but I'm not gonna lose my friend, not after what we've been through together.'

I let him know I was stronger than he realized. He didn't like it.

Salaam turned up. Now there was something for Amy to do. Violetta was missing her mum and didn't want to go back to London on her own so she came back with me. I just wanted to get home, remove myself from all these associations. I left Amy in a good place. It was how it always worked: when she saw me in danger she had to fix up, snap out of herself. And vice versa. We always kept each other going. When I kissed her goodbye she was sitting with Salaam, he had a guitar, she had a pen and paper. Good things were happening again. Maybe even new music.

CHAPTER 28

Amy returned from St Lucia with no new album. She'd made attempts at recording music with Salaam, but she didn't like any of it, though some of it was included on the *Lioness: Hidden Treasures* album after she passed away. She would've *hated* that. After eight months in the sun, exercising, looking after people, completely free from drugs, she wasn't exactly a shiny new penny but she was so much stronger in every way. There was also a willingness in her to accept who and what she had become: a very rich, very successful pop star. It was as if she'd finally *realized*. She'd declare, with a laugh, 'I'm a self-made millionaire-ess!'

It was early 2009 and a new home had been organized by Mitch and Raye – nothing to do with Amy as usual. It was a rented mansion house in Hadley Wood, a suburban area just outside north London where rich bankers and millionaires live. I'd been living at my mum's, or at Chantelle's, or at Jeffrey's Place. In Hadley Wood there were bedrooms for Amy, me and the boys with a spare room for Violetta, who lived there on and off. It was away from central London, pretty much in the countryside. Where Amy had never wanted to live. To me it was a statement house: seeing as you *are* a proper pop star, you should live in a big house in the country. The whole set-up was everyone else's dream, not hers.

When we first moved in there was loads of snow. We walked around the local woodlands and I lobbed snowballs at her head, because she lobbed them at mine first. She had on high heels and a Pringle dress in the snow, tottering around trying to be this self-made millionaire-ess pop star, the two of us laughing like big kids.

Her new reality was civilized: no drugs, no parties. Mitch would visit, her aunties would visit, Mitch's sisters, beautiful Aunty Mel and glamorous Aunty Rene, who looked very similar to Cynthia. The kettle was always on. Amy was drinking but it wasn't all the time, it wasn't like St Lucia, it was normal. Her PA Jevan brought her food shopping round every Monday and there were bottles of pink champagne for her and crates of Red Bull for me. Around one in the afternoon she'd have a glass of pink champagne. Mitch disapproved.

'Ame, it's a bit early to have a drink.'

'Dad, I'm a grown-arse woman, a self-made millionaire-ess, are you saying I can't enjoy the life? I can't have a glass of champagne in the afternoon? I'm not drunk, I'm not obliterating myself, I'm not smoking drugs.'

Mitch and I exchanged looks: *is this gonna be a problem?* She'd have breakfast, scrambled eggs and salmon, be all dressed up, standing there in this beautiful, grown-up's house. It didn't *look* like much of a problem. Her life couldn't all be yoga and green juice, though she did plenty of that too.

She bought a Land Rover, even though she couldn't drive. Life had changed, she had her own car, her own drive and now her live-in security were her drivers too. They moved Amy to Hadley Wood to keep her out of London, to keep her out of trouble, but they didn't think it through. Every day, by six o'clock, she'd be in the Land Rover being driven the forty-minute journey to Camden, to the reopened Hawley, the Mixer, someone's house. She was trying to fit into these pop star shoes at the same time as wanting to kick those shoes off and still be the scallywag running around Camden Town. Sticking her in Hadley Wood was pointless.

It was the first time paparazzi weren't allowed to live outside the house, there was a court order preventing it. But they would follow us from down the road all the way into London and back to Hadley Wood. The journey home was hilarious; we knew all the little rights and lefts they didn't know. We'd deliberately go the wrong way, motorbikes skidding on the motorway. We'd lose them and the boys would high five in the front. 'Fuck them tossers!' It was some of the best fun we had.

Camden doesn't change but we weren't seeing Pete Doherty or the messy, *messy* people and we'd only go for a few hours, Amy just trying to find her feet again. No one came back to Hadley Wood, we wouldn't let it happen. If we went up to the Hawley's private room I wasn't nervous about her looking for drugs but I was nervous about other people offering her drugs when she wasn't that person anymore. She didn't do crack or heroin for the last three years of her life.

Drink was enough for her now. Most of the time she was like a normal person who'd go out drinking till she was drunk. She was trying to live her old, normal life before fame, but finding out it didn't exist anymore. Whenever we left the Mixer there were always paparazzi and fans, crowds outside. It would scare her and upset her. It was like she was seeing it all for the first time. When it happened before she'd been off her head, so she either wasn't aware or she was fearless. Now it made her act like a kid: she'd lie in the back of the car, on my lap, suck her thumb and start crying.

'Why are all these cameras and people here? I hate all this, why are they always there?'

She wasn't going to Camden to destroy herself, she was going to be a normal young woman – she was still twenty-five, about to turn twenty-six years old. She wasn't taking drugs anymore, the madness was over. She wasn't 'Amy Winehouse' even, because she wasn't performing. But ultimately, she couldn't be normal because she *was* 'Amy Winehouse'. She was still the tabloids' number one target and the paps were always there, waiting. She'd see the pictures the next day – and she looked at the papers every day – and there would be a picture of her blinking, captioned: 'Amy drunk in Camden.' It annoyed her. 'I'm drunker *now* sitting at home in my jogging pants!'

They just wouldn't leave her alone.

She was indoors a lot. Sometimes happily so, in the kitchen with her mum and her aunty, she had her cats from Prowse Place, she loved the boys and me. But the house didn't suit her. Mitch said at one point, 'D'you wanna buy this house?' 'No way!' she scoffed. 'I don't wanna live in Cyprus.'

It was like a Greek villa – a huge red-stone house, carpet in the bedrooms but every other room was floored in beige-white marble. There were huge marble pots in corners, nearly the size of Amy. A marble-floored hallway went all the way to the back where there was an enormous extension. The huge dining room was the length of the house with beautiful curtains and a really long table that a king would sit at, though we never went in there. That dining room became where the cats lived; there were kittens now too and they climbed up the curtains every single day and ripped them to ribbons. They were *the* most expensive curtains and they used to hang in the cat litter, swinging in the shit. When Amy left she laughed about it. To replace the curtains cost over £100,000.

Sometimes a new-born kitten would die and Amy would be in bits. She was teary a lot, a resurgence of emotions, like her heart was coming back to life. She'd go upstairs, empty out a Louboutin shoe box and I'd have to put the dead kitten in the Louboutin boxes. And dig holes in the garden. It was a ritual; we'd have little funerals, she'd say, 'We have to bury 'em right.' It wasn't even her garden!

A team of cleaners came round twice a week: two Polish men, six Polish women. That didn't work for Amy either. She loved cleaning, tidying up and she needed it. But she could never have cleaned the house herself, it was too big. On the third, top floor was another huge room with flip-up skylights, four sofas in an L shape and a massive TV. That's where we spent most of our time. It had a side room with recording equipment. She sang Carleen Anderson's version of 'Don't Look Back in Anger' many times in there. I thought she'd end up releasing it.

She had no work in her diary, did maybe two private gigs, but she was starting to write music. A song called 'You Always Hurt the Ones You Love' about her and Blake. To me, it was the best song she'd ever written in her life. She thought so too. It was typical Amy – clever lyrics, a ballad, like 'Love Is A Losing Game' but ten times better. She'd take a statement you've heard a million times, like 'you always hurt the ones you love', and nail it, expressing what that really felt like more than anybody ever had. With a genius melody. The song was so beautiful, referring to Blake as a lion, Amy as the lioness, a reflection on animalistic love between the male and female entities.

Then there was a song called 'Sailor's Pride' about Blake – she always called him her sailor. A song called 'Four Wheel Drive' was about their relationship being a car crash. She went through so much with Blake *after* she'd written *Back to Black*.

Salaam visited but they never managed to put this stuff

down. She played piano when she sang these songs, some of it ended up on *Lioness*, but it was just mucking around. She'd get nervous and drink too much before he arrived, even though she'd been sober for four days beforehand. Then she'd feel deflated when nothing really happened. There was a fear in her – that she didn't have what she used to have, that she'd lost her magic. There was also frustration and a lack of confidence.

She turned down a few offers of work. Eminem wanted to record a duet but she didn't fancy it. She hated his latest album, *Relapse*. 'When I heard that album it made me wanna relapse!'

Of course Island wanted another album and Amy felt that pressure. But to me it wasn't important right now. She should've just been upstairs with her guitar, music as therapy, concentrating on being sober, not thinking about whether it'll win five Grammys or not. It was the beginning of outside pressure for the next two years. The last time she wrote an album she was *normal*. A heartbroken young girl, with a pen and a guitar, drunk on her kitchen floor. And now she had this benchmark to deal with.

'What am I supposed to write about now?' she said to me. 'I don't have a normal life anymore. Shall I write about how famous I am and leave me alone? I need to fall in love and have my heart broken again before they get anything out of me.'

I was a sober person trying to work out how to stay sober so I was still struggling myself. I got really into cooking. I'd do big roast dinners as a way of encouraging normality, doing family things for me, Amy and the boys. Amy didn't do a stitch of it, she'd be smoking her little Vogue cigarette and drinking her pink champagne. When it was cooked she'd say, 'Hand it all out to the boys!' – her way of being the mother she always wanted to be.

I'd always been intent on being skinny ever since I got my

record deal and saw myself on video; people constantly scru-
tinizing what you look like fucks you up. That happened to
Amy too, of course, under a spotlight so much bigger than
mine. Now, it was an everyday thing for me not to eat carbo-
hydrates and just not eat that much. I was never dangerously
thin, I was just a skinny boy and liked staying that way.

When you come out of rehab and start eating properly you
start to put on weight. People said to me, 'You look great,
you've got an arse.' If you have issues around food and body
image like I did, all you think is, Hang on, is everyone telling
me I'm fat? What d'you mean 'well' – you mean fat! If you're
an addict, you often replace one addiction with another. I
couldn't drink, I couldn't take drugs, what could I do? So I ate
and developed bulimia. And, being me, I got really into it.

We knew so many people with food issues, bulimia, anorexia. They used to be seen as 'girls' problems' but we all know
better today. Bulimia is disgusting, making yourself sick is horrible, you brush your teeth afterwards and just wanna forget it
even happened. I'd done it once before and now I was doing it
loads. I'd do it in private, in the top floor bathroom of the
house.

One time Amy overheard me: 'You're throwing up. Great
way to stay thin, innit?'

She was jibing me. I felt terrible because I'd always encourage her to eat healthily: 'Please don't eat all that shit and go
and be sick.' I was supposed to be the person who led by exam-
ple, the miracle poster boy for not drinking. I was embarrassed
and felt like a fraud. I told her I would never do it again because
I didn't want her to do it. And I never did. I just stopped.

But those problems never stopped for Amy.

Bulimia is complicated. It's not only a form of self-control
and having something to obsess over, it's self-harm. Bulimia is

like a ritual, it punctuates your day and there's all this emotion that goes with it: an extreme high when you're eating and then an extreme sense of relief when you've got it out. Before the relief there's panic – you've crammed the food in and know you've only got a certain amount of time before you have to throw it up otherwise you'll start digesting. And throwing up hurts. People can rupture their oesophagus.

It came and went with Amy and now, in Hadley Wood, it was very much there again. The boys were asked to bring back buckets of KFC, or battered sausage and chips with jars of mayonnaise. It's a very personal thing and I never screamed at her about it; I'd only ever say, hoping, 'Amy, you've really gotta try and get a handle on that.' She knew it anyway. The drinking and the bulimia went together and when they were both bad, she'd get so frustrated. Which always led to smashing stuff up. She'd launch her laptop across the room. She smashed a laptop every week.

One night, Amy had had too much to drink and Violetta was with her in the kitchen. I was lying in bed and could hear them shouting at each other.

'Amy, why are you drinking so much?!'

'I'm not fucking drunk!'

'Bullshit, are you lying to yourself or are you lying to me?!'

It was a proper scream-up. I came out of my room and peered my head around the door. Neville was peering round his door. All of a sudden we heared *Smash! Smash! Smash!* And Violetta shouting, 'Oh, you think you can smash plates? I'll show you how to smash plates!' *Smash! Smash! Smash!*

Me and Neville piled downstairs and the pair of them were now pissing themselves laughing, rolling on the floor and firing plates and cups and saucers across the kitchen like at a Greek wedding. Next morning, I went down, was about to make breakfast, and the whole floor was covered in broken china. There was literally nothing left – no plates, no cups. Everything had to be replaced.

At the back of the house in Hadley Wood was what Amy called The Kebab House, a summer outside kitchen at the end of the garden. We were always cooking dinners there; Amy would make the best potato salad you've ever tasted. We were young, we needed to see people; Amy wanted to be sociable so we'd invite people round, Naomi, Catriona, Chantelle. I'd shoot round to Waitrose with the boys, get everything we needed. Amy would be so excited, because it was normal.

Grimmy came round, he'd just got a new job on Radio 1 so Amy immediately wanted to open a bottle of champagne. Any excuse. She'd always end up having a little bit too much to drink but it was an attempt at being civilized.

Kelly Osbourne came round a good few times, she never disappeared from Amy's life. We'd sit in the giant living room and, as a recovered addict herself, Kelly was so pleased things were sane – the drugs were gone, I was sober. She'd say, 'Amy I'm so proud of what you've done and Tyler, look at you, you look so *well*.'

Amy was starting to reflect back on her life in a way she'd never done before.

'I can't believe all this has happened to me,' she said. 'I can't believe I've been married and divorced.'

She started laughing, in hysterics. 'I mean, what the fuck, I used to be a crackhead!'

'I know Ame, trust me I know!'

'Seriously Tyler, no jokes, I was an *actual proper crack-head?!*'

It was like she genuinely had no memory of some of it. She would look at the internet, read the papers, see herself screaming at the paparazzi and say, 'My god, what was I on?!' She definitely wasn't worried about that happening to her again.

'We were young, shit went crazy didn't it, Tyler? D'you remember when you used to drink vodka like water?'

She was still up and down, she'd go from hard nut to teary in a flash. One time she was really crying, talking about how we were both addicts.

'Tyler, I'm so sorry, I can't believe I put us in those situations with them people, it was dangerous, something could've happened to you, to me.'

Especially with those boys who made the video of Amy smoking crack – they could've stabbed me in a heartbeat. I told her it didn't matter, it was over now. She talked about the drug dealers; there were loads of dodgy motherfuckers and it really upset her, what she'd put me through. What she'd put her family through. There was genuine regret.

'T, I spent about 500 grand on drugs, it's a mug's game, I could've bought a house, I could've bought *you* a house.'

People on the outside think she never got better. Most people don't know she stopped taking drugs for years because the tabloids lied about it. She couldn't see this clearly in St Lucia. The Caribbean was where she woke up from the bad dream but was still in a daze. Now, she was wide awake, even talking about Blake like an adult. She'd say, 'We loved each other too much, put me and Blake in a room, bombs start going off.' There was recognition that drugs ruined her and Blake. Nothing survived it.

Blake was out of prison, he had a kid now and she was genuinely happy for him. She talked to him on Skype sometimes. Blake was sober and sober Blake was a nice guy. We'd talk too.

Being chased by the
press on our way to
the Hawley Arms.

Amy attending court
with Raye.

St Lucia; Amy with the orphaned girl she became close to.

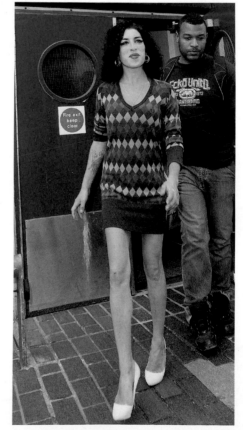

At the airport on the way back from St Lucia.

Above Andrew (left) and Neville
(right) who were constantly by
Amy's side.

Right Out in Soho in the summer
of 2010.

OPPOSITE PAGE
Inset left Climbing into a car
outside The Good Mixer pub.
Main picture Out in Camden.
Inset right With Violetta a
few nights later.

Leaving the studio after recording the duet with Tony Bennett.

On stage in Serbia, shortly before the tour was cancelled.

Amy's funeral.

How I'll always remember my Amy.

He'd say, 'How's it going, T? You don't drink anymore, well done son, I'm the same. We've got the all-or-nothing mentality, you, me and Amy. With us it's do it until it kills you or don't do it at all.'

Amy went to see Blake up north for a couple of days; the boys went with her. She booked a hotel. I thought that maybe she was going to have some closure. Then she brought him back to Hadley Wood. I wasn't there that day, I was on my way back when Amy rang.

'Blake was here, nothing was going on and my dad came in and went mental! He was screaming at him to get the fuck out the house, he caused some scene I tell ya. Blake was really embarrassed.'

She found it funny, like her dad was kicking out the naughty boy, being an old-fashioned dad, which is what she always wanted. She loved that he'd done that, went on about it for days. To her, being told off was like proof of love, that someone cared. Fair play to Mitch.

Sometimes in Hadley Wood she'd be bored, though, when no one from the outside world was around. So, for something to do, she'd visit the posh neighbours, unannounced.

CHAPTER 29

Amy was trying to keep things real like she wasn't famous. In her head, she was a 1950s housewife. After her lunchtime glass of champagne, she'd announce she was off to 'visit the neighbours'. So I went with her.

The Hadley Wood neighbours were very polite, very posh and their houses very plush. Amy would sit at their swanky kitchen island. Sometimes she'd take a bottle of wine round. Or she'd ask for a drink. They knew who she was, they knew she wouldn't want a tea or a coffee, but you could see them thinking, *Do I give her a drink, do I not give her a drink?* I'd want to *die*. Sometimes she'd be a bit drunk already, stumbling in and out of their homes in her high heels and low-cut dress. They were definitely thinking, 'Why is Amy Winehouse sitting in my house?' She would take them a gift, usually one of the big marble pots from the house which weren't even hers because the house was rented.

Nearby was a family with a daughter our age and Amy used to go round daily. It must've annoyed them – she'd just turn up. I'd go round and plead with them. 'Please, *please* stop giving Amy drinks at one o'clock in the afternoon.' They were a lovely family; there was a brother and Amy ended up having a fling with him, which wasn't sensible. She was trying to create friends, be neighbourly, convincing herself she was 'socially' drinking, like a normal person.

Her twenty-sixth birthday came round in September. She still hated birthdays, anybody who really knew her would've known that. An avalanche of flowers arrived, sent by Island Records, the most extravagant *bouquets*. It was Mariah Carey level, some of them in big, square, expensive modern glass pots, about twenty of them. We put them in the dining room with the cats and the shit. Then a van with even *more* turned up.

'Do they think I'm Princess Diana or something?!'

All Amy wanted to do was drink champagne all day until it was over.

Mitch came round to wish her a happy birthday and he scolded her, like he did with the holiday in Mustique.

'Amy, there's about ten thousand pounds' worth of flowers there, you should appreciate people sending you these beautiful things.'

'You have 'em then, Dad. Take 'em! Or, I tell you what I'll do with the flowers . . .'

She went into the dining room and launched a good two or three of these flower pots at the wall, glass smashing everywhere. Mitch was *really* pissed off. It was him that loved all that showbiz nonsense, Amy didn't care about any of it. None of this was normal. And what Amy needed more than anything else was normality. She didn't need to write an album; she needed to go shopping and clean her own house and go where she liked on public transport like everybody else.

She said to me one day, 'I miss getting on the tube.' She was sick of sitting in her eighty grand Land Rover in traffic all the way to London. I thought let's do it, what's the worst that could happen? We got dropped off at the nearest tube, Cockfosters, me and Neville and Amy. The tube wasn't busy, she looked like Amy, her hair was up, she wasn't in disguise. As we got closer to London the carriage filled up. Amy was so famous every person did a double take and I could see it on their faces: it's obviously not her, it *can't* be her.

Amy was laughing, she whispered to me, 'They don't believe it's me, brilliant, I can actually walk around!'

Neville was the one feeling edgy as he was responsible. We got to Camden Town, got off the train and people went berserk, shouting, crowding towards her, they hadn't seen her out in public for so long. Amy wasn't scared, she thought it was hilarious, but Neville was freaking out, 'We've gotta get out of here, we're gonna cause an accident!'

We ran up the escalators, got to the top with our travel cards. It was packed and Amy just jumped the barrier, like a lad. Me and Neville had no choice but to jump the barrier after her. We ran outside, where there were more people cheering. Amy was in between me and Neville, we were holding a hand each, running through Camden. People were screaming and laughing and taking pictures, running after us. We got to the Hawley and Amy collapsed in a seat. 'Brilliant!' It was the most fun she'd had in weeks.

We functioned well together in Hadley Wood. Her family were really pleased we were living together again after so long. They knew I'd take care of her. I was a good cook and she'd always ask me, 'Darlin', can you make me scrambled eggs?' One day, Mitch was there watching and said, 'Oh, why don't you two just get *married*?'

Me and Amy were smiling: we just weren't like that, we were brother and sister. Mitch said it a few times and I knew what he was thinking: *She's nuts, you're nuts but for some reason when you're together everything's alright and if you got married the rest of us wouldn't have to worry about her anymore.*

One night, towards the end of our time in Hadley Wood, Amy's drinking was bad and she was in her bathroom, crying, feeling lost in this gilded prison.

'Tyler, I hate this world, I just want things to be normal. Please, *please* can me and you just get married and have kids and have a life without all this shit?'

It broke me. She was desperate, trying to solve her problems. This wasn't her joking about Marlon and Brandon the gangster twins anymore. She meant it.

'Ame, you know I love you but I can't have kids *now*. I don't even know what I'm gonna do with my life. And I don't have your sort of money.'

'T, it doesn't matter, *I've* got money, I've got a house . . .'

'But none of that's mine! I do wanna have kids one day but I need to be a man first and provide.'

I would never have wanted to be known as 'the guy who lives off Amy Winehouse': I'd be back on the drink within days. And she knew it. I thought about it for days afterwards. If she did have children would that have made everything alright? What if it didn't? Then you add a whole new dimension, of her not being well enough to be a good mother. Problems don't always go away when you have a kid. Sometimes it's the opposite. There was no doubt in my mind she would've been a brilliant mother, a natural, but she just wasn't ready.

I've made my peace with it now but it really upset me. I'd do anything for her but it was a lot to ask: give up your life to be a husband and father. I was twenty-seven and I was just learning how to be sober, never mind anything else. I was only starting to find out who I really was and what I wanted to do. Possibly write again. Be a singer again.

I'd even been working in a studio in New York with the producer Benny Blanco, a friend of Neon's. Amy had encouraged me to go. 'You need to write.' It went really well, there was so much opportunity out there, Benny had just signed a ten-million-pound publishing deal. A&R men were going to sign me. It was my second chance. I rang Nick and he was so excited. 'You're back!'

And yet the whole time all I was worried about was Amy. I called the boys: she wasn't in a great place. I told Benny I had to go back and he was stunned. It wasn't Amy asking me to come back, she'd been the one encouraging me to go. I sometimes wonder where my life would've gone if I'd stayed. But I've made my peace with that, too. I already knew, by then, fame didn't suit me at all. If anything major had happened to me I probably would've ended up drinking again, doing drugs and being insane.

A few people started coming back into Amy's life; the protective cocoon was beginning to crack. Sometimes if we were in Camden, we'd end up staying in a hotel. We were outside the art gallery space Proud Galleries one time and Sheridan Smith was there. We were made up, we thought *Two Pints of Lager and a Packet of Crisps* was genius, we watched it all the time and Sheridan was our favourite. Amy introduced herself and it was apparent straight away she was one of us, working class; she could've been a posh actress for all we knew. We all piled into someone's house and got Sheridan to do skits from *Two Pints*. Amy kept telling her she was amazing and Sheridan wasn't having it.

'You're having a laugh, you're Amy Winehouse, I'm just this TV actress in a funny show.'

Sheridan started to visit Hadley Wood and they had a genuine friendship, had proper conversations. It was good for me too as I could go to bed knowing Amy was safe.

But even so, things were getting messy. Amy was starting to

swig Night Nurse to get to sleep, like I did when I used to drink. I'd give her a shot sometimes because I didn't want her to have the whole bottle. I'd noticed she'd started to sip it in the middle of the day. Night Nurse is dangerous if you don't use it properly. You hallucinate. People sleepwalk. It's from the opiate family and it's full of paracetamol, maybe sixteen doses in a bottle. Overdose on that and your liver will fail; people can top themselves by accident.

I was asleep in bed and Sheridan was shaking me awake.

'Tyler, you need to get up, there's something wrong with Amy . . .'

I jumped out of bed, ran downstairs, Amy was in the kitchen and all six rings on the gas stove were alight. When Sheridan had come up to me the rings weren't even on yet, she just thought Amy was being erratic. But now Amy was holding dinner plates over the burners, 'drying' them, orange and blue flames licking around the plates, a tea towel was catching fire. I threw the tea towel in the sink, pulled Amy away. She dropped the plates, she was angry, slurring, stumbling. 'Fuck off T, I'm doing the washing up.'

I got Sheridan to check her bedroom, where's the Night Nurse? She came down with an empty bottle.

Amy was now completely incoherent, lying on the floor, actually foaming at the mouth. Sheridan woke the boys and they called an ambulance. I was in the back of the ambulance with her and the paramedic wanted to know what she'd taken.

'She's been drinking, maybe had some Valium, but she's drunk all this Night Nurse.'

'How much?'

'As far as I know the whole bottle.'

That's all he needed to know. She went straight into intensive care at The Private Clinic in Harley Street. I stayed in the waiting room with Neville and Andrew. I didn't think Amy was about to die but I was shocked, nothing like this had happened in so long, in maybe a year and a half. When she was awake and stabilized I went down.

'Amy, for fuck's sake, did you really drink all that Night Nurse?'

'I don't remember.'

'You can't keep doing this!'

'I'm alright, calm down T, you're being dramatic . . .'

'You're in intensive care, you don't grasp the situation!'

It was the beginning of Amy feeling invincible. Because no matter what happened, she'd wake up either in her own bed or in hospital and she'd be alright. The seriousness never crossed her mind because there was always someone looking after her – me or the boys. There she was in intensive care saying, 'Oh, they're just being extra cautious.' There were situations where she was rushed to hospital and had no recollection of what got her there. And she never thought any of these situations would go seriously wrong.

It can happen to anyone, but when you're famous and you've bodyguards you're *too* looked after. And you're learning, as an addict, that there are no consequences. You get pulled out of situations. You literally don't have to *watch yourself*. Because other people are doing the watching. I include myself, but what choice did I have? She was my lifelong friend, I couldn't *not* look after her. But when you put all these things in place, you take all personal responsibility away. When you're not even responsible for getting yourself to *bed*, that's dangerous.

The very things that were put in place to save Amy were part of the reason she wasn't saved, in the end.

CHAPTER 30

You can't tell an addict what to do. Ultimately, they can only help themselves. Amy would still never go to rehab because there was no part of her that thought she was an alcoholic. Her idea of an alcoholic was *me*. 'Rehab', the song, haunted her, it followed her around. It defined her in some ways.

The Private Clinic in Harley Street isn't rehab, it's a private hospital, a real hospital, but it's also a lot like a hotel. Most people are there for plastic surgery. Amy went there many times from Hadley Wood, for alcohol withdrawal, but she was only in intensive care once, after the Night Nurse nightmare. It wasn't long before this particular hospital became her second home. After days at home drinking on the sofa, it was her who'd suggest she go, sort herself out – it became her security blanket. Again, being picked up whenever she fell. Management didn't want people to know she was going there so she'd go discreetly, with the boys in the Land Rover.

She loved it there. It has a spa. A gym. There's room service, like a five-star hotel. Nice menu, nice drinks, you can order alcohol. She'd do that when she was better. She'd stay there for a week, ten days, sometimes three weeks. She'd be hooked up to a drip and she got used to these professional techniques. When she was lying on the sofa at home, drinking, I'd tell her she was destroying her *body*, not just her mind, and she'd say, 'Oh why can't I just be put on a drip at home?' She meant it. If I'd said, 'OK, we'll organize it,' it would have been organized. Fame and privilege again. It's like when George Best had a liver transplant and went back on the booze: he was 'fixed', so now he could keep drinking. It's all about tricks and potions to help you become a more successful alcoholic. Pills for heartburn. Amy drank a Dioralyte rehydration sachet every day, counteracting the dehydration from bulimia, which can lead to heart failure.

She started to build a relationship with the hospital. More protection. She already had the boys, who were paid to be there, and now there was this place she could go to at any time – again, running away from her home environment. The boys went with her to the hospital too, sitting outside her room on chairs.

No one needs to be in hospital for three weeks for alcohol withdrawal. She turned it into her version of rehab. In the first few days of brutal withdrawal it would never have crossed her mind to have a drink. And of course they wouldn't have given her one. But she was in there for so long sometimes that by the end of her stay she'd really treat it like a hotel, like she was on holiday in hospital. We used to go out for lunch. To the fish restaurant on Marylebone High Street. We'd even go to the Hawley, not often, maybe four or five times, but she'd get drunk – and go back to hospital.

This wasn't fun to me. I was sober, she was in hospital for *alcohol withdrawal* but she couldn't be stopped. I stayed over a couple of times in hospital, sleeping in the chair in her room. She felt safe there – a hotel where she'd be medically looked after. Sometimes it was just where she slept.

*

Barbara Windsor lived round the corner from the hospital on a mews. Amy had met her before through Mitch and they really got on. So we'd visit her from the hospital, slip out the side and go round to Barbara's, for an hour or so. It was like popping round to your aunty's in East London. There was a big, square living room with a coffee table in the middle. Amy sat on one sofa, Barbara on the other, they'd have a chin-wag while I was in the kitchen with her husband, Scott. Amy told him, 'Tyler's a recovered alcoholic like you,' and he talked to me about addiction and sobriety.

Barbara knew Amy had come from hospital, was very aware of her problems and we'd all talk about how Amy would become like me and Scott, that she'd get there too. Barbara was very supportive of that. They both made us sandwiches, Barbara always made sure I had a cup of tea and sometimes Amy asked for a drink. Barbara was tee-total too but they had drink in the house for visitors. She'd ask Amy, 'Are you sure?' And say to me on the fly, 'Is she alright to have a drink?' almost asking for my permission because she didn't want the responsibility. I'd just say, 'What can you do?' Amy could get a drink anywhere if she wanted one. It wasn't like she was going round there to get drunk, far from it; it was always one drink, half a glass of wine. Though it was awkward sometimes. We'd be sitting there talking about sobriety, Amy talking about how proud she was of me, Barbara talking about being proud of Scott and them both being proud of me, while Amy was drinking her wine! But Amy had asked politely and I also have manners. If I'm in a grown-arse woman's house, who's making me a sandwich and a cuppa tea, I ain't gonna cause a scene and make Barbara Windsor feel bad, am I?

Barbara was an old-school, been-there-done-that character and Amy had so much respect for her, she could really be herself around her. I'd hear Amy say, 'The press never leave me alone,' and Barbara would sympathize, 'Oh, I know all about it, Amy!' She'd do that laugh of hers, she was brilliant. Sometimes Barbara would get her *EastEnders* scripts out for a run-through and Amy always wanted to play Barbara's Peggy Mitchell. Barbara loved it and she'd do Pat Butcher. Amy being Amy with her accents and impressions got right into it.

There was a proper connection between them, they were similar people – not only because they were both tiny with big beehives. Barbara always looked well and was very mothering of Amy; I always used to think maybe Amy would be like her in forty years' time. And it reminded me of seeing Amy with her nan. When we left, Barbara always said to me, 'Look after her, Tyler.'

Amy was living in her own alternative reality. She was a real sun worshipper and whenever it was sunny she'd go out the back of the hospital to this little courtyard for a sunbathe. It wasn't even part of the hospital. To get there you walked through the hospital kitchen. The staff would put some kind of stretcher out and she'd lie on that with her glass of champagne, sunbathing, covered in baby oil. Every now and then a fella from the kitchen would pop out for a fag break and see Amy lying there, topless, dripping in oil. She'd say, 'Gi's a light, darlin' . . .' and he'd never know quite which way to look. For the non-famous that behaviour would be totally unacceptable. Years ago Amy would've thought that was outrageous.

Once she went to the Hawley and got so drunk she forgot she was supposed to be in hospital and ended up back in Camden, at Jeffrey's Place. The flat had become the biggest nightclub in Camden and was falling to bits, wallpaper hanging off, a hell hole. She went back to the hospital raucous drunk at one in the morning, fully dressed up, make-up on, with this entourage bowling in, me and these two big security guards, you couldn't miss us. And she went to bed. After that night they said she definitely needs to go home.

Everybody knew who she was. The nurses loved her, especially the Irish nurses, they were her hospital mates. Amy created a little world for herself in there, a good life; she was like a mum in the 1950s, hanging out her washing and having a chat over the garden hedge. That's all she ever wanted. She even used to wash her underwear in the sink and hang her fancy bras and knickers up around her room.

Over time she'd start saying she wanted to get better, get healthy, put on ten pounds. She'd go to the gym and rebuild herself. By the time she left she was glowing. There are paparazzi pictures from around then when she looks a million dollars. And she was *in hospital*.

One time I went to visit and she wasn't in her room. I panicked and found the Irish nurses.

'Where's Amy?!'

'She's in surgery.'

'What d'you mean?!'

'No, no, no, she's fine!'

Amy wheeled around the corner on a trolley, attached to a drip with two blood bags either side of her body. I was horrified.

'What's happened?!'

'Calm down, I've just got my tits done!'

She hadn't even mentioned it. For the last two years she'd stuck chicken fillets down her bra, those plastic fillet shapes, to fill herself out. She used to have big tits and it bugged her they were gone, she'd lost so much weight with the drugs. At the end of a night out, sometimes Amy would be lying on the sofa, the living room strewn with a detached beehive, a pair of high heels and two chicken fillets turfed out of her bra.

She looked spaced out – she'd had morphine. I was furious, she was still a recovering heroin addict. She was still taped up so you couldn't see anything and she wanted to show me the results. I tried to stop her, 'You've just come out of *surgery*.' She was high as a kite on morphine, most people would be lying on the bed drooling. She jumped out the bed, with the blood bags still either side, pulled the bandage down and showed me her tits.

'They're good, ain't they?'

She still had tubes in them attached to the blood bags so it was zombie film horrific.

'Ame, they're amazing, get back in the bed, there's blood dripping on the floor, you need to lie down . . .'

Typical Amy, she just did it on a whim while she was there. Cost a fortune. But it did what plastic surgery is supposed to do, it gave her confidence. We went bra shopping when she was back home. I saw her catch herself in mirrors and she was happy with herself. For a long time people only saw her looking awful in the papers, ill, a mess, and it had an effect on her. She'd say, 'People think I'm ugly.' She'd call *herself* ugly. Once we were both in the girls' toilets in the Hawley and Amy and this girl were in front of the mirror doing their make-up. The girl said, 'Oh my God, you're the absolute spit of Amy Winehouse.' She obviously thought she'd insulted her. 'But obviously a lot prettier.' Amy didn't say anything but it really upset her. Now, she was starting to feel comfortable about her appearance. At last.

We moved back to London. Amy had made it clear her dream was not suburbia, it was owning her own house in Camden. Mitch took charge of finding one, she wasn't involved at all, which pissed me off. If they'd let her be in charge of finding her own dream home she would've loved it, like anyone would. So while management were finding the house and getting it ready, we moved into a flat in Bryanston Square in Marylebone. It was an apartment conversion in a swanky square of tall, terraced townhouses, just round the corner from Selfridges. It wasn't huge, three bedrooms – for Amy, me and one security – open plan kitchen and living room, with sash windows. It suited her more – it was cosier and she could clean it herself.

As it always was when we went somewhere new, things got better again. The flat was always tidy, she was back to being a clean freak. She laid her magazines out on the coffee table: *Hello!* magazine, *OK!*, crossword puzzle books and *Vogue* – she had a subscription to *Vogue* for years. She still went to Camden but she was less rebellious, more calm and together. She was looking after herself, including getting her teeth fixed, she'd ruined them with crack and heroin. She was back to writing shopping lists of all the girly stuff she loved: bubble baths and face exfoliant and strawberry shampoo and apricot scrub. She went to the gym in the Langham Hotel nearby, ordered takeaway salt beef from a Jewish place, Reubens, round the corner on Baker Street. She spent a lot of time watching TV, especially *Misfits*, the show about the council estate kids with superpowers – we loved that. There was a conscious effort to not drink *all* the time.

Amy had a proper relationship with her doctor by now and was taking beta blockers as well as the sedative Librium, a drug for alcoholism which keeps you level, stops you having a seizure. You can't drink when you're taking Librium, the combination can not only cause severe drowsiness, it can make you black out when you're fully conscious. It can even kill you.

Amy was trying hard and, most of the time, she was pulling

it off. She'd be sober for two, three weeks – a long time in comparison to when we lived in Hadley Wood. She seemed to recognize now that she drank too much. She'd always say about getting sober, 'If you can do it Tyler, I can do it, because no one's ever drunk as much as you.' I knew I was her role model when it came to sobriety: it wasn't like I was some righteous, post-addiction yoga evangelist, I was still exactly the same, I just didn't drink. She'd never acknowledged there was any problem whatsoever back in Hadley Wood, so this was a new perspective. She was looking forward to maybe becoming like me.

She was isolated, though. She was usually indoors, with only me and the boys. There were barely any work commitments so when something came up she had social anxiety. Which made her want to drink. She had a sponsorship deal with Fred Perry and got involved with the designs – I saw the sketches; you can still find Amy's designs in the Fred Perry stores today. She loved Fred Perry and didn't do any endorsement deals with anybody else. There was a shoot for her collection at Bryan Adams' house near the Kings Road. Even though she knew him from Mustique, on the way there she was really anxious.

'I need a drink.'

'Well don't go then. If you don't feel up to it today I'm sure they can move it.'

I calmed her down, tried to make her see it wasn't a big deal – it was Bryan, it was at his house, it wasn't a big studio production. We got there and Vicky from Bryan's house in Mustique was there. We had no idea and she was as lovely as ever, 'How are you kids?!' Amy calmed right down. Then we were taken into another room and there was a *crew* in there, eight or ten people. Amy just froze. We walked out.

'I need a drink.'

Everyone was scared she would kick off. Instead, she retreated.

I knew the only way this could work was if everyone got out of the room. I told Bryan, he cleared the room and started taking pictures. Amy was over by a windowsill looking anxious, standing like a mannequin, no Amy personality whatsoever. She was all done up, perfect hair and make-up, in these classy clothes she'd designed herself and she just looked terrified. I felt so sorry for her. I had an idea: I'm going to use her tactic and *do our thing*.

I asked Bryan to put some Frank Sinatra on. The music started, I went over to the windowsill, put my hand out and she knew straight away what I meant. *Let's dance*. We started slow dancing, my arm around her, waltzing. Vicky was watching and smiling at the door. It was so far removed from Mustique two years ago when we were both a mess. We were no longer a mess. They had no idea what this moment meant for us. Bryan turned the music up anyway, really loud, and we danced to Frank Sinatra for twenty minutes, 'I've Got You Under My Skin', 'Cheek to Cheek', with her head resting on my shoulder. It was so special, just me and Amy, dancing like lovers, like a husband and wife doing the first dance at their wedding.

Bryan came over. 'Shall we do the pictures?'

We got the pictures done.

Mark Ronson came over to Bryanston Square a few times. He took seeing her so together in his stride, never mentioned Henley or the Bond theme, he was too wise to bring all that up. This time they were back to how they used to be, two music nerds sitting and talking about music for hours, bands from the 1960s I'd never heard of. Amy talked about her next album, what they were going to do. That retro sound they'd created for *Back to Black*, Amy definitely wanted to do that again. That was still the music she lived and breathed. She was getting back into her hip hop too, like she was coming back to herself, listening to Nas and Mos Def. She talked to Mark about setting up a supergroup: her, Mos Def, the American rapper Common and American hip hop dude Questlove from The Roots. She Skyped Mos Def a lot. They were all up for it, she was so enthusiastic, Mark would produce. It sounded brilliant. It was exhilarating to me, hearing her ideas – this musical genius whose talents had been dormant for so long. And a huge sign she was on her way back to full health.

Then, out of nowhere, me and Amy had a massive bust-up.

CHAPTER 31

popped out for a Starbucks and a walk one day, came back to Bryanston Square and Amy was sitting on the sofa, drunk on wine. She never started drinking in front of me, she'd wait till I was out. I was so deflated. She'd been getting herself sorted out, been down the gym, was starting to make music, had her teeth done. I'd been optimistic again.

'*Ame*, what's happened, why?'

Her response was nothing new.

'I'm just bored, Tyler. I'm depressed. I just felt like it. Life's boring, innit?'

Something flipped in me.

'Oh, why can't you just fucking *appreciate* what you've got?'

It was the first time I ever said anything like that to Amy. I was pissed off. It was all coming out.

'D'you remember when we were kids? And we both loved music? And we both had dreams? You've *done* it Amy. You've smashed it! You're a global superstar, you've sold millions of albums, you've won *Grammys* . . . You're so fucking *ungrateful*.'

When I look back on this as an adult I know I was in the wrong, even if she shouldn't have been drinking. This was actually about me and *my* problems. I carried on.

'I'm here all the time, I'm trying to help you get sober, help you get to the place where *I* am. And you're telling *me* life is boring? You're telling *me* you're depressed? I'm the one who's not drinking, I'm the one who didn't get their dream but I muddle along, don't I? *I* wanted to be an artist. If I was sitting here in your shoes, someone who's got everything they ever wanted, I'd be the happiest fucking person in the world. I never got to do all this because I've been *too busy looking after you.*'

She looked at me, calm as you like.

'Well Tyler, maybe you should've picked up a guitar for once in your life.'

I lost it.

'Fuck you, Amy. *Fuck you.*'

We had four security on rotation at this point and the one we called Grandad, who was maybe sixty, was living with us. He was there in the corner going, 'Woah! Calm down guys, you don't mean it, what's happening? You love each other!'

I'd seen Amy be an arsehole, I'd heard her deliver a one-liner that would cut your throat. But she'd never done it to me. If she was a boy she would've been punched full pelt in the face. I walked out the door, stormed down the stairs and by the time I got to the bottom I'd rung Tom Wright, my Camden pal.

I wanted to destroy myself for a few days. I knew drink wasn't an option for me, so I'd do coke instead and I could always find coke in Camden. You don't normally do cocaine on its own without drink, it's like sniffing a line of anxiety, but I was determined. I made sure everybody around me knew I was with Tom so Amy would know. And worry about it, thinking she'd caused a catastrophic situation. She'd blown a fuse in me I'd kept under wraps for so long.

Tom was running a night at Koko so we went there. Amy's name was coming up on my phone every three seconds, she was leaving me messages, 'I'm so sorry.' I ignored it all, I wanted her to suffer, I wanted to hurt her.

The next day it hit me: *I'm the poster boy for sobriety, what have I done?* I rang Chantelle and Naomi, they told me Amy was ripping her hair out with worry. I rang her, said 'Ame, I'm alright,' and hung up. Then I felt so screwed up I rang her back.

'Amy, I'm sorry.'

'I'm so sorry too.'

I told her I didn't mean what I'd said, I just didn't want her to drink anymore and now I just wanted to come home and get in my pyjamas and watch *Misfits*.

So I went home. We hugged. Amy ran me a bath and gave me a Librium. Grandad told me afterwards he'd never seen her in such a state. She hadn't started drinking again to hurt me, my sensible head knew that. I'd put my life on hold for her but I *chose* to do that. I was just so sick of hearing it: 'I'm bored.' She'd done everything *we* had ever wanted to do and the chances of it happening to anyone is one in a hundred million. It had been waiting to come out of me for a long time. Because I never mentioned anything to do with me, ever, or what I did for her.

Amy still had her Lioness record label but she didn't take it seriously. Dionne, her goddaughter, was signed to it. So was Juliette. Everyone knew Juliette had a great voice but I think Amy also signed her because she felt bad: she knew Juliette felt shunned out of Amy's life. It's why I'd never get involved in business with Amy. And this was *all* business.

One day she was randomly ringing people, like drunk people do. It was foul Amy with her phone on loudspeaker. She rang Juliette, who didn't answer and Amy was annoyed. She said, 'I feel like we only speak now when it's something to do with her record deal.' Then she rang Lauren, who she hadn't spoken to for three years. Lauren wouldn't have known Amy's new number, there'd been so many new numbers, and just answered her phone.

'Who's this?'

'It's Amy.'

'Amy?'

'Yeah it's Amy . . . how are you doing Lauren?'

Lauren started screaming at Amy, freaked out that she was calling her from a withheld number and angry that she hadn't been in touch for years. I heard them on loudspeaker and then I heard Lauren say, 'How dare you ring me Amy, you don't exist in my life anymore!' I heard every word and started shouting, 'Put the phone down!' because I knew how Amy would react. I grabbed her phone, turned it off. She shot off the sofa and ran to the bathroom. I was two steps behind her. She went straight in, slammed the door, I heard the lock go and I heard the smashing: *Smash! Smash! Smash! Smash! Smash! Smash!* I was standing with Neville outside the door. We were panicking. 'Open the door!' Eventually, when she was silent, we got screwdrivers and took the whole door off. She was slumped over the toilet, she'd cut her arms to pieces.

After that, Amy drank herself stupid for days. Eventually, I carried her over my shoulder, with Neville, into a black taxi and took her back to the hospital. And she'd been doing so well up to then. Lauren had no idea of the consequences of her words, how could she? She was so far removed from Amy's life by then.

It was hard for Lauren and Juliette, to watch their best friend go off and only see her in the newspapers. They'd read about 'Amy's best friend Kelly Osbourne'. I knew that would hurt, it built up for years. Juliette was also a talented singer, with a proper R&B voice, she had aspirations to be an artist too. So watching what happened to Amy could've been hard for her: all that success and then, in Juliette's mind, throwing it all away.

The situation was confused and everyone had their own take. Mitch felt they were never there for Amy. And I agreed. But I heard they felt ostracized and thought they were being kept away from Amy. I don't think that was the case. The truth as usual is more complex. They loved Amy and I just don't think they could cope with the daily level of drama and harm that had come with Amy's new life. I'm not blaming them, I just about managed to cope myself.

They were sent out to St Lucia and they didn't know each other anymore. Amy said to me, 'Where have they been? I ain't seen 'em.' To be fair, they could argue they didn't want to be around when she was on drugs, maybe they thought that would be seen as supporting it. I worried about all that myself. I'd think, am I enabling her, just by being here? No. Because I was constantly telling her that it was killing her. I went through hell with those thoughts. With addiction, you can just leave someone to fester, alone, hoping it makes them come to their senses. But you run the risk they might die. I wouldn't take that risk. Juliette and Lauren chose what they thought was tough love, by leaving her, and I chose to stay as close to her as possible. This wasn't someone just drinking a bit too much, it was full-on crack and heroin addiction. I couldn't live with the thought that, left on her own, Amy might not make it.

As an addict, Amy had opposing forces inside her, battling it out for supremacy. She constantly fought against her addictive nature. That's not typical of a person who *isn't* trying to get better. She was *always* trying. There were only three times in Bryanston Square when she relapsed. She was more likely to be helping someone else. She'd pick Dionne up from school to help her friend Julie. She met a homeless girl when she was out and brought her back to the flat. 'She's got nowhere to go, she's sound, I want her to stay till she sorts her head out.' I was dubious: a random homeless person? They'll sell stories on you. She was very quiet, she wasn't an addict, she slept on the couch for ten days, went out during the day and then just didn't come back. Amy gave her money.

We were friends with Kavana, the 1990s pop star, who we'd met years before in Omega Works. He'd been signed to Simon Fuller like I was, a good-looking boy, a great singer and now he was nuts, a serious alcoholic. He was ten years older than us, in his mid-thirties, he still wanted to be an artist and that ship had sailed. He randomly called Amy one day and I was horrified. '*Please*, don't invite him round, he's a lovely boy but he's a mess!' She invited him anyway. She wasn't drinking, I wasn't drinking and he drank himself into oblivion. She helped him, got him an appointment with her own doctor, took him to the clinic, he got put on medication and she paid for it all. She always had a heart for someone who was nuts because she was nuts herself, had a natural empathy for mental health problems. These weren't the actions of someone hell-bent on self-destruction.

When she was sober she'd still want to go out and do things. She wasn't going to sit indoors in her joggers and watch *Misfits* for the rest of her life. We'd go out to Soho, she'd drink virgin cocktails and she loved it. She'd say it was great to go out, get dressed up and just be a young person again.

I encouraged her to enjoy her money. She loved shopping, she was a fashionable girl. We'd go to Selfridges with a personal shopper and she'd spend fifteen grand, there'd be bags and bags of shoes and underwear all over the living room floor. She still didn't know anything about her money. She was always given cosmetics and skincare freebies – it was *all* free, hundreds of pounds' worth. Amy loved a freebie, she'd say, 'Clear the shelves, Tyler,' and we'd end up with bags of free Clinique and

Dermalogica. Sometimes she'd insist on buying me a shirt. I'd tell her I didn't want it and she wouldn't listen. 'It'll look lovely on you, I'm getting it!'

Mitch would come round, see the bags and be furious. He'd take the shirt she'd bought me out the bag.

'Three hundred quid, that's a nice shirt, Tyler.'

He'd see the men's skincare stuff, have a nut-do about it and I never told him it was free. He knew I wasn't a freeloader; I knew he didn't see me like that. He knew that if I asked Amy for a hundred grand she would just transfer it to me, which I never did. He just didn't like this money being spent. It was frivolous to him, unnecessary.

One time she was having a glass of champagne in the kitchen, rabbiting on, and Mitch called her out.

'Maybe you shouldn't have another drink, Ames.'

She looked at him. 'Maybe you shouldn't be on a salary anymore, Dad.'

It was such an awkward moment, it winded him. She shouldn't have said that in front of me. He didn't say a word. When someone's paying you, it's very hard to stand up to them. Especially if they're an addict. Even if you're their father – and confrontation with Amy in front of others was rarely Mitch's style. But if that was me and my mum there wouldn't have been a silence, there would've been, 'You can stick your money up your arse!' And, 'You can pour that drink down the sink!'

Amy was in charge, she held all the cards. And with that came pressure. The pressure of following up *Back to Black* was one thing, the pressure of bankrolling a team of people was another. I was one of the few people close to her she *wasn't* bankrolling, that would've corrupted everything between us.

Money can fuck people up just as much as fame can. It skews your whole life, changes the people around you. It divides people, causes resentment, messes with trust, creates paranoia and alters reality in every way. Amy was still so young and she had to deal with all of that.

She had put both her mum and dad on salaries, which anyone in her position would do: if you could afford to sort your family out why wouldn't you? Her mum had MS, she wasn't well, Amy wouldn't have wanted her to work. She would justify her dad's salary to herself: 'He can't be a cab driver any-more.' I'd say to her, 'You should be proud of yourself for doing that, Ame.' Even if Mitch had turned himself into Amy's Famous Dad, was now a touring singer himself, with his own deal and his own money. Her mum, dad and family all had access to her company cards, had access to cabs on her account.

To live the life of 'Amy Winehouse', though, cost a fortune. She paid for Raye and her live-in security and her PA. All of Amy's band were on retainers, they got paid to be Amy's band even though there was no band work to do. That's very expensive. It also meant not only were they not working with Amy, they weren't allowed to work with anyone else. So not only did she feel pressure, she felt guilt, knowing what she was responsible for. And knowing how what she did, or didn't do, affected so many people.

Management was starting to imply Amy needed money, which I thought was bollocks – royalties were always coming in from *Back to Black* – but they were worried about the rate she was spending it. Even though her life was basic, she lived mostly in solitude and didn't travel anywhere. Other than the shopping trips to Selfridges, she wasn't going out spending; it's not like she went to The Ivy every night. In fact, she never went to The Ivy *once*, she'd send the boys out for pie and mash. Mitch always told her, 'You've got enough money to live on for the rest of your life, if you're sensible.' Even if the word sensible never applied to Amy. But when you think about it, even beyond the salaries: the repairs to Omega Works. The Hadley Wood curtains. The Private Clinic. The rents on those enormous properties. And she wasn't working. But because she wasn't spending any money on herself she didn't realize her life cost so much. I got the impression she never even thought about it.

Money was now another serious problem.

CHAPTER 32

Mitch started to confide in me. He was worried: what if Amy never works again? Never goes on tour again? What if she never writes another album? One time Jevan brought the shopping round from Waitrose, like he usually did. All the ham and general supermarket stuff was the Essentials basic range. Amy kicked off.

'This ham's shit!'

Jevan was under orders: 'Your dad said we should cut down.'

I thought, *Really*? What are you going to save on five packs of ham when you're bankrolling a village? There might have been enough money for Amy to live on for the rest of her days if she was living in her little flat in Jeffrey's Place and running her life herself. Instead of every single day for three, four years paying for two twenty-four-hour live-in security men and insanely plush homes she never chose for herself.

Raye came round Bryanston Square with paperwork and was, for once, pushing Amy to sign something – he'd usually pussyfoot around her. She was making meatballs.

'Amy, you *need* to sign this.'

Her record deal and her publishing advance had happened a very long time ago. But this was a new publishing advance, from EMI, through Guy Moot. Amy was staring at the piece of paper.

'I've got a two million pound advance.'

'Yeah I know, innit? But we do need to sign it for cash flow.'

As far as I know, when Amy passed away she left almost £3 million: the newspaper reports claimed after-tax assets of £2.94 million. She didn't write a will and her full estate went to Mitch and Janis. I had no idea about those numbers then, but I always used to feel that whenever management said 'She needs the money,' they were talking about feeding the huge machine around her – them included. I'd think, *No*, you *need the money*, everybody else *needs the money*. I saw so many people benefit financially from Amy. She paid for Dionne to go to Sylvia Young's. Paid for Alex Foden's rehab. When Amy was in a bad way, the wife of one of her business team was overheard at a dinner table saying, 'I don't give a shit if she drops down dead, I just want that fucking villa in France.'

Mitch had a go at Amy for staying in the hospital so much, 'using it like a hotel!'

And then we moved into an *actual* hotel.

The rental ran out on Bryanston Square. Mitch had now found Amy her dream home, in Camden Square, but it wasn't ready to move into yet so Amy needed a temporary home. She was always at the gym in the Langham Hotel anyway so we moved in there for two months. Which wasn't exactly cheap either.

She was mostly healthy, even if she was still obsessed with being thin. She'd get up and have a breakfast of lemon juice drinks and boiled eggs. She'd spend a good three hours in the gym, cycling on her back for her stomach muscles all the way through a movie. She got into buying fitness gear. Sometimes she'd be running on the treadmill *all* day, she'd say, 'If I don't run five miles I'll go nuts, it sorts my head out.' She'd go to the spa, have a body massage, a facial, have her hair done, nails done – she was rebuilding herself, the girly Amy I hadn't seen since Jeffrey's Place. She was learning about coping mechanisms, for staying sane. And ultimately, drinking yourself into a stupor gets boring.

But she still didn't want to give up the concept of alcohol. She'd say, 'I'm not saying I'll never have a glass of champagne again but I don't want a drink right now.' Cool. She was toying with the idea of having a glass of champagne like a normal person, which wouldn't necessarily lead to some terrible situation, like it always did with me. But it would always lead to her getting drunk. She'd say, 'Oh, I've had such a nice day, I can have a glass of champagne can't I, Tyler? I don't wanna get drunk, just have a glass and listen to that new album . . .' She'd have a lot more than one glass. But it wouldn't lead to smashing stuff up.

When we went downstairs to the hotel bar she'd have a glass of wine with dinner, an attempt at being civilized. She just didn't want to let it go. Only once in the Langham did she get in a real state, over my parents coming over.

Amy loved my mum and Danny, to her they were what every man and woman should be. They came into London at the weekends now, we were already there and I wanted them to spend some time with Amy. I wanted to show her off as well – look how well she's doing, she's stunning – I was so proud of her.

They were on their way when Amy got a call.

'My mum's coming round right now, she wants to see me, with her other half, how's this gonna work?'

My mum and Danny and her mum and her other half, it was proper chalk and cheese. Janis was lovely but she'd talk about superficial things, small talk, which Amy never really did. They were just so different. She'd say to me, 'I love my mum but I can't talk to her the way I can talk to your mum, if I was that honest with my mum she just wouldn't be able to handle it.'

We all sat down at the dinner table together and Amy was anxious. It was all so awkward even *I* was thinking, *I wanna drink*. I was talking to Janis much more than I was talking to my mum, trying to distract Janis from what I could see, which was Amy keeping on leaving the table, leaving the table, leaving the table. Every time she came back she was drunker and drunker and drunker. After being sober for weeks. It was causing my mum anxiety and now *she* was getting drunker and drunker and drunker. Amy was sneaking drinks at the bar, downing shots. Janis didn't even seem to notice. I walked Janis out to the car, went back in and Amy was slumped on the table. I said we'd better get her upstairs, I'll call the boys. Danny said, 'Fuck all that, come 'ere Ame,' slung Amy over his shoulder and carried her upstairs to her room. Now Amy was laughing.

We got her to sit up and then she slumped over on the floor. Danny kept saying, 'Is she alright?' I told him she was fine and he wasn't having it. 'What d'you mean she's fine? She's lying on the floor, she's not fine!'

She was *really* drunk, not nasty, just slurring. It made me realize how far removed I was from reality, that a person passed out on the floor was normal to me. But it *was* progress compared to what things were like before, with the crack and the heroin and the cutting herself to shreds. She just needed to go to sleep and she'd be alright. But the next day she was awful. Back to full-on drinking. Which led to going back to hospital. But that was *once*, in two months. In the weeks before we left the Langham it was gym, lemon juice, sobriety and going to a nice restaurant on Marylebone High Street with the boys. Enjoying summer.

Summer 2010.

CHAPTER 33

The house in Camden Square was nearly ready – this beautiful white townhouse, with a studio and a gym downstairs, all renovated. Amy was bored one day in the Langham; I could see she was thinking about drinking so I distracted her.

'Let's go to Selfridges, your favourite, and get some Le Creuset dishes and plates and cups and saucers and a really nice ashtray.'

The most important thing was the ashtray, one of those big, glass, diamond-cut, proper old-school pub ashtrays that you can fit 400 fags in. We always said having a cup of tea and a fag was how you bless a house.

Amy bought pots and pans, nice toasters and two of those big glass ashtrays. We were with a personal shopper as usual and this time she had a message for Amy.

'Usher's shopping too and he'd like to meet you.'

When we were teenagers we loved R&B and Usher was a god to us. He was in men's clothing, we walked up and he started singing 'Rehab' to Amy. Then Amy started not just singing but doing the dance to his first single, 'You Make Me Wanna . . .', in the middle of the shop, the two of them just looking at each other, laughing.

It was a great day. Amy was so excited about her Camden

house and kept saying, 'I wish we could just move in now.' The house was ready but all her stuff was still in boxes, it had been in boxes since St Lucia. I said, 'Why d'you need to have your tweezers out anyway? The house is ready, it's your house, let's go!' She rang Mitch and he said to wait because of the boxes, as if she needed a bunch of minions to put her books on shelves and why wouldn't she want to do that herself anyway? It took the joy out of everything. She didn't even get to choose her own kitchen and she was fit and healthy. She ignored her dad.

'We're moving in!'

We got the Selfridges stuff sent round, got the keys and went up. Amy was ecstatic. She'd never even seen the house in real life, she wasn't involved in the buying process at all, only Mitch was. But it was Amy's actual dream, the big house in Camden with a basement. We walked along the hall, kitchen first, with black and white checkerboard flooring, a big gas stove, marble-topped table, windows looking out to the front and *two* SMEG fridges side by side. Further along the hallway on the left was the living room, which was stunning – sash windows looking out over Camden to the back, a huge fireplace, a huge TV above it, inset shelving either side, a little bookcase and two massive sofas. The sofas were identical, dark blue and velvety, really comfy. One was by the window, the other one out in the room with the best view of the TV.

Then she stopped in her tracks, beaming like a kid at Christmas. There, with a wall all to itself, was the jukebox. It was like she'd never seen it before; she didn't remember when she got it in Prowse Place. The vintage AMI jukebox, white and red with a glass and metal top full of 1950s and 60s vinyl singles. It was bigger than she was. She actually kissed it, hugged it, her tiny arms barely managing halfway round it.

At one end of the hallway there were stairs going down to

the gym and the studio, at the other end stairs going up to the bedrooms. There were boxes everywhere, marked 'Living Room', 'Kitchen', 'Band Equipment', 'Bedroom'. We got a new ashtray out, sat down, had a cup of tea and a fag. I wanted her to appreciate the moment.

'Look! Look at what you've done. You own a massive house in Camden that you've always wanted, you've got a studio downstairs, a gym, everything you need.'

She got emotional, welled up. She'd mentioned Blake when we were walking around, she barely ever mentioned him. She didn't well up because she was upset about him, she welled up because she'd moved on from him. And that whole world. This was her new start. She'd lived in all these places she didn't want to live in and now *this*. It had all turned out pretty good, for both of us.

She always talked about 'we'. She'd talk about 'our house in Camden'. People could easily think I was living her life, but that's how we were. It was always our house and she made me feel that way about it. She meant it. Camden Square was about this wonderful new life we were both going to have. With a basement studio where we could jam and play guitar. Just like it was when we were seventeen. That was the day I gave her my Jewish nan's cookbook, the nan I never met who died when I was six months old. It was the only thing my mum had of hers and she always used to say, 'You should give that to Amy.' She was made up, she saw it as a big thing . . . and it ended up on her bookshelf next to the book about my murdering gangster grandad!

She started sorting the house plants, I went back to lugging boxes – and I put my back out. Dale had come round to help, the MD of Amy's band, and she said Dale could fix my back, 'He does that stuff, he's the nuts.' I was lying in the living room, boxes everywhere and Amy said, 'Do that thing Dale, where you walk on people's backs.'

Dale started walking on my back. He's a big man, it felt great, he was working out all the knots with his feet. But then I tried to get up again and couldn't move. I started *crying*. Dale practically broke my back and we had to call an ambulance. On that first day in Camden Square, I had to leave the house on a stretcher and go to hospital. With Amy sitting next to me in the ambulance pissing herself laughing. I was in agony and now she was making me laugh, which made it worse! Typical Amy, she found that *hilarious*.

The first days in Camden Square, Amy was excited about writing again. Not being 'Amy Winehouse', just being a song-writer.

'I'm gonna be in the gym, then I'm gonna sit in the studio and I'm gonna write. I don't know if it'll be an album or anything, but just write about life, like I used to.'

She was getting her alcoholism under control. She wasn't going out much, just enjoying her new house, enjoying her beautiful new bedroom on the top floor, with an en suite, its own little living room and an upright sunbed on the landing before you went in. And that's where she'd sing.

People say crack and heroin ruined Amy's voice. It wasn't ruined now. Her voice was spectacular, better than it had ever been. She'd stand in the sunbed singing old jazz standards like she used to years ago. She'd sing Sarah Vaughan, she'd sing big, long notes, trying to rediscover her voice. Most of the time people never *really* heard Amy sing at her best because she was an addict and a mess. When she was as healthy as she was now she was technically perfect, her lung capacity perfect, all with raw emotion. She was *listening* to her voice, singing the songs from when she learned how to sing. And in the sunbed, apart from the constant buzzing and humming, the acoustics were great, there was reverb and echo. She was enjoying her voice again, after *years*.

Back in the early days of Jeffrey's Place, Amy would get up in the morning, roll her spliff and write her to-do list: launderette, buy strawberry shampoo, clean kitchen. This person was back. Very methodical. She'd get up, I'd make her scrambled eggs and salmon and she'd put on her gym gear. She'd down her greens and electrolytes and spirulina. She had all these little pink weights. She loved pink. She still had her Pink Ladies jacket from *Grease*, which she lived in when she was younger. She'd be in .the gym, sweating in her pink vest and joggers, watching *My Name Is Earl* on the TV above the treadmill for two, three hours a day. Even if she still had the Vogue cigarette on the go. That phase could last a whole month, five weeks. Then she'd relapse, binge and purge and get back on the health trip again. She always had intentions of getting better.

Amy didn't have periods for years because of bulimia and the only thing that ever made her try to stop was the thought that she couldn't have kids. Now she was healthy she'd run downstairs to tell me her period had come on. She'd be so happy about it she'd cry. I got her into health supplements, I ordered tubs of Green Vibrance powder the size of paint pots and bought her colloidal silver water from a Harley Street doctor for the immune system. The kitchen cupboards were full of these expensive compounds, drawers full of electrolyte tablets. She was putting herself back together. Our life was order and cleanliness and organization.

She was still a global household name. She appeared in *The Simpsons* and was referenced in *Family Guy* and *American Dad*, which she didn't know about until we were watching random episodes. She was in a scene in *American Dad* with

Kelly's mum, Sharon Osbourne – we were both shouting at the TV, 'Oh, my God!' Seth McFarlane was a god to us, we used to say we wished Roger the alien in *American Dad* was real so he could be our best friend. Amy would say, '*Puh-lease!* I want him to come round so he can try on my shoes . . .' She fancied Stan in *American Dad*, the chauvinist pig. She'd say, 'If he was real I'd *do* him.'

Amy stayed indoors most evenings and she was quite content. She'd be up on her bed watching television, hair mask in, beautiful nightie on, immaculate. She'd go to bed with a face mask on. I loved it. As much as I dedicated my life to her I needed to do something with my life as well. She was doing so much for me just by being this sane, efficient machine every day, not giving me any stress, any worry. She was starting to talk about the future, about setting up a publishing company for songwriters. She kept on saying, 'Why did I set up Lioness? I've got no interest in making records and selling records, but what I *do* care about is songwriting.' She'd always say she was a songwriter first and foremost; performing she never enjoyed as much, it was too public, made her nervous. Without drink and drugs she was an introvert, much more suited to the solitary writer's life, like I was. She even talked about signing me as a songwriter, that way I wouldn't have to deal with the horrors of fame.

It wasn't always perfect. There were still incidents in Camden Square, times when things were bad. Which is why we still had the boys living with us. For the first period, Amy relapsed maybe every five weeks for three days. Which was still significant progress. There would usually be a reason, an outside trigger. Maybe her mum had come round. She would leave me with Janis in the kitchen, we'd have a lovely chat for an hour and a half, Amy would come back in and I could see she was a glass of champagne down. To take the edge off. Or maybe her dad had come round, or Raye. She found it difficult to talk about work. The pressure. Even though she was singing, even though she was down in the studio a lot. Sometimes, when Mitch or Raye came round, she'd even *pretend* to be drunk, just so they'd go away. We would sit together on the sofa in the living room and she'd watch clips of herself performing, say on Jools Holland. She was stunned.

'Tyler, please don't think I'm being big headed, but I can't believe I used to do that. How did I *do* that? How did I have the *guts* to do that? I was *good*. I need to get back to that . . .'

Pressure. She was thinking, *Who am I? Who did I used to be? Before all this chaos happened?* She wasn't watching herself do her own songs, or videos, she would never do that; I never heard Amy sing one of her own songs, other than when she wrote it, outside of having to sing it, ever. But when she was on Jools Holland she usually did jazz standards and covers. She did an incredible cover of Etta Jones' 'Don't Go to Strangers' with Paul Weller and she couldn't believe she was capable of doing that either. Sometimes she'd go downstairs, try to write or sing, think she was awful and literally punch herself in the head. She was still the insecure geek she always was.

There was still nothing normal about her daily life. Mitch still turned up every Monday morning with cash in a brown envelope for the boys. Whenever we went anywhere or did anything the cash still came out of that envelope. Amy *still* didn't have a bank card. At least the paparazzi couldn't live outside Camden Square as the legal court order from Hadley Wood was still in place. But if we went anywhere they always followed us.

Amy missed being a normal person even more so with the new sobriety. She'd be writing her shopping list and you could see her almost forgetting that she wouldn't be going to Tesco herself. I'd walk out with her list, go to the nearby Tesco garage and feel terrible, like I'd been given the ticket to Disneyland and she wasn't allowed to come. One night I managed to sneak her there – you can slip through a back alleyway. I told the boys not to come. It made her so happy, just walking round the corner, with her mate, like two toerags, no security, no paparazzi. She was low-key, hood up, walking into Tesco at eleven o'clock at night. It wasn't busy and she picked out her things herself. She was absolutely made up. Not a single paparazzo saw us and it was one of the best moments of the year. Forget private jets and touring, this was a special moment: when Amy picked up the fucking mince in Tesco.

Indoors she tried to make a world for herself. She'd brushed paths with one of George Foreman's sons and now she was having cyber dates with him. George Foreman was now more famous for his George Foreman Grill than he was for his boxing so Amy called this guy Grill Face. George Foreman's sons are *all* called George. He was sound, very polite, good looking, like a Ralph Lauren model, and they were always on Skype, flirting. She'd make sure she looked immaculate, 'I'm Skyping Grill Face!' He was in America, there were plans to meet but she still couldn't go to America. They never met; I wish they had.

She started seeing Reg Traviss in real life. She met him out somewhere; his parents ran a pub in Marylebone. He was a handsome boy, charming, nice clothes, good job, the antithesis of Blake. He was a film director – there's always that 'cool new British director' thing and he was the latest. He became better known because of Amy. She went to his premieres and I wondered at the time whether he was into her or liked her because she raised his profile. He wouldn't often come round the house. He'd always say he was still in the edit suite and constantly let her down. And when he *did* come round he spent most of the time talking to me. I got the impression he wasn't that comfortable around her. So I never bought into him. Mitch and Raye did. Reg was a big relief after Blake and they encouraged the impression, in a PR way, that being around him meant she'd sorted herself out, that they were going to get married and have kids. But he was just another dude. No more important than Alex Clare.

I knew Amy wasn't falling in love with him. She was living a healthier life and part of that was to start dating someone again. Since Blake went to prison and even after they were divorced she'd barely indulged that side of her life: she'd had flings but she'd never had another proper boyfriend. And there was the renewed confidence in her appearance. Reg was a bit of a soft touch around her and that would never work for Amy. She wanted the kind of man who – she said this years ago – when you've had too much to drink in the pub and you're getting rowdy, will tell you about yourself, pick you up, sling you over his shoulder and take you the fuck home. That was not Reg's style. She just fancied him.

There were times in the kitchen when he was still talking to me an hour and a half later, 'What was it like when you made an album, Tyler?' – I never found him to be that bright either. Amy would be sitting on his lap, staring at him. I thought, *Why are you still talking to me? Isn't it obvious? You need to go upstairs my friend!* It was as if he was avoiding intimacy so I couldn't help but feel there was an ulterior motive but maybe he thought he was just playing it cool. Nine times out of ten when Amy told me he was coming round, he didn't turn up. She'd be sitting on her bed, full face of make-up, all dolled up, sexy. Eventually I'd go and ask her what was happening. 'Oh, he's not coming.' She looked deflated, like a girl stood up at the prom. She'd go into the bathroom, take off her eye make-up, the beautiful dress. The hair went back up in a bun and the joggers went on. She'd say sometimes, 'Oh, he's just a waster like all the rest of them.' Or, 'No one's interested in me for *me*, are they?'

He made her feel unattractive again and when you've got lifelong self-esteem problems it all feeds in. Sometimes him letting her down would lead to a relapse, just like being frightened of the paparazzi would lead to a relapse. Though I don't think Reg could ever have known the impact it had.

But what led to a relapse more than anything was when work commitments started to be put in her diary.

When she was expected to be 'Amy Winehouse'.

CHAPTER 34

Money was still being talked about in the background. Amy didn't seem to think there was anything to worry about. She certainly never said anything to me. But because of her money situation, whatever it was, her working life was being restarted, opportunities accepted. You could argue it was because they thought it would help her to be busy and she would agree to the work when it was put to her. But what they should've understood is Amy wanted to be busy just sorting her head out and working out how to be sober. Every time a work engagement was put in her diary, by management, it had a detrimental effect on her. Any gig, any appearance, it just tipped her over the edge.

The biggest thing they scheduled was a European tour, upcoming in June 2011. It had been in the diary since the start of the year and I know Amy would have given the impression she was fine doing it at the time. She knew it was important to a lot of people around her. But things, by now, were changing. Whenever Amy expressed doubt she could do it, Mitch would say, 'But you're gonna make six million quid on that tour!' I could tell he thought she was ungrateful, though he never said it: did she know how hard it was for people to make money? It all added to the pressure.

Performance was something Amy just didn't want to do anymore. If some one-off gig or appearance was happening, the entourage would be downstairs, management, Raye, and cars waiting outside. Mostly, whatever it was she was supposed to be doing didn't happen. I'd watch her go from being normal and together and running on the treadmill and eating healthily and having a nice bath in the evening to a breakdown the next morning, caused by having to go and be 'Amy Winehouse'. I knew she wasn't ready because she'd have conversations with me saying, 'I just ain't up for this, I don't wanna do it anymore.' But she felt she *had* to. Pressure. So she'd make the attempt. Go upstairs, get herself ready, try to be the person she used to be.

I'd go downstairs and tell Raye, 'She doesn't wanna do this.' He'd say, 'She has to.'

I'd go back upstairs and she'd be sat on the bed, given up. 'I just don't wanna be that person.'

'Well, go and tell them then, *tell them.*'

'But they'll go mental, my dad will go mental at me.'

She would've been sober for three weeks and now all she could say was, 'I need a drink.' I'd try to find the solution: take a Valium, some Rescue Remedy, *anything,* why don't we sit cross-legged on the bed and pray to the Buddha lord and do yoga? Or, ultimately, why don't we go downstairs and tell everyone to sack this shit off?

'T, I hate this life, all the pressure, the being responsible for everybody.'

'Well, fuck it all off then. We'll just go and live, me and you, in the middle of nowhere, on a desert island, I'll get a job, you'll get a job, we both won't drink and we'll just *be.*'

I was half joking and half meant it. Because I was a recovered alcoholic myself I knew there was only one thing that mattered for her right now: being sober. And everything they wanted her to do would lead to her having a drink. The minute she walked out the door everyone was staring at her. When she got to the gig or the appearance there was either the anxiety of not wanting to *be* 'Amy Winehouse' anymore, or the anxiety of not being able to *do* 'Amy Winehouse' anymore. She'd doubt whether she could even sing anymore. Plus she now hated having to sing those songs.

'If I have to sing "Rehab" one more time, I'm gonna slit my throat.'

We lived in Camden Square less than a year and Amy relapsed maybe seven or eight times. She wasn't drinking all the time, far from it. But she got to the level I was at before I got better: when you're drinking just to seek unconsciousness, just to *escape,* drinking bottles of vodka to pass out on the sofa. Amy would live on the sofa for *days,* asleep most of the time. She couldn't move, couldn't even get upstairs. I used to pick her up off that sofa and shower her. It's the nature of alcoholism, a spiral getting faster and faster and faster. Every relapse is a massive fuck up, a disappointment, a reason to hate yourself, a reason to think you *can't do it.* Which comes with the guilt of failure, which becomes another reason to drink. So every relapse gets worse, a vicious circle. She'd say, like I used to think, 'I'm drinking to forget I'm drinking.' Every relapse would end in Amy going to hospital. In doctors warning her she was getting physically worse. There were doctors' letters in the house saying if she continued to drink she would die. I used to show her the letters when she was off her face and calling me a cunt.

When someone reaches this level of alcoholism they turn into somebody else. *Really* somebody else. Like they're possessed by an actual demon. I called this person The Other Amy. I hated that person. She'd have me up all night. She'd come down the stairs and *kick* my bedroom door open. It could be three in the morning, I'm asleep and she'd be *screaming* my name.

'TYYYLAAAAAAH.'

Amy wasn't an arsehole; this other person *was*. When she screamed my name real fear would shiver right through me. At that point, I'd just want her to drink however much it took till she passed out. Sometimes I'd lie there telling myself to ignore her because it wasn't her.

She was manipulative. 'Tyler, I need a drink!' Which I'd just ignore. 'Tyler, I'm hungry!'

I would fight myself to not get out of bed, I knew it was bollocks. I'd find her on that sofa incapable of reaching down and getting to the wine bottle that was on the floor. She'd test me and say, 'Pass me that.' I'd ignore her. I'd seen other people put a straw in her mouth, just wanting her to go to sleep, because they couldn't deal with her anymore. She'd say, 'If you don't get me that bottle of wine, I'm gonna drink that whole bottle of vodka.' She'd ask me for a bottle of vodka and I'd say, 'Go 'n' get it yourself.' Whenever I could I made sure the vodka bottles in the house were filled mainly with water. I did that a lot. I once gave her a vodka bottle of Evian. She looked me right in the eye with that angry, screwed up look on her face, drinking straight from the bottle and I smiled to myself, *it's water.*

Sometimes she'd call me a cunt and say, 'Why are you here?'

Then when she calmed down, she'd be nice.

'T, will you make me a sandwich?'

'Course I will, darlin', that's all I wanted to do, I just want you to eat something. And then I want you to go to bed.'

Sometimes I'd make her the sandwich and she'd say she wouldn't eat it unless I ate it with her. I'd do the aeroplane thing, one bite for me, one bite for you, she'd turn into a little kid. She'd pick things she knew I wouldn't want to eat, to test me – pure carbs or sugar. Sometimes she'd start crying.

'Tyler, I love you, I can't believe how horrible I was to you just then. I don't mean it, you know I don't mean it.'

I'd tell her I knew what alcoholism does to people, encourage her to forget about it and eat her sandwich.

She'd ask me to make scrambled eggs. I'd stand at the cooker making sure they were really good, put the plate on the table and she'd look at me, put her hand on the plate and go *bang*. Launch the plate off the table, straight into the wall. Eggs and china smashed all over the floor.

Sometimes she'd sit at the table, get her little finger and edge the plate along the table, looking at me. She'd edge the plate and edge the plate, like a child that's wound up, and finally push it off the edge of the table. Sometimes I'd scream at her, sometimes I'd just walk out the room, sometimes I'd get the little dustpan and brush and sweep up bits of broken plate because she might cut herself with it. Sometimes I'd say, '*Fuck you*, I just stood there and made that for you.' She'd start crying, ask me if I'd make it again and promise she'd eat it this time. And I did and she would.

She apologized to me every single time. When she was calm again she'd get little glimpses of what she'd done or said. I didn't tell her everything because she would feel bad and it would lead to more drinking. Though I did tell her more towards the end. 'Do you know you called me a cunt? Do you know you threw this at me?' She threw the diamond cut ashtray at me once, the one we used to bless the house. 'Do you know you told me you wished I was dead?' Sometimes I'd sit there feeding Amy a sandwich in the middle of the night, crying my eyes out.

One night, after she'd thrown something at me across the kitchen table, said sorry and calmed down, she came over to me and took my hand. She walked me into the living room, put a jazz song on the laptop and we slow danced, like we always used to do. I forgave her in a flash. It didn't take away the emotion, or the exhaustion, but seeing that demon disappear again was such a relief to me. My head was bent right down on her shoulder; she couldn't see I was crying.

She was always talking to people on Skype on her computer, on the loud music speakers in the house. When she was drunk it would be loud like you were at a *concert* loud. I'd be lying in bed listening to Amy talking to Nas or Mos Def or whoever, *all night long*, absolutely paralytic and you could tell they didn't want to talk to her.

It was torturous, I was so tired and sometimes I wouldn't sleep for three days. I started letting her think I'd left the house. I couldn't have her kicking my bedroom door open again. I'd tell her, when she'd first relapse, 'Right, I'm off.' The boys knew I wasn't off. I'd disappear out the door with my case, stick it round the side and the boys would put it back in the house without her knowing. I used to take a blanket and sleep on the treadmill downstairs. She'd never go down there. I lay on that treadmill many nights and heard her screaming 'TYYYLAAAH' and then catch herself: *Oh, he's not here.*

She was obsessed with the Robert Rodriguez zombie film *Planet Terror* and she'd blare it out all night long, over and over and over. I could hear her stomping around the living room, *bang, bang, bang*, as I lay on that treadmill hoping I could get at least one hour's sleep so that tomorrow when she woke up I could try again. Get her to eat and stop drinking *today*. And after three or four days it would happen, she would stop drinking.

When The Other Amy was around, other than the treadmill, I had two more places I'd hide. One was on five inches of ledge outside my bedroom window, two storeys up; I'd sit out there and have a fag. The other was a cupboard in the gym, half full of boxes and paper and I'd lock myself in there. I'd sit in that cupboard in the dark and chain-smoke and I felt safe.

It was all so difficult and draining. I'd only been sober two and a half years. I was a trapped person as well. I felt the pressure of being the last man standing, the only person that could tolerate it – or, in her eyes, the only person who cared. Even the friends that had been around, the inner circle, weren't around anymore. They were too messy themselves, at that time, to deal with trying to get someone else sober. Sometimes, in between screaming at her with rage or crying at her with hurt, I'd want to hurt myself and I did. I cut myself, badly, all over my chest, my legs, anywhere she wouldn't see it. I felt so helpless in those moments and she never knew about it.

Occasionally Mitch would come round, look into the living room, see her unconscious on the sofa and say, 'For fuck's sake!' and storm out.

Mitch's TV appearances started really winding Amy up. 'Why's my dad always on TV? Why's he talking about my addictions when he doesn't talk to *me* about my addictions? Why doesn't he talk to me about my problems instead of going on every fucking eggy brekkie chat show and running his mouth to every newspaper that'll have him? He's mugging himself and he's mugging me. You ducked out of my life, Dad. And now you're off with your album, trying to be a superstar.'

I'm sure Mitch would have thought that wasn't fair, he had tried to talk to her over the years but now he was on TV because his debut album had been out since summer 2010. The way he behaved had a huge impact on her.

For the past year and a half I had never given Amy a drink. She wasn't supposed to be seen outside when she was in a state so she'd have to ask someone else to get it for her. She'd ask the boys and they'd refuse so sometimes she'd go herself. The paps would follow her, she'd come back furious and slam the living room door. We were just the bastards who got in her way.

We'd stand there like her three big brothers and she'd say, being funny, 'Right, what have I gotta do, whose dick have I gotta suck for a bottle of vodka?'

To stop her going out to the shops, there was now alcohol deliberately kept in the house on standby. It wasn't on show, she didn't know where it was, but she knew there was a reserve. Sometimes when she kicked off, the boys gave in, rang Raye, said Amy was about to go out and Raye gave them permission because he knew she'd get papped. The alcohol was probably in their room and Amy wouldn't go in there. Sometimes when the boys refused to give in, she'd say, 'Oh, are we really gonna go through this again? Just cut to the chase and go and get it.' Instead of her having to stand at the door and threaten to go to the off licence, go through the motions, play the game.

Amy's doctors were very involved by now. I talked to her main doctor all the time. Sometimes Amy would ask me to sleep in the living room with her and I'd give her a Zopiclone sleeping tablet and she'd fall asleep on my lap. I spent whole nights with Amy sleeping on my lap in that living room, with *Planet Terror* still on a loop. Sometimes one sleeping tablet wasn't enough and I'd think, *Can she take another one?* I had to google it, in case it might kill her. I didn't move; it was like holding a baby when they're asleep. If she woke at three a.m. she could easily say 'I just want a drink,' and you'd be back to square one. But if she slept for a good ten hours, by the time she woke up she'd be sober enough and lucid enough to want to get healthy again.

One morning there was a frantic knocking at the front door. The doctor had been ringing and ringing Amy's phone with no answer. Amy had been out of hospital after a relapse for about three days and she was fine again. Her doctor rushed in.

'Amy, you need to come with me straightaway. We've checked your levels and you shouldn't even be alive right now.'

A test result had come back, not even to do with alcohol, it was about the bulimia. You lose so much vital stuff in your body – potassium, sodium, chloride, electrolytes – it causes palpitations, heart attacks. With every new relapse, the bulimia would also be worse and now it was the worst it had ever been.

She was taken back to hospital.

At some point, Amy would just get bored of being sober again. Then she'd get addicted to her health regime and then she'd get bored of *that*. She was so bored she'd play this game on Facebook, Pet Society, where you create a world. It's for kids. You're a character and you have a cat and you buy material things – shoes for the cat, a bigger house, whatever. When you've played it for two days you get credits and then you can spend them on a nicer pair of shoes for the cat, buy a nicer hairbrush, upgrade the house. But if you wanted to, you could just *buy* credits. Most kids would never buy credits. Amy spent thousands and thousands and *thousands* of pounds on that game. She'd mostly play it when she was sober. I'd say to her, 'Why don't you stop playing Pet Society and live in the real world? This is not normal!' She would ring Jevan two, three times a day and ask him to ask her accountant to transfer a grand. She finally got herself a bank card just so she could top up her Pet Society credits herself. That was a big part of the joy in the game for her, just doing what everybody else does, which is spend their own money.

She retreated into this imaginary world, spending days and days in her bedroom. I genuinely thought, is there something wrong with her? It made me sad. I thought, *Why don't we go out and you can spend thousands of pounds on yourself? Why don't you buy yourself an actual nicer hairbrush or a bigger house? Or give that money to charity?* It was *weird*.

Amy's Aunty Mel, a lovely woman, came round. She sat on the sofa with Amy on one side, I was on the other. Amy was drinking. Aunty Mel was calm but upset.

Aunty Mel told her how dangerous her situation was which Amy didn't want to hear, but Aunty Mel persisted, telling her she needed urgent serious help. Aunty Mel is a beautiful person and it was hard to see her sitting there with her hanky in her hand, and yet being so brave, holding herself together – determined to make Amy understand how worried she was. She was showing so much courage and so much love at the same time, it was almost like Cynthia was there.

I was so pleased. Because it felt like no one ever got involved, except me. Amy said the same thing to her she'd always say to me.

'I'm not going anywhere, Aunty Mel. I'm drinking now and I'll probably stop tomorrow. Won't I, Tyler?'

I said, 'Yeah, you probably will, but one of these times' – even though I didn't fully believe it at the time – 'one of these times it's gonna go seriously wrong.'

Amy still had delusions of invincibility. I used to grab her arms and her belly and tell her she was an incredible human being but her body was just like anybody else's, her tiny little body, it couldn't cope. She knew she had a big problem and she was still in denial. Even though, when she was sober, there was no doubt now in Amy's mind she was an alcoholic. That she'd need to stop drinking forever. In her mind she always thought: *I will do it, just not yet.*

I started to take a different tack: I started to *actually* leave. I told her I'd only come back when she stopped drinking. I thought, *I can't stay here and be exhausted, I can't sleep in the gym. Most of all, she might see my presence as a willingness to just put up with her drinking.* So I wanted her to know: I won't stand for this, when you drink, I'm off.

She begged me, 'Please, *please* don't go.'

'Well, are you gonna stop drinking? No? Not yet? Well, then, I'm off. You ring me when you wanna stop and I'll come back. And I'll help you darlin'. I'm only going to my mum's, I can be back in an hour.'

I'd leave and take my case and feel terrible. Sometimes I'd storm out the door. Though I never left her on her own, never. Neville and Andrew were always there, like her brothers. And when I got to my mum's I'd be in such a state she'd have to cradle me in her arms for two hours.

There was a power in me leaving. It did lead to her being sober. When I came back through the front door with my suitcase, she'd run up and throw herself on me, legs around me, arms around me, like she first did back in Prowse Place but now she wouldn't let go. I'd shuffle through the hallway into the living room and she'd stay like that, legs clamped around my waist, on that sofa. And that's how she'd go to sleep. I was back.

I would've been a *mess* for the last two days. Ringing the boys, checking she was alright, listening to her on the phone, drunk, being an arsehole to me. Then we'd have the conversation with the tears and the remorse and 'Will you come home?' I went through this process because I know what alcoholism is. So when she ran up to me, legs around me, crying, and said, 'Thank you so much for coming back, I can't believe you're still here, everyone's given up on me,' how could I not help? How could I *not*? I would never have given up on her, never. It didn't matter that she said she wished I was dead. Or that she launched the ashtray at my head. Alcoholics will keep fucking up until they crack it.

The last relapse before the final relapse, it happened again. I left, she stopped drinking, I came back, she ran up to me, legs around me.

'Remember that Sleepy Juice you used to make me? Why did you love me so much? Why do you love me so much Tyler?'

'I just do. *I just do.*'

Why does anyone love anyone?

CHAPTER 35

The American jazz legend Tony Bennett loved Amy; he called her a 'once in a lifetime talent'. He was doing a covers album, *Duets II*, and approached Island: would Amy sing with him? She had a very specific initial reaction.

'Oh my God, my dad will be *livid*. He's gonna hate me, I'm doing it!'

That's how fucked up their relationship had become. In her mind, there'd be a part of him that would be made up for her, but another part that would be jealous; Tony Bennett was one of his all-time heroes. Amy wanted to wind her dad up, because she thought it was funny. She'd been sober again for weeks and Mitch didn't even come to the recording.

The recording was scheduled for March 2011 at Abbey Road Studios. It was the one work commitment Amy loved the idea of doing – she idolized Tony Bennett too. But by the time it came round she was nervous. The pressure. She hadn't done anything like this for a long time and all I cared about was that this didn't cause a serious relapse. I always encouraged her to do these things independently but on the day, last minute as usual, she asked me to go with her.

The car was waiting outside. Downstairs, Raye, a new assistant from management and the tour manager were all waiting. Upstairs, Amy was having a full-on breakdown in the bedroom. She couldn't get herself ready. 'I can't do this, I'm gonna have to have a drink.' I went downstairs and told Raye we should cancel it. He said we can't cancel it. Amy was constantly saying 'I need a drink' and I was constantly telling her that if she needed a drink then she needed to cancel it: 'You've worked too hard, you're healthy, look at you.'

'I just need one drink.'

She was terrified, going downstairs, going back upstairs, stalling. We were getting late. She took a Valium to calm herself down and eventually she got out the door. In the car on the way, she wouldn't let up.

'T, I can't do this, can we just stop at a pub, get me a black sambuca shot?'

'No, Ame, you can do this, you do this all the time, you can do it in your *sleep* . . .'

When we got to Abbey Road the organizers were frightened of her, circling around her on egg shells. That still happened a lot, people always thought she was the volatile headcase they read about in the papers years ago. Even when she was as sober, healthy and immaculate as she was that day.

We went downstairs and Amy met Tony Bennett. He was lovely, charming, and so was Amy, telling him, 'I'm really honoured to meet you.' Amy went into a vocal booth by herself and started singing. It was ropey, she knew it was ropey. I could see her inside the booth, she started punching herself in the head. *Properly* punching herself in the head, moving her mouth away from the mic, muttering, 'Fuck, fuck, for fuck's sake Amy!' With everybody watching.

She apologized to Tony, told him, 'I don't wanna waste your time.'

He reassured her, 'It's OK Amy, we have all day.'

We took a break and went upstairs. 'I can't do this unless I have a drink.'

She realized she'd get nothing from me or the boys so she turned to Raye. I could hear her shouting and giving him a hard time but she got her own way because all of a sudden there was a glass of wine in her hand. I couldn't take it out of her hand, could I? I would never mug her off like that in front of everyone. Me and the boys just looked on, in despair. We'd just spent three weeks keeping her sober. We knew what was coming.

After the glass of wine she went back downstairs and she was calm. I was totally stressed and at the same time thinking, I'm gonna enjoy this moment because it's the last moment I can today. The mood had changed. Because Amy's fear had dissipated, everybody calmed down. She was confident. Her voice was beautiful now. I was sitting next to Tony Bennett's wife, staring at Amy like I did sometimes, like a lovestruck puppy. I'd just fall in love with her, hearing her sing. And this was proper old-school jazz, no attitude like there is in so much of Amy's music. Singing with this lovely, dignified old man, a musical giant, a duet that won a Grammy in 2012. Everyone in the room was smiling.

I also felt sad. I hadn't seen her do the 'Amy Winehouse' thing for so long and this performance to me was a lie because it wouldn't have happened without a glass of wine. The glory of the moment wasn't natural and it felt like a dirty secret that only I knew. Everything was beautiful and nothing would be beautiful in seven hours' time.

Before we left, while Amy was saying goodbye to Tony, she had a second glass of wine. In the car home to Camden I tried to swerve the inevitable.

'Ame, remember that film you wanted to watch, *The Boxer*, let's watch that and we'll get a Nando's . . .'

'No, we're going to the Hawley.'

In the pub she did what she usually did, stand around the

jukebox, drink in hand. People turned up and she went with them to the private room upstairs. By the time we got home she was blind drunk, crashing through the house, blaring music at one in the morning, saying, 'Get me a bottle of wine!' The Other Amy was back, taking pleasure in ruining your life. As usual, she was dramatizing everything, deliberately stomping on the floor, her way of saying, 'Fuck you, I'm drunk, I'm gonna be up all night drinking and I'm gonna be drunk for the next few days and I'm gonna blare my hip hop and none of you cunts are gonna sleep and you're gonna have a horrible time.' The absolute antithesis of the insecure girl who was too frightened to go to the studio and do what should've been the most natural thing in the world for her: sing.

I retreated to the cupboard. And then the treadmill.

Of course, Raye was in a difficult position. Amy was an adult and she was the boss. I felt she shouldn't have been working but once she was there, she'd been determined to sing with Tony. Ultimately, her having a drink got the job done, but that only proved to her she needed alcohol to perform. Three days later, in the middle of hell, that was Amy's justification; she threw it back at me.

'I smashed it, didn't I, you said I did, I obviously *do* need a drink to do it.'

It was becoming clear that this was how things would be from now on. She absolutely believed she couldn't be any good without it. That person on Jools Holland, that person she saw on TV be amazing and gutsy, *she* used to drink before a performance, didn't she?

Her biggest excuse for drinking now was that she was working in the studio. I'd come home after being out for two hours, she'd have a glass of wine in her hand and I'd have my head in my hands.

'But T, look, I'm writing, I'm downstairs in the studio, I don't wanna get drunk, I'm being creative, I'm writing an album . . .'

'I couldn't give a fuck about an album! If you can't do it sober then you're not ready to do it. You need to work out how to be sober, fuck everything else . . .'

We'd reached that stage: alcohol was not an option for her if she wanted to stay alive. She knew it. The doctors knew it. Everybody knew it.

I now had a mantra.

'So, if you're telling me you need alcohol to be "Amy Winehouse" then you can't be "Amy Winehouse" anymore! It's better to live being Amy than to die being "Amy Winehouse".'

Her response was the same every time: 'T, I'm not going anywhere.'

CHAPTER 36

The Tony Bennett duet had caused a serious relapse. After that, the relapses came further apart but when they came they were more severe. Now she was in an extreme one, living on the sofa, usually passed out. She hadn't eaten and she didn't have the strength to *move*. She wasn't even The Other Amy, she didn't have the energy, it took everything from her. It's the stage of alcoholism where you don't even mentally want to drink but you've built a physical attachment where it's like water or air and you feel like you've no choice.

Amy's brother Alex was getting married and she really liked his fiancée, Riva. She had a good understanding of mental health problems and Amy could really talk to her. When Amy wasn't drinking Riva would come round once a week and we'd all have a normal day, make some dinner. Mitch kept suggesting Amy should see a therapist. She'd just roll her eyes. Mitch was becoming familiar with that world; I'd been through rehab and it had worked, so through conversations between myself, Riva and Mitch, an intervention for Amy was arranged.

There had been one intervention before but nothing came of it. Reg was there. Amy was in a bad way but she was still walking around. She came into the kitchen and sat on Reg's lap.

'What do you think Reg? Do you think I should go to rehab?'

'I dunno, Ame. If you think you should? I dunno if I should decide that for you.'

He needed to be stronger with her. On the rare occasions he came round he turned up with a bottle of wine, he had no idea what was going on or how bad she was. If he had told her to go, she would've gone; she'd just *asked* him to decide for her. She walked out the room saying, 'Well I don't need to go then.' I told him: 'You had your opportunity and you blew it.'

This time Amy had been on the couch for days and they all came round in the morning: Mitch, Alex, Riva and a woman and a man from the Priory in Highgate. I came upstairs from a night on the treadmill. I was terrified about how this might go. It was how I felt in Mustique when Ally Hilfiger asked if I wanted her to talk to Amy about rehab. I was polite, while in my head thinking, 'She'll eat you alive!'

We all went into the living room. Amy was on the sofa, awake-ish. She looked around, at her dad and then at me, and the look she cut me I'm surprised I didn't drop dead on the spot. She would never have imagined we'd do something like this, it was so obvious and boring. We'd gone behind her back and I'd never gone behind Amy's back. She looked at us again and half-slurred.

'Are you 'avin' a bubble?'

The woman was in charge and she said, very seriously, 'I'm so and so from the Priory, how are you feeling today?'

I was *cringing*. I felt like saying, 'Oh come on, how d'you think she feels? Her brother and sister-in-law are staring at her, she hasn't had a bath in four days, there are empty bottles on the floor, she's in her joggers, hair all over the place.' But I know there's protocol with an intervention and the woman was making her opening, encouraging statement.

'We're here, Amy, because everybody's worried about you and everybody loves you . . .'

She was so earnest. Amy rolled her eyes; if she'd had the strength she would've launched her out the door. You'd have been better off getting Mick Jagger round! Everybody had to say how much they loved her. Her brother cried, her dad had a little cry. It didn't move Amy one bit. The whole situation was a farce to her.

Mitch said, 'I'm so worried about your drinking, you're my daughter and I love you Amy.' All the obvious stuff. Nobody moved me either. It came to my turn. I didn't need to tell her how I felt about her, I told her all the time. I didn't need to do an intervention, I intervened every single day.

'Ame, darlin', you probably wanna top yourself right now, this is a load of bollocks, innit? But your dad wanted to do this and so did I, what else are we supposed to do?'

Amy said nothing but I started to sense this was the most exciting thing that had happened to her in weeks. She was kind of enjoying it, the fact everybody was there. She finally responded.

'Well, this is a laugh, innit? First time I've seen you lot in a while . . .'

The woman told her we all thought she should go to rehab. Amy turned to me. 'Tyler, I love ya, but you know the craic, you know I can get myself out of this.' Everybody continued encouraging her. She said, 'Maybe I *will*.'

The woman said, 'I think you should come *now*.'

Amy looked at me, laughed and shouted out, 'No!'

Mitch stormed out the living room and his wife Jane went off to comfort him. We all walked out and the woman took me aside, told me it was her job to gauge the room and said, 'You're the only person who's going to have any impact in getting her to do anything.'

Myself and Mitch went back into the living room ourselves.

He started screaming at Amy, he obviously didn't want to do that in front of everybody else.

'What am I supposed to do?! I'm your dad, I've gotta do something!'

But Amy wasn't having it. 'Dad, I can sort it out, everyone's being over-dramatic – an intervention?!' I was on one side of the sofa she was sitting on, her dad on the other and Amy started smiling. She *was* enjoying it.

I started laying it on now: 'There's doctors' letters saying you're gonna *die*. This can't carry on!'

She was still smiling, annoying me, then she said something she knew would piss me off: 'Tyler, you look well fit today, I think you should go on a date.'

It worked. I was furious. 'You're enjoying this aren't you?! You love this, me and your dad sitting here, do you realize what I'm going through every day and you think this is fucking funny?'

She rolled her eyes. 'Oh Tyler, pass me the vodka.'

I lost it. 'The vodka? The *vodka?* You want fucking vodka?!'

The bottle was on the other side of the room. I got up, walked over, picked up the bottle of vodka and threw it, *fired* it, just above her head. It smashed on the wall, glass and vodka everywhere. Mitch looked at me, shocked. It shook Amy up because I don't do dangerous things like that. I shocked *myself*. I sat on the other sofa by the window and started crying. I didn't cry in front of her much and that stirred something in her too.

'Tyler, don't be upset, come 'ere, come 'ere . . .'

I went over to her sofa. 'Ame, will you please just go, *please* just go, for me. What harm can it do? You're gonna have to go to hospital anyway. Fuck everybody else, please, please, please, please, *please* just *go*, for me.'

She looked at me. 'Alright then.'

I gave her a big kiss, went upstairs and packed her bag.

The boys drove us, she got in the back of the car with me. Mitch drove in his own car. She started feeling nervous.

'T, I need a drink.'

'Ame, Jesus Christ, you're on your way to the Priory . . .'

'If someone doesn't get me a drink I'm not going in.'

'No one in this car is gonna get you a drink.'

'I'm not going then!'

She wouldn't stop.

'Amy, you need to swear, on my life, if I get you a miniature – and I'm not gonna buy it, I will come with you to get it – that the second you've drunk it you'll go in.'

She said she would and I trusted her. I thought, *You've already drunk eleven litres of vodka, what difference can it make?* But it was one of the hardest decisions I've ever had to make. For the last two years, I hadn't ever bought her alcohol, given her alcohol, all I'd ever done was pour it down the sink. I'd watched other people give her a drink and been furious. The car pulled up, we walked into this little off licence near Highgate and I had to pay for it because I was the one who had the cash. She drank the miniature, it calmed her down and we went to the Priory.

Mitch had to sign her in officially, sign over her rights to leave for a week. He didn't need her permission but he felt the responsibility and he needed me to make the decision with him. I wouldn't make that decision without her consent. So I asked her. I was standing outside with Amy. Her dad wasn't there.

'Look, we've got to sign you in, your dad won't ask you, he's asked me to ask you, can we sign you in? I'm not gonna do it if you don't want us to. But it'll be no different to being in hospital for a week.'

She stubbed her fag out.

'Right, I'll do it for you, if you stay with me today.'

You're not allowed to have anyone stay with you and they

broke every rule for her. I was allowed to stay that day. She was agitated, apprehensive, scared. They did a test and the doctor told us there was so much alcohol in her blood she shouldn't be alive. Just like every doctor told her. She wasn't even drunk, she'd built up such a tolerance.

When I got home that night I got a call from Raye: the guy in the off licence had sold the CCTV footage to the *Sun*.

'But don't worry,' he told me, 'I'm gonna do a deal with them, give them something else and they won't be able to release it.'

It might have cost a lot of money. He might have given them the 'Amy Winehouse goes to rehab' story instead. After everything I'd done, I could've been in the newspapers in the morning looking like I'd taken Amy out to buy alcohol for her. It was disgusting. I'd made her come in with me to face what she was doing. And this dude had been looking at me thinking, *You're buying drink for Amy Winehouse and she's in a state*. Whereas in actual fact I was her carer by now. And part of that carer role was to get her to a proper rehab for the first time in her life. And buying that miniature for her, on that specific day, was the ticket that got her through the door.

I never believed the Priory would sort out Amy's problems; you can't solve anything in a week. I knew that from experience, as someone who'd been through rehab twice: once for a week, which solved nothing, and then the rehab that worked, for three months. It might even have had a detrimental effect on Amy. When she came out, she looked like the life had been sucked out of her. There was no emotion, nothing, like it had taken a vital piece of her. It had been, to her, a very boring process. It was almost like it just didn't *suit* her. I think she went to appease her father, to tick a box herself, to get everyone off her dick about it. She said to me, 'Well, I've done it now, haven't I?' I think she looked so flat because she'd finally been to *rehab*.

That song again, haunting her. The only difference between there and The Private Clinic, apart from therapy, was that she couldn't leave. But that would've been a very big deal to Amy. The worst form of loss of freedom. Somewhere she couldn't run away from. And once you've been to rehab, even if it's only for a week, it's like a switch goes on – you can't pretend anymore you don't have an alcohol problem. That your goal isn't abstinence. Whether you went to shut everybody up or you went because you knew you needed to, *you went to rehab.*

After the Priory, she was sober and healthy again for weeks. But now the twelve-date European tour was imminent, which she'd long had reservations about. She'd already tried a proper tour by then, back in January, a short five-date tour of Brazil. I didn't go because she was going with Reg and Amy also said, 'I don't wanna ruin your birthday again!' The press said it was a triumph but I heard different from people on the tour when they got back: that she wasn't in a good place, that she was drinking, that she struggled, but they managed to keep it under control, just. You can't believe everything you read. I think a lot of people were trying to create a more rosy picture of Amy around then, doing a PR spin for their own ends. The press also said she earned five million quid on that tour, which should've taken some of the money pressure off, but all these months later it hadn't seemed to. So this new tour was still going ahead.

But when there had been an intervention, doctors' letters saying if she drank anymore she'd die, the Priory saying there was so much alcohol in her blood she shouldn't be alive, I thought someone *surely* must be thinking about cancelling this tour? If that thought did cross people's minds I never heard about it and one thing was certain: by the time the tour came round, she definitely didn't want to do it.

So she sabotaged it.

CHAPTER 37

The European tour was a big one. The first night, in Belgrade, Serbia, Amy would be singing in front of 20,000 people in a beautiful historical park, Kalemegdan, where there's a fortress. Everybody was excited about it, the first gig of that size she'd done in almost three years. When it was first mentioned I'd wanted her to tour again; you can't defeat alcoholism without being busy. She was sober, healthy and getting better then. But now I was scared; it wasn't long since she couldn't handle singing in a controlled studio environment with Tony Bennett. She was only weeks out of the Priory. She was still vulnerable.

There was a tour rehearsal a week before, Amy with her band at the 100 Club on Oxford Street – not for the public, just press and the record label.

We were in the car on the way there. Amy said, 'T, d'you think they'll let me have a drink tonight?'

'Amy, are you mental?'

She said she was only joking. She was starting to get agitated. 'I don't really wanna do this tour.'

'Don't do it then.'

'I'm sick of singing these songs I wrote five years ago, why do they wanna do a tour, why can't they wait for me to write another album so I've actually got something to say? People must be so bored of "Rehab", I know *I* am.'

We were in the club and I saw her talking to management. The next time I saw her from afar she was holding a drink. Same as always, the drink calmed her down. The rehearsal was good, we left, she wasn't talking about the Hawley, we actually went home. With the drink in her that night she might have given the impression she was ready for the tour, but now she was going on and *on* to me about how she didn't want to do the tour and how she should be in the studio.

She was setting it up, the sabotage. The next day she started drinking, a full-blown relapse. And I was sleeping on the treadmill.

Every day management came round and every day they'd tell me I needed to get her to stop drinking. It was like a ticking time bomb, five days before, four days before . . . but every day she sank further into that dark blue, velvety sofa. She'd convinced herself: *If I'm not capable of moving the tour will be cancelled.* She drank until she passed out for five days, in and out of vodka unconsciousness. They'd *have* to cancel the tour.

The day she was supposed to leave, the day before the first show, no one could get her up off the sofa. They left. The message came back that if she was still like this tomorrow, they would take her anyway. The next day would be show day.

They arrived next morning, everything was packed, ready to go. The boys literally picked Amy up off the sofa because they were told to and put her in the car. She was barely conscious. On the drive to the airport everyone was silent, not a word, fully on edge. I sat next to her thinking, *This is so wrong.* Naomi had come round earlier that morning to sort out the dresses and I'd said to her, 'Well, obviously, we're not gonna go.' She said, 'Oh no, they said we're gonna go.' It reminded me of a story that Amy had told me about being literally wheeled

301

onto a plane in a wheelchair because she'd been too weak to walk on earlier tours.

I felt sick to my stomach. Everyone clearly thought Amy would suddenly snap out of it, sober up and perform as well as the press and public thought she had done in Brazil. Amy may well have been telling different people different things at this time but to me her actions spoke louder than words. I knew how much she was dreading performing. I'm sure some people on the tour didn't realize that, she maybe told them she was still up for it because she didn't want to let them down. If they didn't know she was in such a bad place now, maybe that's why they just went ahead with the schedule. And now it was too late, the wheels were already in motion. That's how ruthless the industry is, everything just carries on, regardless. There's too much money at stake.

We got to Luton airport, where the private jets fly from, handed our passports out through the window at security and Amy stirred.

'Where are we, T?'

'The airport, Ame.'

She said nothing, rolled her eyes, tutted and pulled the hoodie she'd been wearing for the last five days back over her head. She was so delirious and weak, the boys had to help her onto the plane, arms around her, guiding her up the steps. Mitch wasn't there, he rarely came on tour, but management were upfront, we were down the back. I don't think they wanted anything to do with her at this point. I gave Amy her withdrawal medication, Librium, to prevent the onset of a seizure. It was always my responsibility. She acknowledged what she was taking, 'I know I can't drink on this tour.' They wouldn't have got the insurance otherwise. She was coming round to full consciousness. She didn't kick off and try and get off the plane, she wasn't there against her will, she just didn't put up a fight anymore. Her fight had been to obliterate herself.

She was watching them upfront, in a different world, the plane taxiing on the runway. They were excited, getting paid to do what they loved again, laughing and eating trays of perfect fruit, like you're always served on private jets.

'Do you like all this shit, Tyler? I hate all this private jet bollocks, this ain't real, this ain't me, it never was to be honest and I don't wanna have to deal with it anymore. I just wanna be at home, or playing pool.'

We got to the Hyatt Hotel in Belgrade. Amy still had no idea where she was: 'Where are we, T?'

We didn't see anyone else for a good eight hours, it was just me and Amy in her room. She wasn't just in a bad way – sick, shaky, withdrawing – she was mostly semi-unconscious. Much of the time she was fully asleep in bed, the result of five days' solid drinking. She should've been in hospital. Every now and again she'd stir, ask me for a drink and I wouldn't even have to respond, she'd just fall back to sleep again. She couldn't get one anyway; management had asked for the hotel phone to be disconnected so she couldn't order room service.

For those eight hours, every hour, I'm getting calls from management. 'Is she alright?'

I kept saying, 'No, she's completely unconscious, there's no way she can do a gig tonight, it's not possible.'

All day they kept ringing me and ringing me and ringing me. No one came to the room to see for themselves, they were too busy preparing for the show. Finally Naomi came in to get her styled, with the new assistant from management, who was trying to gee her up: 'Come on Amy, let's get ready!'

Amy got up and Naomi and the assistant had to dress her as she wasn't capable, this was all a dream state to her. She put herself in the chair in front of the mirror and went to put on her own make-up, like she usually did. Her eyes were practically closed, her head nodding down and shooting back up to try and catch a glimpse of herself in the mirror. She picked up her eyeliner, missed her eye and swiped a big black tick on her forehead. She had no idea if her eye was her mouth or her nose or her fucking toes. We were all welling up. The assistant said, 'I'll help you Ame.' She started doing her make-up for her, tears in her eyes. It was one of the saddest moments of my life, my girl was so unwell. I rang management.

'This can't happen, she's not even *awake*.'

'No, she'll be alright.'

All I could think of was to give her some Pro Plus, liven her up.

Only now Raye came in. We all walked out of the room, into the elevator, into a cab to the outdoor marquee dressing room before the show. I had to go for a piss so I was out of the room for five minutes and when I came back Amy had downed a glass of wine. I know how it will have happened – she would have been convinced she needed one to perform and argued with Raye until she got it. I wasn't there when she did; if I had been I would've stepped in because you cannot drink on Librium.

What was happening to Amy now was what the medics tell you can happen with alcohol and Librium: like she was blacking out while conscious. Five minutes before she was due on stage Raye said to me, 'What have you given her?' I wanted to kill him.

Raye held her by the hand and helped her up the steel steps behind the stage. I saw them, I was standing at the side of the stage like I always did. This time I was crying, dreading what might happen next. Eleven hours ago, Amy had been on the sofa and I'd watched her make not one decision or one move of her own. It was almost as if they'd taken her off the sofa in Camden Square and, seconds later, placed her straight onstage over a thousand miles away.

The show was *awful*. It was nearly five years since she released *Back to Black*, in 2006, when she'd just turned twenty-three, and they'd got her propped up on a stage trying to sing 'Rehab', which she couldn't stand anymore. She couldn't sing, she was stumbling back and forth, fell backwards into her backing singers. Everyone could see she'd been looking after herself, she was a decent weight, with glossy hair and perfect skin. Despite the relapse she was so beautiful that day. But her mind was gone. *She* was gone.

The crowd were booing, drunk, yobby. If I'd had a machine gun I would be in prison. I would've mown down 20,000 people. I fought every instinct I had not to run on stage and carry her off in my arms. A sick girl was thrown in at the deep end and everyone watched her drown in front of their eyes.

That footage went all over the world and made Amy look like a mug. Nothing but a mess. I *hated* everyone for it. Six days before she was perfectly normal.

They rushed us out of there like we had a president in the car. She couldn't remember doing the gig. We went straight into a media circus at the airport. She was rushed past the press, who were baying for headlines, and no one had the bollocks to tell her what had happened. She asked me how it went and I tried to at least warn her it was bad: 'It weren't brilliant, Ame. It weren't your best. But don't worry about it darlin', *you* are brilliant.'

We flew to Istanbul, Turkey, where Amy was playing next, in another park. She was so tired. Only twelve hours ago we were at home in London. Now, we'd done two flights and been to two different countries. We were ushered into the hotel via private back door elevator by two security.

'Welcome to Istanbul, Ms Winehouse.'

She hated all that even more than ever. I was waiting for her to say, like she always did, 'I'm not no one special, mate, my name's Amy.' But she didn't. She was totally confused, she said, 'I thought the gig was in Poland. Have I gotta do a sound-check?' I told her again. 'You've done the gig already darlin'. We've just flown here from Serbia. We went there first.'

'Really? Shit, was it any good?'

She didn't remember being carried off the sofa in London, boarding the private jet to Serbia, doing a gig in front of 20,000 people, none of it. At least she wouldn't remember getting booed or not singing through a single song.

We walked down the corridor to our room, both exhausted. Raye and some others came in and two bottles of champagne appeared, even though the gig had been a disaster. *What the fuck?* Everyone started drinking and then left again, leaving me to deal with everything, as usual. I poured the champagne down the sink, filling the bottles up with fizzy water like I always did. Amy was walking around and I had to hold her up, circling her in my arms. I got her to eat something. We were sitting on the floor, playing the aeroplane game again: one spoon for you, one spoon for me. But this wasn't The Other Amy. She was like a child who'd been abandoned in a world she didn't recognize.

I finally got her to bed and locked the door. The room was unbearably hot – it was Istanbul in summer – but I didn't open the balcony shutters. If Amy walked out there in the night she could have fallen over the side; we were right on the top floor. They never thought about details like that either. I took my Pro Plus and stayed up all night, checking she was breathing, holding her in my arms, knowing she was safe, listening to the Muslim prayer just before sunrise from speakers outside the mosque.

The next morning, I started distracting her. That's another

withdrawal tactic: when you think you need a drink, if you distract yourself for ten minutes, it'll become fifteen minutes, half an hour. I had her sunbathing on the balcony, I was ringing everybody – we wanted soft drinks with electrolytes, Lucozade – but no one answered. The next show wasn't until tomorrow and everyone was having a day off driving around Istanbul having a ball.

I got a message on Facebook that morning telling me a mate in London, Greg, had died of an accidental overdose. He was a messy dude, into drink and drugs; I'd known him years before. I didn't tell Amy about it but I was upset. It felt like an omen: that's what will happen to Amy. My whole life seemed to be about alcoholism and dealing with addicts.

'Cancel the tour,' I told Amy. 'Tell them.'

She was awake by now, her mind was clearing, and all the good thoughts were coming back.

'T, I wanna go home, I wanna get sober, I wanna get healthy, I wanna put on half a stone. Fuck the tour.'

I thought: *Brilliant! There you are again, yes Amy, come on!*

She had an idea. 'Let's just stay here for four or five days, get a bit of sun, relax and then we'll go home.'

Excellent! 'Call Raye.'

She called Raye, told him to cancel the tour. Inevitably, Raye called me and told me we needed to talk. I went to meet him downstairs.

'Tyler this is a nightmare, cancelling the tour at the last minute. It's important she does this tour, she needs the money. You need to tell her. You have to do whatever you have to do to get her to do it.'

Raye knew what cancelling the tour would mean for Amy's finances and reputation as an artist but I told him what he needed to hear. It was the first time I ever put my foot down with him. I was so sick of it all.

'I don't give a fuck. My best mate is upstairs, she's getting sober, she wants to be sober, she wants to be happy, she wants to be *fucking alive* and that's all I give a shit about, so *fuck* the tour. I don't give a shit if she never writes another song, I don't give a shit if she never goes on stage again! You don't know what I've just been through since she had that wine at six o'clock yesterday, you don't know what I went through last night, worrying she would sling herself off the balcony, and now she's in her room, she's sunbathing, all she wants is to be sober and that is all that matters, so you can go fuck yourself Raye.'

He was furious that I'd talk to him like that. Raye's massive and I really thought he was about to punch me. I walked away. I was done with them all. I understood alcoholism: when you're an alcoholic, there is nothing more important, there is *nothing else*, other than being sober. Forget *this this this this this*, that's all you have to think about: *be sober*.

Amy cancelled the tour. People were fuming, saying behind her back that she was selfish, they'd been looking forward to the tour. Amy noticed it. That added to the pressure, that she'd let everyone down.

The boys went home and we stayed on for four or five days. Everything was civilized. I thought about that terrible gig in Serbia and how it was perceived by the world, that Amy must've been fucked up and on drugs, still, these past three years. But what I saw that night was an actual mental breakdown. She always cared about her band but none of the rest of it mattered to her anymore: those songs, the performing, the thousands of people. It wasn't just the five-day relapse, the exhaustion and the medication. It was like she just couldn't have cared less anymore. Like she'd gone *fuck it*.

On our first night in Istanbul on our own, we were sitting on the balcony, it was almost sunset, she'd eaten, she'd had a good sleep and she was happy. She was talking about having a few days in the sun, going home, staying sober, getting herself together and not doing these big tours anymore. She hadn't been sure about that before and now she *knew*. She didn't even beat herself up about Serbia, there was no shame, she was just glad the tour wasn't happening. A corner had been turned very quickly, in less than twenty-four hours; she was now calm, peaceful, together.

She got up. 'I'm gonna give Reg a call.'

It was all lovely because it was all normal. She went to make the call, I slid her tablets over – 'Remember to take these' – and went out for a walk for hours in the sweltering heat. That's how confident I was she'd be alright.

I'd never been to Istanbul before. I was sitting in this square feeling so good about everything. Reg was coming over, we'd all have a holiday in the sun. After days of stress and fear, the worry about what was coming next was finally gone.

It was 20 June 2011.

CHAPTER 38

Back in Camden Square, after Istanbul, Amy was sparkling again. She was sparkling *before*: on the flight home I had my laptop out and clean freak Amy grabbed it – 'Gimme that, it's filthy!' – got a tissue out, with a bit of spit, and cleaned my laptop, meticulously, for ages. That's what 'tragic Amy Winehouse' was doing less than a week after Belgrade, where she played what reports were calling the worst live show ever seen in Serbia's history.

I sat on the plane smiling. Perfectly healthy, beautiful Amy, who could replenish herself like no other. She'd be reborn in five days. I don't think people ever realized how beautiful she was. I thought, *We're going home, she wants to get well, everything's sweet.*

She was sober for the next month, on the treadmill, rebuilding herself. For months now she'd been saying she was getting bored of drinking anyway. I held on to that. When I saw Amy get bored of something, whether a guy, a TV programme, it was over, dead, that was her nature. There was nothing fun for her about drinking anymore. Five days on the sofa, that wasn't fun. Her thinking was starting to shift. I *knew* we were turning a corner.

We constantly talked about the future, the next journey together, sober. Because we always did shit together. I was

310

sober, she was sober. I encouraged her all the time: 'Come on, get on this bus with me! Cos it's alright actually.' She was just a few steps behind me and she went through a *shitload* more than I did.

For the last three months, she'd been taking steps towards getting her independence back. She talked about making sure her company was back in her own name instead of her dad's, about ringing Margaret her accountant to make sure she had all her bank cards. We talked about the day when she wouldn't live with two security men anymore. About getting back to the person she was when she first left home, when she first got her independence, when she was so alive. Before everything went haywire. When Amy was given the freedom to be herself, she flourished.

We talked in detail about how to be sober. She *absolutely* believed she could do it. She recognized it was the little things she needed in her life again. The basics. To do things for herself again. She still never made decisions for herself.

'They're still completely in control of my life,' she told me. 'I understand why my dad took control of my company, I understand why I've got two babysitters living in my house, I was a bit of a mess, wasn't I? Fair play. But I'm not anymore. And it's not helping me now.'

She wanted to write in the studio – not necessarily write another album, just come back to herself, music as therapy, like it is for anyone. And if they'd just left her to do that, in a year's time maybe she would've written that next album. Nobody made her write *Back to Black*, she just lived her life.

She was now very serious about setting up her publishing company for songwriters and talked about asking Nick Shymansky if he knew any good writers.

She asked Raye to come round so they could talk about it

as a real proposition. As it was a business conversation I went out, as usual. When I came back, Raye was still there, though he left within two minutes. The vibe wasn't good. She told me Raye wouldn't agree to her idea. He didn't think it was a good investment and didn't want her, in his mind, to waste money. The European tour had just been cancelled, it probably cost Amy and therefore *them* money. She took it very personally, she was upset.

'For once this is something *I* wanna do. I think I'll ring Margaret and just set it up myself.'

I was disappointed for her but I was also pleased to hear her say she could do something *herself*. It tied in with everything she'd been saying for months: 'I'm gonna take control back of my life.' She got more and more annoyed.

'Why have I not got enough money to start a publishing company? They're always spending money on shit I don't wanna do and now they're telling me I've got no money to do what *I* wanna do?'

By this point I could barely hear what she was saying because I sensed she'd had a drink. In fact, I *knew* it. After a month of sobriety, after Istanbul, I just didn't think this was going to happen again. I went downstairs and had a fag in the gym cupboard, just wanting to be by myself. When I came back up, Amy was very casually drinking a glass of wine. I looked at her, horrified.

'*Ame?*'

'Yeah?' And then she actually said it: 'It's only a glass of wine.'

I lost it.

'Only a glass of wine, are you mental? Fuck the publishing deal! Is this the reason? That you think you're entitled to a glass of wine? You're just using this as an excuse!'

I walked out of the house and didn't come back for hours. When I did, I went straight to my room, packed my bag. She was now drunk but not yet a mess. I was charging around my room, filling my case and she came to the door.

'Tyler, please don't go . . . .'

'No! I've told you, you *know* that I'm not gonna be here, I'm not gonna let you do this and I'm not gonna be a part of this.'

She picked my stuff up.

'Put it back in the wardrobe, I'm *fine,* I'm downstairs, I'm writing, I'm recording, I'm doing what I'm supposed to be doing . . .'

'I don't give a shit if you're recording, I don't give a shit if you write another album! All I care about, Amy, is that you don't drink, *you can't drink anymore.* And you don't even want to! Are you just gonna give in that easily? D'you think it's that easy? That when you fancy a glass of wine you don't have to fight it? That's the *nature* of this thing. You have to find a way to swerve it. Four weeks ago you sat with me on that balcony in Istanbul saying you didn't wanna drink anymore, you just wanted to go home and be in your studio and in your gym and playing pool. That's what you wanted. So how can you be *here,* again?'

'T, I'm alright . . .'

I finished packing my case. I knew that in two, three days' time it would be a nightmare again; she'd be on that sofa, going back to hospital. It only *ever* led to that. I left, rolled my case down the road like I always did, to the pub on the corner where I'd book an Addison Lee to my mum's. It was ten, eleven o'clock at night. Sitting at this bench, I got this feeling. I didn't think anything was gonna go wrong, but I still felt that if I just left, I would regret it. I always just left and I was usually calm when I did. When I said all those things in the bedroom, my voice wasn't that loud, I wasn't screaming. I thought, *No, it's not enough. I need to go back.*

313

I picked up my case and went back to the house. As I approached I could hear her music blaring, The Specials' 'Ghost Town'. I could hear her in her top floor bedroom singing along. I'd been gone for an hour, she would've thought I was *gone* gone. I went upstairs. She was singing, I could tell everything was perfect in her soft-focus world. I slammed her laptop lid down. Turning Amy's music off was more powerful than punching her in the face. I'd *had enough*. Even as I was standing there just looking at her because I loved her and adored her little bones more than anybody else in the world.

I said everything I needed to say. She didn't want to hear it but she *did* hear it. And she let me say it; she knew it was important for me to have my diatribe. She heard my mantra one more time.

'It's better to be alive being Amy than to die trying to be "Amy Winehouse". *Fuck* "Amy Winehouse", it's a character, *fuck* that persona!'

'T, I'm not going anywhere.'

'Unless you stop drinking *right now*, I'm going.'

'Well, fuck off then.'

'Well, fuck *you*.'

And then I left, knowing I'd see her again in a few days.

I went to my mum's and the following day she rang, at lunchtime.

'You alright darlin'?'

That's when I went to the field and we talked, and she told me all the things she wanted for me in life. Mostly, to finally fall in love. She promised she'd stop drinking the following day and I believed her. I always knew when to believe her.

'T, please come home.'

The following day, I went home.

*

I walked up the wide, stone steps to Camden Square, put my key in the door and stepped inside with my case. Andrew was in the hallway on the phone. He gestured to me to stay where I was and not go upstairs.

I wasn't worried. I'd only been away two days. I thought Amy was asleep and everything would be like it always was: I'd be back, she'd stop drinking, we'd carry her into the car, take her to The Private Clinic, give it a week of withdrawal and she'd be fine. So it was all cool. I went into the kitchen and made her a cup of tea. Tomorrow we were supposed to be going to Nick Shymansky's wedding and we wouldn't make it now, Amy would be in hospital, which was a shame because we'd been so excited. She'd even laid her dress out for it on the living room sofa alongside my suit, all ready. Today was also the wedding anniversary of my mum and Danny and I smiled at the thought, such an epic day for all of us, five years ago now.

An ambulance turned up. Andrew told me to open the front door. I let the paramedic in and Andrew took him upstairs to Amy's room on the top floor. This had happened countless times. I started going through in my head what to pack for the hospital, because I knew what she was like. Once she started getting better she'd want her hair conditioner, probably the strawberry one. I was calm and ready to do the usual when the buzzer went.

A second ambulance.

My head just went . . . bang. *Something's not right.*

Andrew told me, 'Stay downstairs.' I opened the door to another paramedic and I knew. I just *knew*. My stomach flipped. This wasn't standard procedure. I didn't even look at him. I just ran, I ran so fast up those stairs to my girl, *ran, ran, ran, ran, ran* up the stairs. I couldn't breathe. I legged it past my room and up to Amy's where Andrew was already blocking the doorway. He stood there like a brick wall. Andrew's a big fucker. I fought him to get into that room. I pushed him, I punched him, I wanted to *kill* him to get him out of the way. He took it all. He said nothing and did not budge.

I was still trying to break through Andrew when the first paramedic walked up from behind him. He leaned over Andrew's shoulder and said a sentence to me that I've never repeated until now. Ever. The sentence that ended my world. Delivered so calmly, so matter of fact, it cut through me to the bone.

'I'm sorry, mate, but she's long gone. She isn't even warm anymore.'

It sounded so cold to me, the way he said it.

'What? What? *What?!*'

That's all I could say. I went blank. Numb. Sick. Dizzy. I fell down.

I got back up and ran down the stairs. Away from what he'd just said. Away from my worst nightmare coming to life. Away from the one thing that I thought would never happen. The one thing I would not survive. No way. *I'm not strong enough to be without her.* I ran outside and collapsed on the steps outside the front door. I looked up into the sky and I *knew*. She was *there*. I felt it and it killed me. My Amy. My girl. She wasn't upstairs. She wasn't there. She was gone.

She'd left me.

I don't remember the next hour. I rang my mum first, apparently. The police arrived. I wanted to run and I wasn't allowed to leave. I'd run out of fags and I just wanted to smoke but a policeman said, 'You can't leave – procedure.'

And then the world came: the media circus. All the cameras, all the journalists, all behind this police tape on the other side of the road. People, hundreds and hundreds of people, all of

London it felt like. Just staring. Watching. It was different for them. They didn't see Amy as real. It was like the scene in court with Amy behind the glass but a billion times worse. Now Amy's death was drama to them, entertainment, gossip. Some would have cared. I was sobbing, I was lost, and they watched me like an audience watching a film.

I'd never thought anything could go this wrong and especially not now. Not when she'd been getting so well, when there was nothing wrong with her head, when she was normal. The people watching this, the people who were about to hear it on the news, all over the world, they would never have believed it. I know they thought it was always an inevitable decline, that she was just another self-destructive fuck-up. When the truth was all she'd talked about for weeks, months, was sobriety and the future.

I had to go to a police station to go through the events and I was smashing things up, crying. The police were lovely: they let me leave for fresh air and I walked to the shop, for water and fags. It was now two hours after I'd been sitting on the steps outside the house and the newspapers had a board up already: 'AMY WINEHOUSE DEAD.' They said it was a drug overdose. Fuckers. She was three years clean of all drugs and they just wrote what they wanted to believe.

I went back into the police station and comforted myself with one single thought: I wouldn't be around tomorrow. I didn't wanna live without her and it calmed me down. There was a way out and I'd be with her. I was gonna end my life. I was gonna kill myself. I was gonna relapse: drink, drugs, fuck it.

I walked out of the police station and my mum was waiting outside. She didn't put her arms around me at first. She just said this: 'Listen to me, boy, you need to be alright. You need to fucking *be alright*. I do not wanna be in the same position as Mitch tomorrow morning.' And in that moment, I thought, *Fuck. I can't go through with it, can I? I've gotta deal with this.*

There are no words. You don't get over it. Ever. It's a scar you carry forever. You cry and you cry. You catch your breath, then you start howling and crying again. You pass out from crying and the relief of that level of exhaustion is almost beautiful, pure escapism and it stops hurting. You wake up and for a few seconds you've forgotten, like it hasn't happened, until it hits you full pelt in the face and it physically takes your breath away. And you cry again. And that's it, for days and weeks. You throw up, you're dizzy, your legs give way and you just pray someone will switch you off or knock you the fuck out so you can stop and not think. But they don't. And you can't. You just have to deal with it.

And my life became simplicity. Just remember to get up. Remember to eat food. Remember to brush your teeth. Grief is a fucked-up thing. I'd get angry at Amy. I flipped one day walking down the street. Why have you LEFT ME? How do I exist? How do I cope? It was always me and you. Always me and you.

Me and you.

CHAPTER 39

The last months of Amy's life were so close to the end but it never felt like it. That's the hardest thing to process. Even the traumatic times, in between the weeks of sobriety – the Tony Bennett relapse, the intervention, the Priory, the cancelled European tour – it always just felt like the next thing that was happening. That we'd get through it. I knew the severity of the situation – my whole mission every day was to keep Amy sober – but I could never have foreseen the way her life would end, never. Not *then*. The coroner's verdict was 'misadventure' through high levels of alcohol. A large part of that was the stress her body went through with bulimia; it wrecks your cardiovascular system and her body wasn't strong enough to cope. There were no illegal drugs found in her body. The very thing I'd feared most would happen when things were at their worst, the reason I watched over her all night for years, *happened*: she just stopped breathing.

I know I kept Amy alive. Members of her family said that to me: if I hadn't been with her, she probably would've died a lot sooner. Over those last months, when I started to leave as a tactic, I feel like I let her go. I've tortured myself about that. I should've withstood *all* of it. But if I kept her alive, does that also mean I prolonged her agony? I don't think so. She really was only a few steps behind me into sobriety, she *was* turning that corner, she just needed more time and serious professional help. The kind of help I could never give her myself. During those last months she was even talking about seeing a therapist. It wasn't me saying it anymore, it was *her*.

All I know is that I just had this instinct the day I met Amy that I had to look after her. I always felt it and I always tried to, as a young man often overwhelmed by not only her chaos but my own.

After many hours in the police station the day Amy passed away, a friend of Chantelle's who wasn't involved in Amy's life said she had an empty house in West Hampstead we could use, so the friends could all be together. That's where we stayed for a few days: me, Chantelle, Naomi and Catriona, who popped round. Phil Griffin drove us there. As soon as we arrived I threw up. And threw up. And threw up. We spent the night crying, putting the kettle on and – apart from me – pouring drinks. I could barely speak. Phil arrived the next day with fresh clothes for us all from JD Sports; we'd brought nothing with us. No wonder Amy called him Daddy Phil.

I spoke to Nick on the phone. He still wanted me to go to his wedding. Of course I couldn't. I felt I was seconds away from a mental institution. Phil suggested a walk and we all went together. I was striding ahead, everyone behind me, they all thought I intended to kill myself. I stopped at a pond and someone came up to me. 'The family want to see you, they're worried about you.'

That afternoon I went round to Aunty Mel's. I was terrified. Frightened that if I really connected with what had happened, accepted it, I'd lose my mind. I'd only been three years sober. I still had anxiety and depression and one of my biggest fears had always been that I'd end up in an asylum.

I was ushered into the garden and Amy's whole family was

there: all her uncles, aunties, cousins, about twenty-five of them. They circled around me, put their arms around me, every single one of them. I burst into tears. I sobbed, and sobbed, and sobbed in the middle of this circle. I lost it in a way I'd never lost it before in my life. I was crying so much I couldn't *breathe*.

We all sat down together on garden furniture, Riva next to me, Alex, Janis, Mitch, Jane. Riva said, 'Let it out, let it out.'

'But . . . I was supposed to look after her, that's what I *do,* I'm supposed to look after her.'

Those were the first words out of my mouth, the first words I'd properly spoken since it happened. One of the most torturous moments of my life. They all told me I couldn't have done any more for her and couldn't have been a better friend. And how it always gave them comfort knowing I was always there, looking after her. Mitch even said to me, 'Tyler, I know you know her better than me, of course you do. I'm her dad, but you're closer to her than anybody. I'm so sorry.'

I was absolutely exhausted. I felt so let down, by life. And the way things had gone. I'd put so much energy into something and it didn't work. I *didn't* save her.

The next day everyone congregated at the house Janis now lived in. I'd never been there before. Aunty Rene, who used to visit Hadley Wood, was there all glammed up, just like Amy's nan Cynthia. Mitch asked me to go with him to pick out the coffin. We did that in a blur. He asked me to choose the first song they'd play at Amy's funeral and I chose Our Song: Carole King's 'So Far Away'.

People kept saying to me, 'Stop smoking and eat something.' I must have been smoking 140 fags a day. I couldn't stop. I didn't even use a lighter; as soon as one was nearly finished I used it to light the next one. Kelly came round. It had been a long time since anyone thought of her as 'Kelly Osbourne', she'd been a good friend to Amy, always stayed in touch. We were all invited to write letters to be placed in Amy's coffin. I sat in a corner, writing and sobbing.

The funeral was held three days after she died, at Edgwarebury Cemetery. We all left from Janis's place. I was in a car with Kelly and Chantelle, driving down these country lanes, which for a half a mile were lined with fans and the world's media. The same as it had been outside Camden Square when the ambulances turned up: hundreds of photographers all professionally set up like you'd see at a film premiere. Once again I was living through a personal nightmare that was being viewed by the world as entertainment. There was no privacy. They were even standing on ladders outside the cemetery walls.

Kelly insisted on holding my hand as we walked in. Juliette and Lauren came. Mitch hadn't wanted to invite them because they weren't in Amy's life anymore, but I persuaded him: I knew Amy would've wanted them to be there.

It was a Jewish ceremony and I didn't know the rules, didn't know where I was supposed to go until Riva pulled me up to the front with the family. I sat next to Reg who was there in the traditional 'husband' seat. Mitch gave the eulogy, full of funny childhood stories. There was a black butterfly flying around and everyone was saying out loud, 'That's Amy, she's here in spirit!' It landed on Kelly's shoulder and Mitch made a joke.

'She knows where the money is.'

People laughed. I didn't. Or couldn't.

Then he spoke at length about setting up the foundation. There were loads of press there, it felt like a public event and Mitch's speech was printed in full in the newspapers the next day. He closed the eulogy with: 'Goodnight my angel, sleep tight. Mummy and Daddy love you ever so much.' I heard my mum, rows back, breaking. Then 'So Far Away' started.

Doesn't anybody stay in one place anymore?

It would be so fine to see your face at my door . . .

It *killed* me. And then, as we left, we had to walk up to the coffin one by one and place our hands onto it. I couldn't do it. I kissed the coffin instead, walked away, got to the door, and collapsed. Phil and my mum had to carry me outside.

My mum said, 'Are you alright boy?'

'No. I'm not, and I'm not gonna be alright for a long time.'

She looked at me, distraught: 'We should've done what you always said we should've done. We should've put her in the van and taken her away.'

Mark Ronson was there. He was just so sorry, there wasn't much to say. Bryan Adams was there and he looked at me as if to say 'you poor bastard'. He knew the chaos and the stupidness and the struggle. He finally met my mum and said to her, 'Don't forget what you did for Amy, too.'

There was a wake in a synagogue. Darcus was there. He came up to me and said, 'Aw, man, I heard you were in a bad way, I heard you were close.' I couldn't speak. Grimmy was there, he just gave me a hug. Drinks were organized. It didn't even cross my mind to drink. I knew if I picked up one thing, drink or drugs, that would be the end of me. People from the record label were there, all these people doing and saying the bizarre things you say at a wake. I felt different and separate from everybody else. I lasted five minutes.

Round the back of the synagogue I found a metal stairwell, and I sat there to smoke and be on my own for two hours. For some people it was like a showbiz event, for label people and acquaintances who just weren't close to her. I felt crippled.

People had come up to me and said, 'We've lost our friend but it's like you've lost your wife.' But she wasn't like my wife, she was my *life*. Because what is life? It's love and your purpose. What you do every day. And I'd been with her, pretty much, every hour of every day for years and years. And it stopped. *It all stopped.*

Amy never wanted me to have a tattoo. She told me she regretted having so many. But within weeks of her passing I had her name tattooed over my heart: Amy Jade. It always felt like the right thing to do. I still touch it when I talk about her. I wanted her on my heart, forever; it's the only tattoo I'll ever have.

For the first year, I couldn't be on my own and I wasn't left on my own. I had a tiny flat in Camden where I was supposedly rebuilding my life and I went walking for fourteen hours a day. My friends walked with me, or followed me, and one of them would always stay over. I didn't sleep. In the rare hour I did, I had nightmares about trying to get Amy to stop drinking. In my dreams, I kept saying to her, 'No, you have to stop drinking because this time it's different Amy, you died this time. You *died* this time.'

It was months, maybe even a year, before we all went back to the cemetery in Edgware to see the headstone unveiled. It's beautiful, a black marble monolith with pink lettering – because she loved pink and always wore her pink ballet slippers – and a monument to Amy and her nan. The idea mostly came from Mitch and the family loved it. The inscription reads: 'In Loving Memory of Cynthia Levy and Her Beloved Granddaughter Amy Jade Winehouse.' Cynthia had a stone there already, where her ashes are, and Amy's ashes were put there too. They're together, as it should be. The design includes an open black marble book, with names in pink of all her family and friends. I was in too much of a mess to get involved in the discussions about the order of the names, but to me the final decision on the non-family side doesn't reflect the importance of people in Amy's life: Reg, the boys, me, Naomi, Jevan, Catriona, Chantelle, Violetta, Raye, Mark, Salaam, Dionne, Amy's band, who she loved.

But it's not somewhere I ever go. It's just a tombstone. Amy isn't there.

A week after the funeral, I went back to Camden Square for the first time with Mitch. We went up to Amy's bedroom and he took the top pillow from her bed and said, 'You have the other one.' I took the pillow and I saw, on her bedside table, a photo frame with four photos in it: two of me, one of Mitch and one of Cynthia. They were the only photos to be seen in her bedroom.

I've still got the pillow, it's creamy beige silk. It stays in a black holdall and sometimes I'll bring it out and hug it. There's a few other things I keep in the bag with it: a beehive of Amy's, a pair of pink ballet slippers, a headscarf, letters and notes she wrote to me. Some things smell of Amy and some things smell of crack, still. That's a smell that doesn't go! The pillow, though, that doesn't smell of anything anymore. It used to smell good – she was a good-smelling person – it smelled of strawberry shampoo. I also keep a lock of her hair. And a handful of things I asked for when the rest of the family were going through Camden Square, and someone from management was taking an inventory of her possessions. I have her drumsticks. A necklace. And a pair of tweezers with two little love hearts where they tweeze. I love those tweezers, they're so *her*.

Over the past decade I've tried to analyse why Amy had the problems she had in life and some of it, in my view, is that certain people are just wired that way. Wired differently. Amy was special, unusual – whatever word you want to use, she was not an ordinary person. There was no childhood abuse in Amy's life, nothing sinister, nor in mine, but of course your upbringing and your family fundamentally affect you.

A few weeks into writing this book, in spring 2020, my biological dad passed away. I'd spent a lifetime thinking my parents' divorce didn't affect me and it was only when he died I realized it *did*. Profoundly. I missed my dad. I used to ring him every single day, leave messages on his answer machine. Me and Amy had so much in common and one of those things was we both needed our dads. And our dads weren't there. I got my talent and my intelligence from my dad; Amy got her passion for music, maybe even her talent, from her dad. He played her Billie Holiday and the jazz standards when she was just a kid.

When we were teenagers she was like Cinderella in the basement with a stepfamily upstairs, and that influences somebody. We both always felt different and became reclusive. I was like no one else around me, reading Shakespeare by myself in hard-nut Canning Town while the other boys were out robbing cars. I was always closer to women. I grew up with an army of them in my dad's absence; my mum raised me by herself and I idolized her. I find it a lot easier to build healthy relationships with women than I do with fellas because of that. Just like Amy I didn't fit in – and as soon as we could leave home, we were offski.

Certain people just want to run away with the circus. Certain people in their early twenties are just hell-bent on destruction and danger and having *too* much fun. That's rock 'n' roll too. When Amy fell in love, started taking heroin and crack, you could say that was just being young and wild. If she hadn't become famous, she could've gone down that road anyway, she could've easily been someone like Blake. In your twenties, you're working yourself out, you're still a kid, you don't really know who you are. But by twenty-seven she was starting to fully grow up, mature and grow out of all that chaos.

There was no destructive side to Amy at the end of her life. She didn't have a death wish, that wasn't her problem at all. A death wish is not the same thing as alcoholism, addiction and not having what she really needed, which was normality.

For me, the biggest problem Amy had, of all of them, was being famous. Not every individual who becomes famous will have the outcome she did. But if you're a certain kind of person, the kind of person who values freedom above everything, it's a fast track to disaster, because of how much fame imprisons you, how much it inhibits ordinary life, how much it strips reality away from you. And if your self-esteem is shaky, which is the case for so many creative people, you have to deal with how you're perceived, how you're judged and how you're ridiculed. Amy was all of those things. And all of that is incredibly unhealthy.

I blame being famous for how lonely she became; it cut her off from people and society, it stopped her being treated like everyone else. Everybody saw her as something other than just Amy. I blame the system that's put in place around you, how you lose control over your life, how the machine keeps turning whether you want it to or not. I blame the effect fame had on the people around her, so she couldn't trust anyone anymore – her boyfriends, her friends, even her dad couldn't be normal around her anymore, he couldn't just be her *dad*. But I can see now, as an adult, that even though he was dazzled by her show-biz world, he was probably just as head-fucked by everything that happened to her as the rest of us. I'm sure he wishes, like I do, that Cynthia had still been around, not least to give him some proper support. Even though she would've had Mitch by the earhole *and* Amy by the earhole, she would've had plenty to say about everything. I've often wondered how that might have played out: the admiration and respect Amy had for her nan meant her words would've carried tremendous weight.

Amy was definitely someone who should never have been mainstream famous, who should've done a few small gigs a year, in places like the Jazz Café in Camden, while living a low-key, comfortable life. And she would've become a mother, which she always wanted to be. And her kids would've been her ultimate masterpiece.

In the last two years of her life there wasn't much of a life going on. No people, no work, staying indoors. The worst environment if you have a tendency to drink. As her drinking escalated, more and more people couldn't deal with her and her life became lonelier and lonelier. It was like a permanent lockdown with no way out of it. The only thing that was ever offered to her was to be 'Amy Winehouse' again. Go on tour. Write another album. No one gave Amy the option to opt out.

The human experience isn't supposed to be about adulation. No one is supposed to be any more important than anybody else. There are billions of us. And we all want the same things: to fall in love, be loved, work, have a purpose, live in the real world alongside everybody else. Love and admiration coming from people who don't know you is no substitute for that. It's an illusion, a projection of what they think you are or what they need you to be. And it is all absolute bollocks.

Amy was just a person who had a few problems like we all do. Maybe more than others. But what happened to her wasn't inevitable. I've clenched my teeth many times when I've heard people say it was: 'Oh, she was always gonna die, she was a crackhead, a fuck-up, a loser.' I've heard that in pubs and had to be pulled back from confronting some stranger, thinking, *You don't know her*. One of the hardest things for me when she passed away was I got the impression from people who *did* know her that even *they* thought this was inevitable: Nick, Juliette, Lauren. The look on their faces said it all: *Oh, Tyler, you poor bastard if you didn't think this was always gonna happen.* But they didn't see what I saw. She wasn't a mess who never tried to sort herself out. She *did*.

But in the last few months she'd often tell me she was tired. When I asked her questions about her life, when she'd had a few drinks, when she wasn't The Other Amy, she would be straight with me.

'I just don't want this life, Tyler. Would you ever wanna be famous, really? I *hate* it. I'm *bored* of it. And I'm tired.'

She used that word a lot, through those last relapses: 'I'm tired, I'm *tired*.'

Like she was tired of *life*. At twenty-seven years old.

I think back sometimes to my council house in East London and my mum giving me a fiver to get to Sylvia Young's every day. And meeting Amy. You never know, do you? What one chance meeting can do. The life it can lead you to. That kills me. We were only in the same class because neither of us could dance. Life is complicated and nothing is forever. The older you get you start to see things in different ways. Everything you go through is all just a memory and a journey. Jesus Christ, the shit she taught me. The lessons I learned. The emotions I felt because of her. She was a force. A little tornado, a thunderstorm. And in leaving me, she really made a man out of me. You have to grow up. That was a gift from her. And she keeps giving to me still, she's teaching me, still. That the beauty in the simplicity of life, *that's* what actually matters.

I miss her. I miss her so much. I love her. She's my girl, she will always be my girl. And despite all of the madness and all of the trauma she put me through, I still love the bones of her. I just *do*. And I'm so grateful, I am *so grateful*, to have known that little nutter. Because no one knew her like I did.

I am the luckiest boy in the world.

Acknowledgements

This book wouldn't have happened without the following people. It's been a hell of a journey. Thanks to Ingrid Connell at Pan Macmillan for believing in me and giving me the opportunity to tell my Amy's story. Kevin Pocklington at The North Literary Agency for always being real with me and having my back throughout this process. Chloe Roberts: I can't thank you enough for understanding from the very beginning how important it was for me, spiritually and emotionally, to get this off my chest. Sometimes there are things you just have to do, and none of this would've happened without you. Nick Shymansky for the memories and being a great friend. What can I say? You're a mensch. Sarita Borge for kicking the whole thing off. Shane O'Neill for looking out for me and Amy, and for knowing what I needed to write this book. I couldn't do it on my own and you found me my buddy, Sylvia Patterson. Shareena Harnett for her hard work and dedication behind the scenes. You're the ultimate problem solver. Richie and Mary McTigue and the bales of hay on the farm where I lay, thinking and thinking and writing and thinking some more. Until the cows come home. Sylvia Patterson: you absolute fucking legend. You know I have no filter and without you I would've been writing this book forever. We've had an incredible, intense, emotional experience together. You bled this out of me, I opened up to you in ways I never have, and you found realness and compassion in the words. There's a bond between us now: me, you and Amy.

1: *Top* © Sylvia Young, *middle and bottom* © Nick Shymansky. 2: © Nick Shymansky. 3: *Top* © Nick Shymansky, *bottom* Ian Dickson/Redferns via Getty Images. 4: *Top left* © Nick Shymansky, *top right* David Butler/Shutterstock, *bottom* Ian Dickinson/Redferns via Getty Images. 5: *Top* Diane Patrice/Iconic Images, *bottom left* Tim Whitby/WireImage via Getty Images, *bottom right* Jo Hale/Getty Images. 6: © Harvey Brown. 7: *Main* Alan Davidson/Shutterstock, *inset left* © Tyler James, *inset right* GTCRFOTO/Alamy Stock Photo. 8: *Top left* WENN/Alamy Stock Photo, *bottom left* Fiona Hanson/Alamy Stock Photo, *right* WENN/Alamy Stock Photo. 9: Peter Macdiarmid/Getty Images for NARAS. 10: *Top* Will/GC Images via Getty Images, *bottom* Shutterstock. 11: *Top* Splash News, *bottom* WENN/Alamy Stock Photo. 12: *Main* EDB Image Archive/Alamy Stock Photo, *inset left* WENN/Alamy Stock Photo, *inset right* EDB Image Archive/Alamy Stock Photo. 13: *Top* Jeremy Selwyn/Evening Standard/Shutterstock, *bottom* EDB Image Archive/Alamy Stock Photo. 14: *Top* Ringo, PacificCoastNews.com via Avalon, *bottom* Anonymous/AP/Shutterstock. 15: *Top* Danny Martindale/WireImage via Getty Images, *bottom* Steve Parsons/Alamy Stock Photo. 16: *Top left* © Harvey Brown, *bottom left* © Nick Shymansky, *right* © Tyler James.